This Time It's Personal

A Monster Kid's History of Horror Memories and Experiences

B Harrison Smith

Published in the USA by
BearManor Media
1317 Edgewater Dr. #110
Orlando, FL 32804
www.BearManorMedia.com

Softcover Edition
ISBN-10: 000
ISBN-13: 978-1-62933-900-9

Printed in the United States of America

DEDICATION

For every "weird kid, horror kid, movie kid" out there.
Keep being that kid. The world needs you more than ever.

To everyone else…whatever you do…
"Don't. Fall. Asleep."

Table of Contents

I'm too lazy to look it up but I wanted to know how you got into the horror genre?

2h

By not being lazy.

18s ✓

FOREWORD BY
ADRIENNE BARBEAU

I love making horror films. I don't like watching them.

I've never seen *Psycho* or *Frankenstein* or *Dracula*. I thought *The Exorcist* was sort of laughable. But the scary movie that really put paid to the genre for me was *Halloween*.

I saw it for the first and *only* time on the night I announced my engagement to the director, John Carpenter. He was screening it for the studio execs and a few close friends.

When it was over, John's arm was bruised from my fearful clutching, his leg was battered by my hand striking out in terror every time I jumped, and my friends Tom Atkins and Garn Stephens, who were meeting John for the first time (and who both went on to star in *Halloween 3: Season of the Witch*), were asking if I shouldn't reconsider accepting his proposal.

So if I don't like being scared and if I avoid horror films at all cost and...oh yes...since I happen to be someone who doesn't understand why anyone would see a film more than once (okay, I've seen *Three Days of the Condor* and *All The President's Men* twice, but that's it for me), well, why am I the one writing this foreword for Harrison?

Because in the twenty years since I've been appearing at horror conventions – we called them autograph shows way back then and the same small handful of fans would follow us from town to town – I've seen the genre take on epic proportions, the fan base grow to equal those of any major league sport, and A-list Hollywood actors scramble for parts in movies they wouldn't have been caught dead in two decades ago. Pun intended.

The conventions I attend these days have tens of thousands of people coming up to my table to tell me how their lives were affected by the movies they watched. The movies they still watch over and over again. The movies their mom or dad showed them when they were way too young to be watching, and the movies they show their kids, who are way too young to be watching.

Horror has arrived—and no one loves it more, or knows more about it than Harrison. Consider yourself lucky – he's sharing his fascinating journey through the celluloid world of terror with all of us - and you've got a front row seat.

INTRODUCTION

Did you ever have a fantastic cinematic adventure? I am talking where you EXPERIENCED a film, not just watched one. Where the audience cheered and laughed as a collective group. They applauded, gave an ovation or went nuts in the aisles at some standout moment? If the answer is YES, then savor it because that kind of thing has been going away for some time. You were given not just an experience, you were given a memory. It might have been something profound enough that it changed your life or it might be a fantastic story to just share with others.

That is what the true "movie-going experience" should be. The 2020 pandemic was like a cancer in an already sick body…eroding our social experience, pushing us further away from each other and from the things that bind us as a culture, nation and species. Technology has always been a problem, transitioning the theater experience to our living rooms and now to the palms of our hands and into complete isolation thanks to air pods and other instruments of seclusion.

Movies help to make our memories. They remind us of days gone by. They reflect our times, our history and often give hints of things to come. They are not to be reduced to tiny screens and viewed with 30-second skip markers to just plow through to "the good parts." Movies are made to be enjoyed, loved and shared in our viewing experience.

If you disagree, you wasted money buying this book or you could forge ahead to hear me, and a lot of others make my statement irrefutable. You may have missed out, but you're not alone.

There are enough movie review books, websites, and online videos. The last thing pop culture needs is another movie review *anything*. The Internet created a false belief that comments constitute actual reviews. There is a big difference.

I created a whole podcast called *Cynema*, dedicated to critical thinking and demanding the best of our entertainment. It was inspired by the worst motion picture ever made: *Jaws the Revenge*. I stand by that criticism.

Stephen King did a thorough history of horror with his *Danse Macabre*. He tackled old time TV, film and literature. His deft handling of the subject, his love for certain films in the genre made it a fast and enjoyable read. That was 1981 and he had not yet peaked in his popularity (has he yet?) so the book is missing quite a bit since then but it's a fine entry level into the genre.

Eli Roth threw his weight behind his *History of Horror* on *AMC*. Aside from a healthy budget, he locked in A-list talent to interview and of course a number of the faces of 80s horror to make, what I feel, is a pretty definitive documentary on the origins and evolution of the genre.

Onset of my *Camp Dread* with star, Danielle Harris.

Roth, however, loves ultra-violent horror. While he is a fan of my *Camp Dread*, I know he has a soft spot for 1983's *Sleepaway Camp*. So much, that there is an urban legend that he fired someone from one of his sets because that person did not see the film.

When I was approached by a financier to do a documentary on the history of horror, I balked. What else was there to say after Roth's superb handling of the material? You can also go online and find everything you want to know.

Some of it might be bullshit, but the old stories of behind the scenes antics, secrets and trouble allow you to fill the gaps with online digital putty. There was no fire in my belly to do a video documentary. What do I do? Trot out many of the same horror faces and have them repeat what they told Roth for my project or what they've said in countless interviews or on the convention circuit?

I took to *Twitter* and floated some questions to my followers and fans. The overall online reaction (I have at the time of this writing 24,000 followers and still no blue check mark) was Roth did a great job overall and gave fans something to enjoy. His focus on heavy-hitter-horror and the over-the-topviolent horror seemed to be a common observation. There was nothing wrong with it, and after watching, I thought that there are so many other films never mentioned. These are the films that get ignored or overlooked and many have just been forgotten.

I became a full time, professional genre filmmaker in 2009 with my first film, *The Fields;* a semi-autobiographical thriller based on my childhood experience on my grandparent's farm. It starred the late Oscar-winner, Cloris Leachman and Tara Reid. The film was personal, as I felt the best horror—the horror that scared me the most, was horror that hits on the personal level.

While I will discuss *The Fields* later in this book, it was important to show the scenes where my grandmother (Nanny) stayed up late to show me classic monster and horror films. Thanks to Nanny I knew Karloff, Lorre, Lugosi, Price, Cushing, Lee, Chaney and more by the time I was eight years old. Nanny was the living Internet, telling me how they did certain effects, stories about the actors (I knew Lugosi was a heroin addict long before Tim Burton made his *Ed Wood*).

I got invited to horror conventions to speak and promote my growing list of films. The nice part about being behind the camera is the anonymity one can enjoy at these events. Often I would stand near the tables of the horror stars to listen to the fans as they approached the tables of their idols. Aside from some gushing, the common thing I heard almost every time from hundreds of fans was the memories these people had when they first saw their star's films. They could tell where they were, what era of their life, what person they were dating. They brought their kids with them to pass down these memories as some sort of horror legacy or heirloom. The signed photos, the merchandise— it was about owning a memory.

It was more than fan worship. These films connected to people on such a powerful, emotional level. Some got choked up when they described events from their lives or how a certain film or star got them through a bad time, and that resonated with me as a person, not just a filmmaker. They got the chance to tell their idols how they *felt*.

Horror was also an escape from a turbulent childhood. I spent time with Nanny and Pappy because their home was safe harbor from some pretty nasty domestic shit going on at home. Godzilla, The Wolf Man, Dracula, Dr. Phibes, creatures and demons…they were comfort. I wanted to live with "The Brady Bunch," and to live next door to "The Addams Family."

Horror has again become a paragon of "what's wrong with this country." It cycles around to being a scapegoat every so many years. Children now grow up with a tsunami of content, most of it homogenized and vanilla. I feel a dose of the macabre is healthy for kids in their emotional development; however just vocalizing that runs the risk of one being "canceled" these days.

Let me give you an example and then I will get moving with this book because most of you likely don't read the introduction anyway. You count the pages and say, "Fuck it, I'll come back to it."

But you never do.

The Fields premiered in my home town of Stroudsburg, PA at the old Sherman Theater where I grew up watching *The Shining, American Werewolf in London, Creepshow* and laughed my ass off almost all the way through 1979's *The Amityville Horror.*

It was a sold out house just under 1300 people. A number of the cast attended and I headlined as I guess this was my "Hometown boy done good" moment.

The Sherman Theater where *The Fields* premiered and where I saw so many terrific horror films growing up

The movie ended and the lights came up for a Q&A session. We got through the initial softball questions: "What was it like to work with Cloris? Was Tara nice? Where did you film it in the area?" It was small town "Entertainment Tonight."

Then this lady stood up. You knew she was not throwing a softball question. The way she took the mic seemed to say, "Now it's MY turn." She made sure everyone was listening.

"Aren't you embarrassed to have a story like this? Didn't your parents get you any kind of therapy for going through what you did?"

It was a public attack, a direct attempt to get her talk show audience applause moment. "My daughter," she looked down to a girl who might've been 14, sitting in the theater chair. The girl looked like she wanted to crawl under it. She was mortified. All we needed was the girl to silently mouth "Mom!" and shield her mortified face with one hand.

"My daughter," she continued, "is now terrified to look at a cornfield because of this film. We were not prepared for this kind of movie. We thought this was a family film because it was about your life and you grew up here."

A few stifled laughs greeted her soapbox moment. You could tell it was not the response she wanted. She expected to get applause—leading some kind of outrage crusade against me, the film and the cast and crew onstage. It was her "gotcha!" moment.

I asked if she saw the poster with the rating outside when she bought her tickets. She did. Did the artwork alone convey any sort of family film? Did the synopsis in the program (which lay in her seat) not give a clue? How did she find out about the event because The Sherman website and the local paper both made it clear this was a suspenseful, psychological thriller?

I guess this translated into being my fault. I stood up, took the wireless mic and walked to the front of the stage. Would I apologize to her and her daughter? Would I make excuses for my family? I said this:

"I believe that horror and porn are the purest of the movie genres. Both have one simple objective: to stimulate and excite. Neither has a religious, political or societal agenda."

That got some laughs and a few claps somewhere out there. The spotlights were in my eyes. I couldn't see her from where I was standing. It didn't matter. Public speaking never scared me.

"Do you like *Disney*?" I asked.

'Of course. We love *Disney*." She was indignant.

"You saw the new Jonas Brothers movie? The one in 3-D?"

"We OWN it," she replied fast and proud. "We watch it a couple times a week sometimes."

"Did you like the part where the boys come out on stage with those hoses between their legs and spray white foam on the faces of all those tween and teen girls?"

She had to think about it. "I don't remember that."

Sure she didn't. Instead of clubbing her like a baby seal with her own DVD, I moved to shut this nonsense down. She'd hijacked enough time. *Disney* owns *ABC TV*, I told her and the crowd. "You all watch "The Secret Life of the

American Teenager," where they regularly discuss unmarried pregnancy, oral sex and other stuff like that? They say they're "a different kind of family." I guess so." Some laughter and applause.

"*High School Musical* teaches through fun poppy songs that if you're physically attractive, life is great. The fat kids, the sullen ones, the ones facing depression, terrible family lives…we don't see those kids. I think they send them off to some *Disney* concentration camp called *Mouseschwitz.*"

Okay, I was pushing it. It's never good to invoke The Holocaust, but come on, "Mouseschwitz" was too good to let go. More laughs and more applause. "Horror," I continued, "unlike *Disney*, doesn't pretend to be something it's not. What you see is what you get."

She wasn't listening.

"*Disney* pretends to be family oriented, when instead they are a marketing, merchandizing machine designed to sell you and your kids a lot of stuff. They sexualize young kids under the pretext of family entertainment. They invoke eating disorders in this plastic life template they crank so many of their films and TV product with."

Now I got some real applause and a few whistles. I was like the preacher under the revival tent at the end of 1988's *The Blob*. The Horror Preacher.

The mother shook her head. She was done and motioned to her daughter to stand and join her. They were leaving.

"Kids need a dose of the macabre," I said before she got away. She was trapped in the tight aisles. She still had a jacket and purse to fish out of the cramped seating and her daughter had to do the same. "We have helicopter parents afraid to let their kids skin their shins. They think they can protect them from all the bad things in the world and the truth is, they can't." I was serious and not mocking her. "I would never wish upon a kid what I went through, but horror, ma'am, was my escape. When watching the plights of some of the people in those films, my life didn't seem so bad."

She wasn't having it. Her voice bled into the open microphone she didn't shut off and everyone could hear her hissing to her daughter to get up. They were going.

"I identified with outcasts like The Wolf Man, The Creature from the Black Lagoon or Frankenstein's Monster," I continued. "Most of all, I have the memories of so many great late nights watching "The CBS Late Night Movie, Chiller Theater" or Saturday creature features and Doctor Shock out of Philadelphia with my Nanny." I ended it by saying that everyone in that theater just watched a valentine to my grandparents. It wasn't a horror story, it was a thank you, and they were no longer here to see it.

Standing ovation.

The woman gathered her daughter and walked out. I never got her name and I never saw her again. I suspect she never watched another one of my films after that. I doubt she'll be reading this book.

Horror helped to save my childhood. I never once thought of bringing a gun to my school and shooting people. I didn't think of raping or murdering. I wasn't inspired to kill animals or desecrate cemeteries. The Columbine killers cited Warner Brother's *The Matrix* as an inspiration to make it into the history books and parent nightmares. Last time I checked, that wasn't a horror movie.

To be clear, I did not nor do I now believe *The Matrix* bears any responsibility for the tragedy in Littleton, Colorado. As much as people don't want to admit it, that falls on the two boys who carried out their massacre and their parents who were in charge.

I wanted to visit The Isle of Evil in 1967's *Mad Monster Party* and learn Doctor Frankenstein's secrets and fall in love with his beautiful secretary, Francesca. I fantasized about partying with Dracula, The Werewolf, The Monster and more during those days and nights when my parents were screaming at each other and we often were sent away when things got out of hand. I took my monsters with me. I was Godzilla in my snowsuit, breathing cold winter vapor for atomic breath, destroying large snowplowed mountains that stood in for skyscrapers.

I convinced friends there were giant Kaiju monsters slumbering beneath the slate mountains surrounding our small town of Bangor, PA. I built a "Monstress" out of wood, with a drawn paper face and an old tank top for a dress. I was going to animate her with lightning and make her come alive like Dr. Frankenstein. Instant girlfriend!

These are memories. I have a lot more. Many of them are related to horror and the best part is I made it contagious, converting some friends over the years who said they hated the genre.

That is what this book is all about.

When Linda Blair grabbed that crucifix in *The Exorcist* and did what she did, we were shocked, but it wasn't out of context. It was a horror movie. It was called *The Exorcist* and it was based on a best seller of the same name and content. It wasn't a family film that took a dark turn.

I was shocked, though, when the purity ring-bearing Jonas brothers heaved those fire hoses out onstage between their legs and pumped their white foam all over those underage girls. That shocked me more than "Let Jesus fuck you!"

Horror doesn't have to be all guts and gore. It doesn't have to be *A Serbian Film* or *Cannibal Holocaust* every time. Those films and others of their kind are just a sub-genre of horror and don't solely represent it any more than *Friday the 13th* defines the genre. Horror is what connects with YOU.

It's always personal.

You do know what you're getting when you look at the posters and see the previews. The filmmakers aren't hiding anything from you. Horror is transparent.

Disney and other "family" companies can't all say the same.

If this offends you, then you don't know horror. You do not understand it.

With the star of *The Fields*, the late Cloris Leachman.

Grab a flashlight, button your jacket and let's head out into the dark night and walk with me down this memory lane.

THIS IS HOW HORROR MOVIES START

Halloween 2019.

I was doing a "trunk or treat" with my SUV at the bottom of my driveway. In between children wearing masks begging for candy, a headline caught me on the front of *Yahoo News*. It was from the *Associated Press* and it read something like: *The Return of SARS?*

SARS. Hadn't heard that since 2004. There was the MERS outbreak but that got contained pretty fast and never got here, at least anything major to my knowledge. I read the article. Lab workers in some unknown Chinese province in a town called Wuhan were sick. Nurses and doctors at nearby hospitals were sick with pneumonia-like symptoms that resembled SARS.

It went on, but a hoard of costumed urchins swarmed my vehicle and I forgot about it.

As we got closer to the end of the year, the situation worsened. Some Chinese doctor took to social media to warn shit wasn't right and then he vanished and his warnings were censored by the Chinese government. He later succumbed to this SARS-like virus.

The US and its media conglomerates were focused on Trump's first impeachment. I think he mentioned something about this "Chinese virus" in a State of the Union, but again, on this side of the world, that wasn't our focus.

It was like a horror movie. They always start out with some small, obscure threat that grows into a monstrosity. By the time we got to mid-January, 2020 the news was chattering about its new given name: COVID-19.

Cable news pundits started the blame game. Some called it a hoax. Trump called it a hoax and was on his way to downplaying the potential for this new coronavirus to fuck some serious shit up.

1

We now know, through recorded phone calls with Watergate journalist and writer Bob Woodward that Trump knew just how bad this was and was going to get. A master bullshit artist himself, the Mayor of Amity Island, sounded a bit wracked in the conversation. He knew.

Below is a piece of the recorded transcript from Feb. 7th, 2020, with Bob Woodward and Donald Trump. [1]

Donald Trump: (00:16) It goes through air, Bob. That's always tougher than the touch. The touch, you don't have to touch things, right? But the air, you just breathe the air and that's how it's passed. And so that's a very tricky one. That's a very delicate one. It's also more deadly than even your strenuous flus. People don't realize, we lose 25,000, 30,000 people a year here. Who would ever think that, right?

Bob Woodward: (00:41) I know. It's much forgotten.

Donald Trump: (00:42) It's pretty amazing. And then I said, "Well, is that the same thing?"

Bob Woodward: (00:46) What are you able to do for-

Donald Trump: (00:47) This is more deadly. This is 5% versus 1%, and less than 1%. So this is deadly stuff.

I flew to San Francisco at the end of January 2020 to the SF Sci-Fi Indie Fest for the debut of my horror film, *The Special*. When I got off the plane and passed by International Arrivals, there was staff in Haz Mat suits, bio suits, spraying down these giant, tarped areas. I text back home: "There's some bad shit going on here," and sent the pictures to prove it.

The opening to George Romero's *Dawn of the Dead* came to mind after I got home as *FOX News* and *CNN* started working themselves into a lather over this growing international threat. It was spreading. Pundits, doctors and officials were alternating between arguing over this plague and downplaying to calm the public. I bought ammo, stocked up on medicine and essential supplies for a possible zombie apocalypse.

---

1   https://www.nbcnews.com/politics/donald-trump/trump-told-bob-woodward-he-knew-february-covid-19-was-n1239658

1979's *Dawn of the Dead* opened with a public in panic playing out in real time on television. Scientists and professionals were engaged in name calling and conspiracy theories while the politicians told the public there was nothing to fear and even said the stories of the dead walking were hoaxes.

There was a little Mayor Larry Vaughn from *Jaws* in this emerging pandemic and the public was quick to make that connection as Trump told the country we had 15 cases or something like that, the numbers were going down. Only they weren't and this global pandemic had all the makings of a real life reboot of *Stephen King's The Stand*.

"Amity, as you know, means friendship."

Then—the lockdowns. Italy fell. Europe fell. Wearing a mask turned into a political issue and the virus was given license to mutate and kill. Trump threw much of the responsibility of dealing with this national crisis on his automaton, Damien Thorn-esque son-in-law and his "Pray it away" mannequin Vice-President.

This is how horror movies start.

The US stock market crashed. Hospitals were overwhelmed. The *Q-Anon* roaches came out into the light, and declared the virus a hoax—a ploy to reduce the population and a result of 5G technology masterminded by none other than Bond villain, Bill Gates.

You couldn't write a better horror movie. The deniers compared the virus to the flu, calling its mortality rates acceptable and nothing near the virulence of other diseases. They crowed of 99% survival rates, but in China a news clip showed the amazing construction of a hospital in ten days. When I saw that footage, I replied, "That's not a hospital, it's a morgue."

China was and still is lying on the origins of the virus and its mortality rate. Trump was in over his head, unable to get proper testing, unable to coordinate government departments and agencies to follow basic contact tracing. By April the bottom was out of the tub and until a vaccine came along, all we could do was allow the wildfire to rage. In the meantime, the media and an unequipped

President rationalized that it only hit the old and infirm. This wasn't true, even by stable genius, virus expert standards.

We needed sunglasses out of John Carpenter's *They Live!* No one wanted to put them on but we did have a few who could see.

Those are my memories of the first few months of COVID and they are linked to *Dawn of the Dead, Invasion of the Body Snatchers, The Stand, They Live!* and *Jaws.* The collapse of Hollywood created a dearth of content and that's how I got to make *Where The Scary Things Are*, a monster horror that got acquired by *Lionsgate.*

As the pandemic raged, people stockpiled basic necessities that they didn't need to do. They armed up, buying weaponry and went into bunker mode, waiting any day for the purge to begin as the virus ripped from coast to coast. That's how horror movies start—small, little things, out of the ordinary grow into monstrous things that envelop and alter our worlds. No one listens to the scientist, the expert, the one with the experience until it's too late. Whether zombies or sharks or even disaster movie earthquakes, or towering inferno skyscrapers, no one listens to the Brody-style characters who want the beaches closed.

Then you think it's all over. You go down a whole other horror road to *Friday the 13th, Halloween* and *A Nightmare on Elm Street.* You think it's done. The vaccine arrived, the monster was vanquished.

The eye opens just before the screen goes black. The Boogeyman sits up. The dead boy leaps from the lake into your boat. An evil cackle is heard as the screen fades to black. The thing had offspring or mutated itself into something else to survive.

Enter Delta, Lambda and at the time of this writing, a third variant.

COVID is the worst horror franchise ever.

WHAT GOT YOU INTO HORROR?

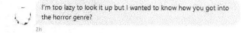

I'm too lazy to look it up but I wanted to know how you got into the horror genre?

2h

By not being lazy

18s ✓

The historical context around a film, particularly in horror, is paramount. Horror reflects the times in which it was made. This is why remakes of *Friday the* 13th and *A Nightmare on Elm Street* failed. Times changed but the monsters didn't. This is the fate of the classic *Universal Monsters* of the 1930s and 40s. More on this later. You'll see, I'll pull it all together.

First, some personal history context.

My early childhood was spent in "Southside" Bangor, PA in a half-a-double until I was four-years-old. My first experience with death was a gerbil that my mother and I buried in the backyard. I took a black crayon and drew on the driver side door of our neighbor's brand new, cherry red *Mach One Mustang*.

I owned up to it and my mother took me to the people who lived in the other half of our double and made me apologize to their faces. Fortunately for me, crayon washes off cars. You could say that was my first brush with death as I was amazed the car's owner didn't kill me.

I watched "HR Puff 'n Stuff "and wanted my own Freddy the Magic Flute. My mother ordered one off the back of *Cocoa Krispies* for fifty cents. I looked one up recently on *eBay* and it was selling for over $1200.00. Mine went into a landfill before Nixon resigned.

The gas crisis was about to hit. Charles Manson and his "family" brought the 60s to a literal screaming halt. "The Brady Bunch" was on prime time television and Vietnam was heading toward its inevitable conclusion as Walter Cronkite helped bring the war into our living room.

There were three major TV networks and color TVs had become commonplace. We had a rotary phone. The car radio had punch keys that you stabbed to change a channel and AM or FM was marked on the dial faceplates. Just like the pioneer days, huh?

My days were spent playing outside on the sidewalk in a "Krazy Kar" or riding a tricycle up and down the sidewalk. I had a crush on a girl named Judy who lived about six doors down. She had to be at least 18 and I was four.

It didn't work out. Her father drove an old van that my mother, for some reason, called "The Pill Wagon." He was fresh off the commune and would always flash me the "V" fingers which meant "peace." As a result, I dubbed him "The Peace Man" and looked for him every day as he came and went. I think he was a house painter.

If you want to get technical, my first real introduction to horror was "The Monster Cereals" from *General Mills*: *Count Chocula* and *Frankenberry*. *Boo Berry* came along by the mid-70s, followed by *Yummy Mummy* and *Fruit Brute*.

At the time I had no idea who the real monsters and their actors were who inspired these cartoon mascots, but damn I loved the cereal.

If there were two people who had the chemistry of Jack Nicholson and Shelley Duvall from *The Shining*, it was my mother and father. They married for convenience. My mother died in 2007 and my father is still alive. I don't want the focus of this book to be about the issues I dealt with at home.

What I can say is when my father was around, he was fun and loved to play fight and wrestle with me and later when my younger brother came along. "Beat me up!" he would challenge us, prompting dives off the couch onto his back, trying to bring him down.

My mother was no Wendy Torrance. She was independent and liked to party. She was heading toward two packs a day for her cigarette habit and she had no plans to be a housewife for the remainder of her life.

These two should've discussed some things before tying the knot.

I lived on a street where people sat on their porches at night. The ice cream truck rolled through during the summers. I can still hear it and see it as it would come around the far corner, by The Peace Man's house, heading down to the part of town where my Barber, Bob Finelli, cut my hair. He had this buzzer that tickled the living hell out of the back of your neck. I would scrunch up and wiggle in the chair every time. My mom would have to stand by the chair to make me hold still.

An old man lived over Finelli's Barber Shop. He liked to be called "Whitey" for his snow white hair and Charlie Weaver mustache (I'll bet most of you have to *Google* who that was). He made me hot cocoa and would bring it down when I visited the shop.

It was a different time. Cars were big. Gas was still leaded and sold at around 35–40 cents per gallon. My father traded in one of his muscle cars for this little orange *Datsun*. He felt between the Vietnam War and rising issues in the Middle East, cheap gas wasn't going to stay that way. He ditched his gas guzzler showroom, mint condition sports car for this little thing that had the neighbors laughing at him when he parked on the street in front of our half of the double.

My grandfather fought in World War II and was convinced that the Japanese made superior cars because they had new factories built for them after the war and US factories were almost a hundred years old. He was "Pappy" to me and he was married to "Nanny." You will hear a lot about them later on.

I was so young and remembered very little of the problems between my mother and father at this point as a boy. It got worse when we moved to East Bangor in 1972, just short of my fifth birthday.

Did I paint a decent picture for you of what life was like in this little town? Do you have at least a little feel for the historical things going on around this oblivious little boy? I hope so, because it's important in understanding the horror films that will come our way as we continue our walkabout.

I loved the TV show, "The Munsters." They didn't scare me, and this was before I knew about Frankenstein's Monster or any of the *Universal Monsters*. All I knew was I liked the show and thought it was funny. Were Fred Gwynne, Al Lewis and Yvonne DeCarlo my introduction to the horror genre? Maybe. The problem was I had no idea what they were spoofing. I was only four.

The show was in syndication. I remember walking down the moving van ramp, mimicking Herman Munster's goofy laugh and shake after he smashed through the front door of 1313 Mockingbird Lane in the titles. I ran the theme music through my head and walked all jerky and laughed like Herman down the ramp, then scampered up to the truck and did it all again. Anyone watching would have thought there was something wrong with the Smith kid.

Before I made the move to East Bangor (Only 10 minutes up the road, if that) there was one incident on Southside Bangor that will connect with my horror future.

I mentioned that I had a tricycle. It was red with white hand grips. I would pedal up and down the sidewalk from corner to corner. Nowadays many parents would be horrified to know my mother was inside the house, no eye on me, satisfied that I wouldn't go into the street or get snatched. Everyone knew everyone, but Springwood, Ohio was also one of those towns and we know how that shit turned out.

It was a summer evening. I was up several houses to the corner by myself. There was an old couple, The Wilson's, who would sit on their front porch and give me lemonade or cookies if I passed by. I was heading toward their house when this lady who lived in the house at the corner stopped me. She was fat and in those 70s polyester shorts, polyester tank top and these slip-on sandals. She had around five kids and she was always in hair curlers.

She was loud. You heard her yelling and when the ice cream truck came she would scream at her kids to move their asses or they would miss it. She saw me bike by her porch and ran after me. "Give me a ride!" she screamed. She laughed at her own silliness and before I could do anything, she jumped onto the back of my little tryke.

Her weight popped the front into the air and spilled her off the back. She slipped in those shoes, I think, and she fell flat on her back. Her head hit that cement sidewalk with a crack! She screamed. I mean SCREAMED, wailing, calling for her kids. I cried. I yelled for my mother. The Wilson's came off their porch.

The woman's kids ran out of the house. Some yelled at me, asking me what I did. I just cried. I don't remember saying anything.

I saw blood leaking from the back of her head and seeping into the cement under her splayed hair like a ghastly halo. Neighbors crossed the street. Someone got my mother, because she was just there. She was training to be a nurse at that time and helped tend to the crying lady. The Wilson's let her know they saw the whole thing and how the woman tried to hijack my bike for a ride.

What the hell was she thinking? This was the first horrific image I can remember. Blood leaked out, she let out dramatic wails and screams—I got all that at the age of four.

The other image of "horror" was finding my gerbil dead in its aquarium. I know she had babies and she ate one or two, according to my father. Then she died. I found her—eyes closed in the cedar shavings. That might be the first time I wrapped my head around the concept of death. My mother tried to help by removing the rodent, explaining death to me and then wrapped her up in a tissue. We buried her in the back yard, under a maple tree near my decrepit swing set. I cried a lot and can still see dirt covering that white tissue.

I got my first bee sting in Bangor. It was a wasp, flying near the front porch of our neighbor's house. I thought it would be a good idea to catch it. I snatched it into my hand and it promptly stung me. I screamed, let it go and then knew: don't touch those fuckers ever again.

God built the wasp pissed off. There was nothing close to the construction of the insect that invites someone to want to catch it. Its eyes looked pissed off. Its coloring was that brown, black and the abdomen was tipped, and encased their stinger. They're in direct contrast to a butterfly that almost seems to say in their flutters: "touch me!" Not the wasp. They don't flutter, they hover, they glide, and it looks uninviting. That's how stupid I was. I grabbed it anyway.

That story will work its way into my film *The Fields* when I have the character of Steven (me) describe his mother's mean-looking friend. "She looks like a wasp," he tells Tara Reid. That imagery was inspired from the wasp incident I just laid out. I think it's a great piece of dialogue that paints an image of a character we've yet to see. When he says it, you know just what he means.

We moved to East Bangor. It was a single family home. No more half a double. While it was only ten minutes up the road, it would be a whole new world, and looking back, it's amazing I survived my childhood.

Horror would find me in East Bangor on our first Christmas as someone, dressed in a creepy as hell Santa suit and mask walked through the door and plopped me on his knee.

To this day I still don't know who it was.

MAD MONSTER PARTY AND
FREE RANGE KIDS

Rankin-Bass Entertainment was a major influence on *Generation X* and our television landscape. I was first introduced to stop-motion "Animagic" by Arthur Rankin and Jules Bass while living on Southside Bangor. Their breakout theatrical hit, *The Daydreamer* was a mix of live action with stars like Margaret Hamilton and Jack Gilford starring in the wraparound narrative that stitched together a string of animated stories from the fairytale world.

The animated stories brought the vocal talents of Hayley Mills, Terry-Thomas and Boris Karloff. The only one that stood out to me was *The Little Mermaid*, which, to *Rankin-Bass's* credit stayed far more faithful to the original Hans Christian Andersen story than what Disney would do almost thirty years later. Tallulah Bankhead was the voice of the evil Sea Witch and the dark aspects of the story appealed to me.

I was just becoming aware of movies and *Rankin-Bass*, along with the old, classic *Little Rascals* were my first pop culture consumptions. While "Rudolph the Red-Nosed Reindeer" gave *Rankin-Bass* pop culture eternal life, their 1967 theatrical release, *Mad Monster Party* made me a horror fan.

"Animagic" was just stop-motion puppetry, but *Rankin-Bass* had their own unique look and they got *Mad Magazine* artist, Jack Davis, to design the *MMP*

13

cast. I do not remember seeing a single classic *Universal* monster movie for context before the age of five. I was introduced to Frankenstein's Monster, The Wolf Man, The Mummy, The Creature and others through this kiddy matinee film that underperformed at the box office but became a TV classic.

We moved to that new house in East Bangor. My parents were still together but the marriage was falling apart. Our house was on Dewey Street with five other homes and my Aunt Fran and Uncle Paul living only two houses up on the hill.

As my parents' arguments grew, I retreated outside or discovered the bevy of material on TV to get away from it. I don't know when *Mad Monster Party* first came across my radar but I know which character hooked me: Francesca. She was Doctor Frankenstein's voluptuous red-haired secretary with an attitude and beauty mark.

Francesca was my first movie crush and let me tell you why. Even at the young age of five, I was a little horn toad before I knew what horny feelings were.

In the middle of the film Francesca gets into a catfight (complete with sounds) with Phyllis Diller's Monster's Mate. They rip each other's dresses off at the party. A cartoon puppet was stripped to

15

her slip and then fought the woman who did it. I was addicted to *Mad Monster Party* evermore.

The sound of that gold, satin, slit up to the thigh dress pulling off Francesca got my blood racing every time. The problem was I couldn't see it whenever I wanted. I was at the mercy of affiliate channel programming. I learned fast to check Channel 9, 11 or 5 out of New York City. While you would think the film would air around Halloween, I found better luck at Thanksgiving and New Years. No idea why.

I identified with and envied Doctor Frankenstein's (voiced by Boris Karloff) nerdy nephew Felix who got Francesca at the end. I wanted her to fall in love with me like she did Felix. I wanted to live in that castle and hang with all of those monsters. I could envision myself running the stone hallways, walking through that huge ballroom and fraternizing with the zombie help.

I wanted to be Uncle Boris Frankenstein, with my lab full of secrets and the ability to create and destroy all centered on my private island hideaway.

I would build my own girlfriend and she would be Francesca—my masterpiece. These were the fantasies of a seven-year-old-boy. The woman who ambushed me in the introduction of this book at *The Fields* premiere would think they were dangerous. Here was the "danger" of being "free range kids."

"Don't go near the quarries. If you fall down in that water, there are air pockets that will suck you down and you'll drown." I think almost every mother in the Slate Belt Bangor, East Bangor and Pen Argyl areas told some variation of a quarry horror story that incorporated some kid drowning because they didn't heed the warnings.

Nanny did it. While she lived on the outskirts of Easton, she knew about the quarries and every, single, bad thing that happened in them. "Jesus Christ!" she would exclaim. "You fall down in that water, it'll pull you right under!"

Once a booming slate mining area, the Bangor economy fell on hard times in the years after World War II. You could drive along the roads and sees these giant slate mountains around emerald green and sometimes teal blue water below.

By the time I was seven or eight I ran the area with friends Steven, Douglas, John and Nelson. You ever see this meme? It's true.

Summers, weekends, holidays, from 1974-78 I left the house no later than ten in the morning. Then back home for lunch, not home again until the street lights kicked on.

Gone. All. Day.

That's not exaggerated memory. Sure there were times we played in the yard, but there were slate quarries to climb. The East Bangor dam was filled with turtles, fish, frogs and giant snails to catch. The train that ran along the dam was a target for rock throwing or putting pennies and quarters on the track to see if they stretched when run over. We also used to lie on the tracks, ears to the rails to see if they really hummed or "sang" with an approaching train. They did.

We were often miles from home. I swear I was no more than seven or eight when we did these things. We were these little kids, playing deep in the woods, atop slate quarry mountains, down by a vast dam that likely saw some shady shit.

I could have been nabbed, duct-taped and thrown into a trunk and not missed until maybe an hour after lunch or after the streetlight came on. Drowning was the least to worry about.

We scaled two-hundred foot slate mountains to reach the top of the quarries. When you looked down, you saw junked cars, trucks, refrigerators, anything someone wanted to junk. Many landed just feet from the water—rusting skeletons of mechanical dinosaurs stuck in and around the blue-green tar pit. We hurled slate to smash windshields and hit whatever we could. Out there, under that glassy, deceptively calm blue water was an evil force ready to suck us down into its cold hell. Those were how we spent many afternoons.

The picture above is me in my Cub Scouts uniform around 3rd grade, so I was about seven-years-old. My mom would give me two dollars to walk the mile from our house to *Jessie's* general store and meat market. They had a sign in their window that said, "You Can't Beat Our Meat!" I didn't get that joke until fifth grade.

Jessie's was first located at the top of Central Avenue across from a blouse mill. They moved it about four blocks down Central.

I would get Mom a pack of "*Pall Mall* regular in the soft pack" (I still remember the exact order after the store's owner no longer required a note from her giving permission to sell me cigarettes), maybe a loaf of bread or jug of milk and whatever was left over was mine for a candy bar. That all entailed a walk across a busy double lane highway there and back all alone.

19

My favorite candy at the time was *Mr. Bones*. It was *Smarties*-type hard candy in the shape of skeletal pieces and they came in a variety of colored plastic coffins. I wanted the coffins. You needed to buy multiple coffins to get the pieces needed to assemble a full skeleton. The candy was lousy but the concept was cool.

That may not seem scary to some of you, but let me bring in "Bobby." Bobby was the guy every small town knows. He's the one that people whisper to their kids to stay away from because "there's something wrong with him."

He was thin, and uniformed in baggy work jeans, stained, white T-shirt and these high top work boots. He had curly, long hair and black-rimmed shop glasses. He would visit *Jessie's* once a week or so to buy a slab of raw liver. Bobby would take it home and masturbate with it.

"Feels like the real thing," he would tell the old-timers who sat outside *Jessie's* on a bench. I sometimes heard them ask Bobby as he approached the store, "Where's the liver, Bobby? Big date tonight?" They'd laugh as Bobby walked past to get his package or leave with it in hand, undaunted by their taunts.

When the movie *Bad Ronald* came into my life, I thought of Bobby right away. Ronald in that film wasn't much different than Bobby. "Where's the liver, Bobby?"

We would play manhunt and hide and seek in East Bangor cemetery until dark or sometimes after. That was a mile from home as well. I had relatives buried there, maybe that counted as some sort of supervision?

As a Cub Scout, in 1974, I walked from my house to the top of Central Avenue for our den meetings at the old East Bangor firehouse. Meetings would start around seven at night and run until about 830 or so. The summer wasn't so bad, but in fall and winter it was dark for the walk home.

I walked it alone. It was mostly sidewalks along row house after row house. The road leading up to Dewey Street was just a road, no walkways. When it was icy in winter, I would get on all fours and crawl up the hill to get down to my house. We had a shortcut into my yard but the neighbors blocked it off.

We all got little flip flashlights one year with the Cub Scout emblem. I was thrilled because now I had light for the dark walk back home. Sure, there were streetlights, but that little pocket light made me feel better. I would also sing: "Whenever I feel afraid, I hold my head up high and whistle a happy tune so no one ever knows I'm afraid."

We would have Cub Scout fundraisers and one year it was candles. They gave us this cardboard suitcase of scented, animal figure candles (maybe a dozen) and it was up to us to sell them. I walked all of East Bangor, from down by the quarry-side trailer courts to the dam and all the way out by East Bangor Park, and further by myself around eight years of age. I went into people's homes. Some I knew. Some I did not.

Think about it. I was invited into homes when someone promised to get money or wanted to see my candles. No adult was with me. I could've been a tragic story. There weren't even milk carton kids then, let alone the Internet or *Unsolved Mysteries*.

Our bus stop was a good half mile walk from my house. I walked with a friend and her kid sister to the stop. No adults were with us, and that went for the walk home after school.

21

I was a little kid walking the empty roads, rail lines and dam shorelines of East Bangor.

This was what it was like from 1971-78. Three networks, no VCRs, DVDs or computers. You depended on the syndicate channels for your real entertainment. Channels 17, 11, 9, 5, 17, 48 and *The CBS Late Night Movie* would be my portal to horror.

Even the toys of the 70s were dangerous. I burned my arm and hands a number of times with *Creepy Crawlers*—a kit that had kids pour liquid goop into a hot, heated metal block that fused the green shit into rubbery insects and snakes. I had scars all over my wrists. I burned fingertips and inhaled fumes that could've been toxic. What toy designer thought that was a good idea? Someone who hated kids, I'll bet.

Where other kids played *Chutes and Ladders* or *Candyland,* I wanted *Screech;* a game played in the dark with a light up, glow-in-the-dark plastic owl. I can't remember the point of the game, but it was horror for me and I loved it.

Above all, I wanted to be Baron Von Frankenstein from *Mad Monster Party.* I wanted my own "Book of Secrets" that the entire world's monsters would revere. I wanted to create the potion that would destroy all matter.

All of this would come in the form of a junior chemistry kit. It would give me great powers and more. I saw test tubes bubbling with dry ice plumes puffing out of them and beakers over burners. All I needed was a skylight in my bedroom to hoist my potions and formulas into the heavens as lightning streaked the sky. Instead it was a bunch of not-so-safe powders and liquids in cheap  plastic bottles with some glass test tubes and a chintzy microscope.

Being The Baron meant that I had to build my own masterpiece, my own Francesca. I used scrap wood to build a skeleton. My father worked at a bindery and there was never a shortage of drawing paper or huge sheets of white cardboard. I drew Francesca's face on the heavy board, colored in her red hair, and taped it to the stick figure skeleton.

When I stood her up naked, she was tall as me. I stole one of my father's tank tops, a brownish one that resembled the color of one of Francesca's dresses in *Mad Monster Party* and dressed her.

There was an old cement wall in our backyard under a giant maple tree. This was my laboratory. It was here that I pretended lightning struck my creation and gave my wooden Francesca life.

No, it doesn't get creepy and end up with a slab of liver.

I was obsessed with the film. I found a fellow classmate in second and third grade who was a fan too. I overplayed my hand in fourth grade. I knew how to read the *TV Guide*. For those of you with no idea what I am talking about, there once was a booklet you bought at the checkout line or magazine stand or had delivered to your home that gave you everything on TV for the week. I checked it almost every week to see if *Mad Monster Party* was coming around on rotation.

APRIL 18, 1977

Monday
EVENING

shows his hatred and disgust by eating them—sometimes raw, sometimes cooked. He subdues his enemies by biting them viciously with his poison-tipped teeth (he is immuned to the poison). Starring Burt Lancaster as Cannibal, with Joel Grey as his sidekick and chef.

Guest Cast

Little Benny .... Ben Gazzara
Danielle Leroy .... Leslie Caron
Don Travelle .... Moses Gunn
Bo .... D.P. Schneider

⑦**HIT AND RUN**
A team of professional assassins, or "hit men," work for the FBI. Their method: run their victims over and leave the scene in their souped-up, high-performance cars that no one can catch. Starring Anthony George as "Cracker," James Franciscus as "Crasher" and Greg Morris as "Snapper."

10:30 ❷**BUDGET WRESTLING**
③**FIRING SQUAD**
William Buckley debates himself and wins.
❹**NEWS BEFORE 11 O'CLOCK**
⑤**TRAVEL WITH THE STARS**
Rose Marie and Morey Amsterdam go to Puerto Rico.
⑦**KEEP YOUR SHIRT ON**
❾**THE BAITING GAME**
Girls tease boys until they come in their pants.

⑪**HOWDY COWBOY**
Tall tales of the Old West.
⑬**PLANT SWAPPERS**
11:00 ❷NEWS—Snuff/Bogash
❹NEWS—Pitz/Malone
❼NEWS—Krell/Van Scroon
⑤NEWS—Bleminger/Kosh
❾MOVIE—Comedy
"Doctor Gets Sued." (1973) Dr. Mal Practice, a bumbling incompetent, is constantly sued by incapacitated patients, and relatives of patients he has accidentally killed. Somehow, he manages to survive and marry an heiress. With Lorne Greene, Jack Carter and Lauren Bacall. (84 min.)
⑫**MARY TYLER WHORE**
Mary thinks she's being fired because her boss, Madame Ovary, doesn't smile at her for days. It turns out that the Madame has a new set of false teeth she's ashamed of.
11:30 ❷**JOHNNY TALK SHOW**
Tonight's guests include Peter Marshall, Monty Hall, Gene Rayburn and Regis Philbin.
❹**THE BIG HYPE**
The widow of General David Sarnoff celebrates what would be their 75th anniversary. On hand to salute her is everyone from the entertainment world, including Vice-President Mondale. (3 hrs.)
⑤**MOVIE—WESTERN**
"Bend of the Hunter." (1950) A story of re-

see this one

NBC
MOVIE OF THE WEEK
THE BACKBONE FAMILY
8:00 ③ ❹

Multimillionaire Justin Backbone decides to leave the jungle of corporate warfare for the jungle of South Africa and a simpler way of life for himself and his family. Living on just the interest from his municipal bond holdings, Backbone, his wife Nanci, and their children, Lauri and Tiny Todd, buy a plot of land in the South African veldt so that each member of the family can "do his or her thing."
In Part 1 of this two-part movie, the Backbone family buys a trailer, a collapsible swimming pool, and a portable tennis court. Lauri discovers that mixed doubles are taboo in the veldt, and Tiny Todd tries to go into the lumber business by using killer bees as chainsaws.
Starring Brian Keith as Justin Backbone, Barbara Rush as Nanci, Mackenzie Phillips as Lauri, and newcomer Jody Cody, Jr. as Tiny Todd.

24

> *"The Monster Squad "is an interesting one. I don't recall the first time I saw it. It's just kind of ingrained in my memory. This is my "Goonies." It introduced me to the Universal monsters. My family was never big movie people, so I discovered things on my own or through friends. And this is a great gateway horror film.*
>
> Josh G.

My parents divorced and my mother lived with some new guy who beat the shit out of my brother and me while she was at work or not home. That's a whole other, real-life horror, but it does provide historical context to the memories. I was nine years old when he punched me in the side of my head so hard he loosened a molar that eventually came out. I didn't ask for the salt at the dinner table. My mother had no idea, but my brother and I would pray for this asshole to die when my mom's mother made us say our prayers when we stayed over.

Then, one summer afternoon, he fell over with a massive heart attack. He died several months later from heart failure.

Fourth grade was the last year he would be around. One Sunday night while we were with our real father, I checked the *TV Guide* and there it was...*Mad Monster Party* was on that coming Tuesday. The problem was it was on at one in the afternoon and that was smack in the middle of the school day.

I spoke aloud of my excitement for the film and when I got home asked my mother if I could stay home on that day to see the film. Stupid, stupid, stupid! You never talk aloud of something you know you will not get permission. I was nine.

My request was denied. I still had a plan, because there was no way Francesca was getting her dress ripped off with me sitting in Language Arts or at recess. Why couldn't it be on just a few days later when we went on Easter Break?

I went to school that Tuesday morning with a small baggie of *Cream of Wheat*. I took a packet—dumped half in the bag and then fixed myself the rest. I made a very casual reference that I wasn't feel too hot. Did she buy it? She didn't react.

I asked to go to the nurse in the middle of lunch. The movie came on at one o'clock. It was like 11:30 or so when I activated my plan. She checked my temperature. I was fine. Before she could ask if I wanted to lie down, I told her I needed to use the bathroom which was in also the nurse's office.

I went in, pulled out the baggie of *Cream of Wheat*, dumped it into the toilet and made puking sounds. Loud puking sounds. The nurse knocked and asked if I was okay. I ran the water at the sink and opened the door to let her in. I needed her to look into the toilet. She did, flushed it and asked for my phone number. I needed to go home, she decided.

My mom was working, so her boyfriend came for me in his jacked-up 1974 Plymouth Duster complete with fuzzy dice hanging from the rearview mirror. He didn't say much, but he was annoyed. He said my mother wanted me to go right to bed. He had to go out and would leave me home alone until my mom got home from work.

That meant he was going drinking. He didn't work because of a previous heart attack and open heart surgery that made him a disabled veteran. I would be home with 30 minutes to spare and then I would be alone.

Me in the foreground and in the background the TV with no channel switch. The pliers were there I am sure.

He wasted no time leaving. Any problems, call my mom was his direction. His nickname for me was "Little Faggot" because I loved the "weird, gay movies." I didn't watch football.

We had an old 25-inch console TV. The channel dial broke off and we had to change channels with a set of pliers.

The picture above shows me in front of the exact TV at that time. I went downstairs, laid on the couch with a hand-crocheted afghan over me to look sick if anyone came home. There was no remote, so I had to be on alert as I would have less than 30 seconds to turn the TV off. If my mom walked through the door and saw *Mad Monster Party* on the TV, I was dead.

The movie started. Doctor Frankenstein sent out his invites, the monsters set sail, Francesca got her dress ripped off (I got off the couch and sat as close to the TV as I could) and Felix got the girl. No one came home.

Worth it.

My mom came home from work after five. I said I didn't have an appetite as she found me upstairs in bed. She sat down on my bed, still in her jacket and waited for me to confess. I asked "What?" She felt my head.

"Your being sick wouldn't have anything to do with that movie being on TV today, would it?" She felt again for a fever. Nothing. She stared at me, waiting for me to crack. I denied it all. Deny, deny, deny.

She knew. "You'll be grounded over Easter break for lying. No friends. No going out to play. Inside with no TV." Her tone was flat. She was calm. That meant she was pissed, but also I knew she didn't want the guy downstairs hearing her.

She never confirmed it, but she never told him I was faking it. He didn't care if I was sick, but he would've loved to smack me around for making him come to the school to get me. While I never told my mom of his abuse, I think these kind of things indicated she knew something. As said, he never laid a hand on my brother or me while she was around.

It might seem that I went way too long on *Mad Monster Party* and before I share my final memory of this movie, I want to remind you as we walk this road that all of these set up the historical context of the entertainment I consumed. It lays out what was in my life and why I responded to the genre the way I did. I won't be so in-depth for each film.

While my mother's boyfriend's pet name for me was "Little Faggot," I was just "faggot" to a lot of the boys in school. I was the weird kid who liked scary movies. When I saved up to buy my first *Scholastic* book in fourth grade, I got

Dick Smith's "do it yourself" monster makeup book while everyone else got sports, the standard library faire or *Dynamite* magazine.

I borrowed an old fur coat from my grandmother, built a bunch of city buildings out of shoe boxes and used a useless Christmas toy skyscraper called *Earthquake Tower* as the main skyscraper to do a live version of the 1976 *King Kong* before Mrs. Deen's fourth grade class. I played Kong and donned a Halloween *Ben Cooper* company *Planet of the Apes* mask and that fur coat and pretended to scale the stupid plastic model skyscraper. I don't remember if I had a plot. What I do remember was Mrs. Deen giving me the hook ten minutes in and leaving my classmates wondering just what the hell they watched.

> My memories of King Kong were all about my mother. She just loved him; we would sit in the motel quarters (where I grew up) and tell everyone to shut up!
>
> We would cry over poor Kong every time! When we went to Universal, she was in her glory! We rode the Kong ride over and over. They were great memories for me.
>
> Linda Rapattoni

None of this helped my image and confirmed the label of "That kid" which went hand in hand with "faggot." The other guys shook their heads when they looked at me from down the lunch table, their eyes looking right at me. I was *that* guy.

I became best friends with Michael in fifth grade. He might be the first person I can describe as "droll." He had a sharp, sarcastic sense of humor fused with a rapier wit and intellect. Although I was called "gay" and "faggot," I didn't *really* know what it meant other than I was supposed to "like guys." Michael came from a wealthy family and was gay. I didn't know it then and didn't care. This was a decade before he would come out. He made me laugh so hard, I would ask him to stop just so I could breathe, and that's all that mattered.

We shared the same taste in movies, loved old film stars and schlocky horror. Michael loved kitsch and camp. We talked about Doc Shock, the horror host on WPHL 17 in Philly. He went along with my elaborate Godzilla fantasies about a monster buried in the slate quarries around us. He watched *Mad Monster Party* because I told him to and he pretended for years to like it. He stood by me when I hyped the film to my fifth grade homeroom. I talked about it to anyone who would listen, saying it was the greatest movie ever. I neglected to tell them it was in "Animagic" but it was on over the coming weekend and they should all watch it.

A number of them did. Two of the most popular guys in our class made sure to view it. I had no idea I had that much credibility. It didn't matter. Whatever I had was spent that weekend. The following Monday I was verbally assailed. "You didn't say it was a stupid puppet movie!" Another bemoaned, "It's like "Rudolph" ("The Red-Nosed Reindeer") and it was stupid!" The biggest insult: "It's a little kid's movie, you faggot."

There was no coming back from it. Michael was the only one who gave me any props. "The catfight was funny," he chuckled in his monotone, sardonic delivery. "They made cat screeching sounds." He followed that observation with this *Riff Track*-style comment.

There was a scene where Count Dracula takes a hors-d'oeuvre and smells it. He says, "This chopped liver smells fishy!" Phyllis Diller's Monster's Mate corrects him by exclaiming, "It's not the chopped liver, Count. It's the pickled salmon! Yuk!" and points to The Creature from the Black Lagoon standing nearby. Michael recreated the dialogue, only his punch line changed Diller's to: "It's not the chopped liver, Count. It's ME!" He did a Phyllis Diller laugh.

I had no idea what he meant by that. I was eleven and didn't know shit about sex. I was getting a boner because an animated puppet got her dress ripped off.

That's also how the word "Catfight" came into my lexicon. Michael gave it a name. I learned the reason was girls clawed each other, shredded clothes and screeched like cats. You learn something sexist every day.

Francesca's dress ripping joined the ranks of Spanky's mom in "The Little Rascals" short, "Beginner's Luck" losing hers onstage in front of a crowd, or the cute blonde lady losing her skirt in front of a dance party thanks to Curly's antics in *The Three Stooges* short, *Three Smart Saps*.

My brother and I got matching cassette recorders for Christmas that year. I used it to audio record Channel 9's showing of *Mad Monster Party*. I sat in a chair by the console TV speaker, the recorder held up, capturing it all. I was quick to flip the tape, hoping that would come during a commercial and got the whole thing.

My mother's boyfriend, only months from his fatal heart attack, sat half-drunk in our black "pleather" recliner watching me and the movie. He would shake his head once in awhile and give a disgusted, pained smile. He was wondering if my mother was worth it to have such a faggot stepson.

I took the audio tape and drew the film, comic strip-style on the endless supply of paper my biological father would get from his bindery. My "graphic novel" consisted of black and white pencil drawings that were crude and lacked style. I couldn't wait to get to the catfight scene and draw that.

I called *WOR-TV* Channel 9 in New York City to see if they could make a "photo novel" of *Mad Monster Party*. Could they take scenes from the film and print them into a comic book kind of format? No one there that I spoke to knew what I was talking about. Ironically, that kind of thing would be popular for a few seconds in the 80s.

Mad Monster Party would lead me to *Abbott and Costello Meet Frankenstein*, allowing a safe, light passage into horror. *Mad Monster Party* opened the door to explore the *Universal* classic monsters, to learn the names of the actors who played them and appreciate the parodies even more.

No single person would have more impact on my love of horror than Nanny. She would have such an influence that my first feature film, *The Fields* would be all about her. The pic below is of her at our mountain cabin, chopping wood with a hatchet.

That was Nanny.

"BE MORE AFRAID OF THE LIVING THAN THE DEAD."

 Nanny was salty and farm-raised. She spoke her mind, even when it didn't help the situation. She had the mouth of a truck driver and very little scared her. This is why she loved horror movies. They made her laugh. I remember her in her chair, cigarette in hand, illuminated by the blue-gray TV light, chuckling and loving the "horror shows" that we both watched.

Nanny also knew how these movies were made. She introduced me to *Creature Double Feature* and the litany of 1950s schlock aired on the weekend afternoons and nights. She told me how Boris Karloff was placed under pounds of makeup, how his back was ruined by the braces and rods used to make him walk so stilted as The Monster. Those giant boots had lead weights in them. She told me of Lon Chaney and how he filed his teeth, put fish hooks into his skin, glued fish scales to his face all to get the iconic looks he did for his films.

By the time I was eight years old I knew the names of Karloff, Lorre, Price, Cushing, Chaney, Lugosi, Carradine and more. Nanny watched *Mad Monster Party* with me and told me all about Phyllis Diller who voiced the Monster's Mate. That's how I found out Diller was a comedienne and Nanny pointed her out to me on the old "Dean Martin Show" and "Flip Wilson" and our absolute favorite: "The Carol Burnett Show."

I understood parody and satire better—seeing how Karloff resembled his "Animagic" counterpart in *Mad Monster Party* and not only how The Monster's Mate resembled Diller, but also *The Bride of Frankenstein's* Elsa Lanchester. Nanny was living horror education.

32

She filled in a lot of my younger years' horror gaps and was a living, smoking behind the scenes commentary when I watched these films. She also filled in my life, substituting a calm home life as I stayed with her often as my parents' marriage fell apart. Nanny picked up the pieces, and without exaggeration, helped raise me in my younger years equal to, if not more, than my own mother.

My grandfather, Harrison Kline, was nicknamed "Hiney." Hiney took one for the team in marrying Nanny, but to marry her and stay married...God bless him.

Hiney was "Pop Pop" or "Pappy" to me. Pap would often turn down his hearing aid or remove it to tune out Nanny, sometimes with unfortunate results.

"What the fuck did you get a birdcage for?" Nanny screamed at him after we came home from a trip to the store. "I said *BAND-AIDS* you dumb fuck! Not birdcage! We don't even have a fucking bird!"

He bought the birdcage because that's what he thought he heard. If Gladys wanted a birdcage, she was getting it. He followed orders. Life was easier that way.

Pap built a cabin by himself in the Pocono Mountains in the early '70's. It was a little, two-bedroom cottage for him and Nanny to retreat for weekends and holidays. It was in the middle of nowhere above Monroe Lake and that's just what he liked: peace and quiet. Now if Nanny would give him some of that. He did not approve of her showing me "all those scary movies. He's a kid." That's the closest I heard him get contrary with Nanny.

He walked the cabin property with me one evening and showed me a drain field for the coming septic system. It was a large, gravel filled pit with white PVC piping snaking all through it. We stood on the embankment looking down in silence at this giant hole when he turned to me and gave me a smile.

"You know what, Boo-Boo?" (His nickname for me) He pointed down that hole. "I could kill your Nanny and put her down there and no one would ever find her."

I considered what he said. Before I could respond, his face crinkled up, eyes became slits with a smile that wrapped around his head. He had this raspy, deep laughter like the old cartoon dog, Muttley. He tousled my hair as I laughed with him. That was our little joke.

Pap's sick sense of humor didn't take a break over the holiday season. Over the next several years, he would come running into the house after dark on Christmas Eve after

firing shotgun blasts outside, his gun in hand pointing to the ceiling.

"That's the last time that fat bastard is on my roof!" he announced.

I wailed, which sounded the alarm for Nanny, who rushed in like a momma bear. "Hiney, for Christ's sake stop telling the kid that!" Nanny would calm me down by telling me what an asshole I had for a grandfather.

This was the guy who was concerned about the horror movies I was watching.

Our sources for horror movies were Channels 17 and 29 out of Philly, Channels 11, five and nine out of New York and "The CBS Late Night Movie."

Before the cabin, before moving to the farmette where a real horror would play out and inspire *The Fields*, we lived on a rural road in Northampton County. It's here where I remember sitting up late, watching the variety shows Nanny loved: Dean Martin, Flip Wilson, Carol Burnett, and then "Chiller Theater" on WPIX Channel 11. *Chiller* introduced me to Roger Corman, and Channel 48 gave *Hammer* films and Vincent Price.

I would sit up late, Pappy having gone to bed sometime after the news and before "Carol Burnett," with a late night TV dinner called *Libby Land*. It had frozen corn, some kind of processed chicken and some kind of gooey shit dessert in a tin that went into the oven. No microwave ovens then, tin foil over-the-topof a tin serving tray.

35

The Astounding She Monster comes to mind. I hid my eyes behind a pillow and watched some glowing woman walk around and kill people just by touching them. One of them, if I remember right (I have not seen the film since 1972) was an old lady that reminded me of Nanny. The alien woman neck-pinched her and made her scream as she died.

Fiend Without a Face tortured me. Brains with antennae and spinal cords could turn invisible and leap onto victims--sucking out their brains or some shit like that. All I knew was the stop-motion critters were scary and could turn invisible. Again, the old farm couple bore more than a passing resemblance to Nanny and Pap. The invisible things made a heartbeat sound and people groped for their necks, and fell to their knees dead.

I didn't know at the time that making your monsters invisible saved considerable money in the budgets. All I knew was the ability to turn invisible made these things terrifying.

"The CBS Late Night Movie" had a higher quality horror. I don't remember much 1950s drive-in horror on this channel. Scarier, color 1970s grindhouse-style horror came after "Mannix" or "Barnaby Jones." In addition to horror, I got my introduction to the *Planet of the Apes* films which Nanny also loved.

I discovered movie ads could scare me too. While a few over the years would creep me out, the earliest TV spot for a theatrical release was Larry Cohen's *It's Alive.* They showed nothing from the film, played creepy nursery music, and

pushed in on a basinet lit on a black set. Something horrible dangled from the basinet—a small clawed hand and you would hear the baby cry as the narrator told us there was something very wrong with the Davis baby.

I hid my eyes, clasped hands over ears and buried my face in a couch pillow or just left the room. This one haunted me so much that if I even heard the commercial from another room, I plugged my ears.

"Be more afraid of the living than the dead," Nanny would tell me. I think in her mind this was to make me less scared of the movies she loved. She made it clear I should fear whack jobs like Charles Manson in the real world and not some ghost, rubber monster or an actor running around in makeup.

"The CBS Late Night Movie" would introduce me to *Bad Ronald*, an obscure, social horror movie that showed scary things aren't always in the forms of bats, wolves and monsters. Sometimes they were neighborhood faces. Be more afraid of the living than the dead.

Bad Ronald had its roots in the whole Manson fallout. A socially awkward, parentally compromised young man kills a young girl after she taunts him, and mom hides Ronald in a room in the house, sealing him up to prevent him being taken away by the police. Mom dies unexpectedly. A new family moves in, not knowing Ronald is still in his hidden room behind their walls. All you needed were some old men sitting outside a general store asking, "Where's the liver, Ronnie?"

This was a whole new kind of horror for me. Nanny expounded on her incredible knowledge of all things criminal and awful, gleaned from the news and tabloids. She would tell me worse stories, real stories during the commercial breaks. *Bad Ronald* did more than scare me; it made me see the world differently at the age of seven.

Nanny randomly asked during one of the commercial breaks if I knew why we hadn't seen our neighbor, "Old Man Bender" in awhile. She had this thing with affixing "Old Man" in front of the old men she knew. We knew an "Old Man Williams" an "Old Man Shoemaker" and an "Old Man Ralph." She never used "Old Lady," maybe because she was one.

The Benders lived next door. While they seemed ancient, they were likely in their 60s. Mr. Bender was tall, with a full head of *Bryl-Creamed* grey-white hair. He smoked cigars and cigarettes and loved washing his 1963 *AMC Rambler* in a tank top. The car stood out to me a decade later, as Peter Vincent in Tom Holland's 1985 *Fright Night* drove an almost identical car.

Mrs. Bender suffered a series of strokes that left her slow-speaking and with a voice that sounded more like a deep frog croak. Her voice sounded like a special effect, and the closest I can equate is Froggy from the later *Our Gang* comedy shorts from the 1940s. Her croaky voice was slower, thicker and downright scary to a little kid like me. Both she and her husband were smokers.

Nanny and Pappy didn't visit much with people. Pappy worked, Nanny kept house and watched me. Our big social outing was Friday night to "the store" (meaning one of several local department stores all now defunct). Pappy occasionally talked to Old Man Bender about cars or had a beer with him, and watched him wax his *Rambler*. Nanny would bring "things from the garden" to Mrs. Bender and that was about it for socializing.

Only now something was wrong. She decided to tell me during the commercial break of a movie that was scaring the piss out of me. She dragged on her cigarette, shook her head and grumbled, "He's got fucking cancer."

Keep in mind; I was seven, maybe going on eight. My only real experience with death was that gerbil. I asked what "fucking cancer" was and her definition came out like this: "It eats you up inside."

Jesus Christ! He had something *eating* him alive from the inside? My mind went to the brain creatures in *Fiend Without a Face*. She said it would kill him. He was dying and there was nothing the doctors could do. She worried about what Mrs. Bender would do and how she would keep up around the house with all of their property. "Sonofabitch smoked fuckin' cigars." She tapped the ash from her *Taryton* cigarette onto the floor ashtray by her chair.

Bad Ronald came back on and that was it. We were back to the movie and that conversation was forgotten, by Nanny, not me. I went to bed with images from the film, and of something awful eating Mr. Bender's guts.

The following week we went to the Bender house.

Nanny made some stew with vegetables from Pap's garden. Mrs. Bender opened the front storm door and let us in. She wore these black nylons that seemed a little too baggy. Nanny and I came into the living room and sat down. Nanny made it clear we couldn't stay long but Mrs. Bender said we could stay as long as we liked. It was a welcome break from taking care of her husband.

Nanny neglected to tell me that Mr. Bender was dying at home. I thought he was in the hospital. I remember being terrified that a man, who had something eating him alive from the inside out, was somewhere in the same house with me. This was a real-life horror movie. Could the cancer get into me? Could it eat my guts the way it was eating his?

Before you laugh at that, Nanny would tell me old wives tales of "earwigs"- those bugs with the big pincer stems on their ass, and how they could crawl into your ear and eat your brain while they tunneled through to the other side of your head. I grew up believing dragonflies (she called them darning needles) would sew my mouth up with their long abdomens if I told a lie. Now Mr. Bender had this cancer killing him. Could it get me?

I had to go to the bathroom and tried to hold it until we left but Mrs. Bender just kept croaking and Nanny listened, often punctuating the conversation with a "Jesus Christ" or something like that. I asked to go, and Mrs. Bender told me the bathroom was down the hall.

Their home was a little two bedroom cottage-style house with an upstairs that might have been an attic bedroom. I went down the hall and past an open door. It was their bedroom.

Mr. Bender was in there. The curtains were drawn but the daylight still came through in grey, diffused lighting. He was on his back, some kind of tube inserted into his neck. Looking back, it might've been a trach? He was always a thin man, but now he was a scarecrow. His thick grey-white hair seemed thin, flat and greasy, pasted to his skull. His cheeks were sunken, his mouth open and eyes closed. He had no idea I was there.

I could hear him breathing, or maybe it was an oxygen tank? I just remember a tube or pipe entering his throat, surrounded by cotton gauze and tape.

I went to the bathroom and never looked back into the room when I returned. I left with Nanny and that image of Mr. Bender in that bed.

He died a month later.

The Man, Bad Ronald, Charles Manson and The Fields

If you skipped my intro to this book, you missed the background on my first feature, *The Fields* that starred Cloris Leachman and Tara Reid. One of our weekend TV show routines was "The Mary Tyler Moore Show" and Nanny's favorite character was Leachman's Phyllis. Decades later, the Oscar-winner would portray my grandmother in my film.

Nanny and Pappy moved to a small farmette surrounded on three sides by miles of corn. I am not talking a few rows, I am talking IOWA corn deep. My summers were spent at Nanny's house surrounded by these fields.

Gladys and Hiney rented a small three bedroom home in the middle of nowhere because they liked it that way. They had a few acres for Pap to grow his giant garden (that produced way too many tomatoes, squash and beans that rotted every fall) and lots of room for me to play on.

A giant Weeping Willow dropped giant sticks that formed the shapes of dinosaurs and mutated monsters intent on destroying the world. I alternated between being Godzilla and "Ultraman," waging battles against the enemies of mankind in the back yard.

Wintertime was the best time to be Godzilla. I would build large snow Tokyo's and wade through them in my heavy, padded snowsuit. I belched out radioactive breath as my atomic vapor and pretended I was melting down the Japanese army that tried to stop my advance. I still do it on occasion. Thanks to endless Saturday creature feature-type shows, I watched every *Godzilla* movie to date by the time I was ten.

Nanny and I watched "Creature Feature," Philly's Dr. Shock or New York's *WPIX* 11's "Chiller Theater" (the opening to the show was a horrifying claymation, six-fingered zombie hand that rose from some blood swamp while a demonic voice moaned "Chilllllllerrrrrr!") late at night. I'd hide my eyes as she laughed and hooted and explained how they did the special effects and soon I was sitting alongside her without having to hide from the *Chiller* logo.

Doctor Shock came on Saturday afternoons with "Horror Theater" and later "Mad Theater." His real name was Joseph Zawislak, a professional magician. His catchphrase was: "Let There Be Fright!" He hosted guests who brought on animals and he talked of different careers. Doc Shock was known for featuring his daughter, Bubbles, who softened his original Lugosi Dracula image.

Not the first horror host, nor the last (*Svengoolie* got plenty of inspiration from Doc Shock, including his rubber chicken gag) but Doc Shock made semi-scary horror films fun. You knew you were going to be okay because little Bubbles was on the show. I watched her grow up along with me. The formats for his shows changed. *Horror Theater* lasted 13 weeks and was cancelled. A fan letter campaign brought him back and magic tricks and other variety show stuff were integrated into the format. All in all, Doc Shock had three shows: "Scream-In, Horror Theater and Mad Theater."

The good doctor focused on monster movies like *Godzilla* or the cheese-fest Roger Corman *I Was a Teenage...* type of monster films. Sometimes creepy, sometimes scary, they were safe overall. Doctor Shock pretended he wanted to scare, but he was just a birthday performer for *The Addams Family*. What scares me is he died of a heart attack at age 42.

It was during the doc's "Scream-In, Mad and Horror Theaters" I caught Corman's *Attack of the Crab Monsters* with those giant, silly yet simultaneously sleepy-eyed, crabs that talked telepathically.

I would hide my eyes in the couch pillow when Michael Landon transformed into his teenage werewolf, drooling that pudding out of his fanged mouth. The teenage Frankenstein was a bit more ghoulish and pieced together and looked nothing like Karloff's monster. This was before I understood copyrights and trademarks.

IT Conquered the World creeped me out with those floppy, flying starfish, the "Annoying Orange"-faced monster released from beneath it. It was just creepy enough for a little kid, but a few years older and you'd be laughing at that shit. I'm sure the origins of the eventual "Mystery Science Theater" could be traced back to similar programming.

IT! The Terror from Beyond Space was fun and set the stage for *Alien* and the coming Summer of 1979 that would scare the shit out of me. Doc Shock made me cry when he showed *20 Million Miles to Earth*—when Ray Harryhausen's

Ymir, a poor Venusian alien monster brought back to this planet, killed a circus elephant, and then when the Ymir was blasted from the top of the Roman Coliseum by the US Army.

The good doctor introduced me to the giant ants of *Them!* The high pitched sound of their communications stuck with me all through my life. At one point, in my 30s, I was at a state fair and some kiddy ride's guns sounded just like the ants from *Them!* I turned to my brother and at the same time we exclaimed "Them!"

Them! was different. It wasn't played for schlock. It had an A-list name (Edmund Gwenn from *A Miracle on 34th Street*), good script, solid budget and Oscar-worthy effects. Doc Shock didn't heckle it like he did some of the Corman and *American International* stuff.

Creature Double Feature played two odd monster films that stick out in my childhood memories: *The Giant Tarantula* and *The Monolith Monsters*. Channel

29 was known more for the giant Japanese monster movies. While Doctor Shock showed the original 1955 *Godzilla: King of the Monsters* with Raymond Burr, Channel 29 ran the other *Godzilla* films, especially *Godzilla's Revenge* which appealed to me at that time as a bullied kid.

I got my first real brush with death during a late-night viewing of *The Killer Shrews* on Channel 5. If Nanny had not been there I would have died. I took one of those purple plastic Easter eggs, popped it into my mouth. The longer, more cone part of the egg popped off as they were split. It lodged into my throat, sealing off my windpipe.

I panicked, unable to breathe. Nanny was in her overstuffed chair, feet up on her hassock. She moved fast, and it was one of the few times she wasted a cigarette. She grabbed me by the arm and hoisted me up. Her hand clapped me on the back several times to dislodge the plastic egg. She said I turned blue and knew I was choking because I wasn't making any sounds. When the back-slapping didn't work, her index finger and its sharp nail pushed into my mouth, at the side. It felt like she sliced me on the inside of the cheek and throat. The picture below is the exact chair and place in the house where this happened.

Her finger got in there, and dislodged the egg. I gagged, sucked in air. She shook me, forced me to look at her. She was staring in my eyes, asking if I understood her. I nodded, crying fast and panicked. She didn't hug me. She didn't say it was going to be okay. She got up to get me water and let the movie play. Nanny went into her "Jesus Christ, kid, you almost died! You never put those goddamned things in your mouth! You don't put shit in your mouth except fuckin' food!" She went through her entire fear catalogue.

The reality was she was scared. It was one of the few times I saw her so frightened and rattled. There would be two more moments coming.

Back to *Tarantula!* and *The Monolith Monsters.*

They used a real tarantula for the monster. It had this eerie visual effect. It worked and was coupled with this odd spacey kind of sound that the spider made for some reason. I can still hear it.

The mad doctor who created the giant tarantula is what scared me. He was a victim of his own experiments and transformed into this mutant that made me hide my eyes whenever I watched. There was a scene where he woke up in bed in striped pajamas, and it took me back to Mr. Bender in his bed, dying from the cancer that was eating him alive. This was part of the 1950s "Big Bug Era" where either atomic testing or something in a lab was to blame for the sudden growth of insects and lizards. The projection work in *Tarantula!* still stands out and the makeup effects on that mad doctor were really effective for a drive-in monster movie. It also happened to be Clint Eastwood's big screen debut as a fighter pilot.

The Monolith Monsters was a weird one and a boring one. Someone thought it would be a good idea to make a monster movie where the monsters were giant growing spikes of silica. The "monsters" turn everything around them into stone. All I remember was the things growing bigger and falling apart over this western cabin and the characters saying they were turning to stone. They blew up a dam and salt water saved the day.

Maybe this seemed high concept at the time. Maybe the producers thought the public was tiring of giant Praying Mantises, Gila Monsters, grasshoppers and ants. The stones were alien (from a meteorite of course) but even for a young kid like me, this was a snooze fest. Points to the studio system for at least trying something different, but it just didn't work.

The Blob did work. The quick and cheap monster from space flick hit all the right notes with me. A blob of space mucus hitched a ride to earth on a meteorite and ate people by just absorbing them. Nanny told me some big actor named Steve McQueen got his break in the film.

INDESCRIBABLE...
INDESTRUCTIBLE!
NOTHING CAN STOP I

THE BLOB

STEVEN McQUEEN · ANETA CORSEAUT · EARL ROWE

·HARRIS · IRVIN S. YEAWORTH, JR. · THEODORE SIMONSON ₐₙₐ KATE P

FROM AN IDEA BY IRVINE H. MILLGATE   ●   A TONYLYN PRODUCTION · COLOR BY DE LUXE

"The Blob" was different. There was absolutely nothing about it we could identify with. Unlike Dracula or Frankenstein's monster, you couldn't bargain with it; you couldn't reason with it, you couldn't hide from it. There was no limit to its appetite and no limit to how big it could get. It didn't just want to kill you and eat you: it wanted to annihilate you -- dissolve you while you were still alive, and digest you into a gooey pink slime... break down everything that separated what's You from what's Not You until you simply didn't exist anymore.

That's pretty heavy stuff for a kid to come to terms with. I was scared of the Blob itself. I didn't think the movie itself was particularly scary; but I was terrified of the very idea of that hungry, shapeless thing crawling silently through the darkness. I didn't have to wonder what the monster under my bed was... I knew it was the Blob. It also taught me that you could enjoy being genuinely scared and disturbed by something, and that lesson really got me started on the way to becoming a true horror fan.

"The Monolith Monsters" were terrifying for much the same reason "The Blob" was terrifying: they were incredibly different from all the other monsters I grew up with. They were impersonal. Implacable. Unrelenting. Unstoppable. They grew larger than the biggest of the great Japanese monsters, but unlike the kaiju there was nothing lovable about them.

I felt there was something very wrong with a world in which the stones themselves started to grow, and move, and threaten you. Even touching them meant death, and that kind of death meant slowly, inexorably, turning to stone -- in effect, changing places with the unnatural thing that had killed you... and being aware of it as it happened. The worst of it was the scene in the back of the truck, which made it plain to us kids that even children like us were not to be spared.

Most horror and sci-fi flicks of that vintage stopped short of showing children in actual danger, but "The Monolith Monsters" was a disturbing exception. I lost a lot of sleep imagining what would happen if those living rocks ever did land on earth.

Will T. Laughlin

50

I would watch the 1988 remake of *The Blob* over a decade later, as a movie theater manager, not expecting much as the original wasn't high art. Instead I was surprised with a solid cast, great script and fantastic practical special effects. Chuck Russell's remake was an example of what happens when remakes were done right. It could have set the bar low, but instead aimed high and hit the mark. My only complaint was not enough of Candy Clark, one of my favorite genre actresses who got blobbed way too soon. Clark wasn't really a "Scream Queen" or a femme  fatale like Fiona Lewis. Instead, she was this "every woman," the realistic character we can get behind and root for. I was excited whenever I saw her listed in a film. Candace Clark is like Harry Dean Stanton…no movie can be totally bad if Candy Clark is in it. She is one of the most underrated actors in the industry.

Philadelphia was the horror pipeline to our little house in the corn. I had no idea that this little house in the corn would become my real-life cabin in the woods.

It was now the mid-70s. Charles Manson and his family had their death sentences commuted to life in prison. The horrors of their killing sprees were documented in the book *Helter Skelter* and there was talk of it becoming a movie. It would be a whole new genre of horror movie for me. The nightly news seemed to have the Manson Girls on all the time and Manson seemed to have something to say to the American public. I didn't understand at the time that Manson translated into ratings and marketing for the coming TV movie.

Nanny knew what they did and she described it to me in gruesome detail whenever Charlie or his girls appeared on Walter Cronkite or John Chancellor's broadcasts. She started her accounts with a disgusted, mournful, "Jesus Christ…" and then went into the butchering of Sharon Tate, the LaBianca's and "how they wanted to cut out that poor actress's baby but didn't have the time."

Charles Manson was like *Bad Ronald.* He was a monster with a real human face. While the kid from *Bad Ronald* didn't resemble Manson (he was cleaner cut) the parallel was there—the dark American youth thing. I was yet to be introduced to Norman Bates but *Willard* was around the corner thanks to "The CBS Late Night Movie." Some people's kids.

I was at the age of understanding that there were real monsters out there. Death was taking tangible shape. Mr. Bender withering away took things to a new level. I remember *smelling* death in the Bender house. It was a sick smell, whether from stagnant air, or just gases or odors given off by Mr. Bender's body as it went through shut down. The Bender house smelled of soup, pot roast, shit and death.

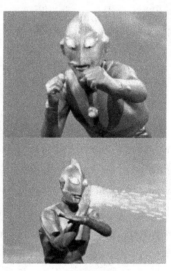

Our farmette was made up of the main house, a small cottage with two bedrooms downstairs and one upstairs in what was likely an attic at one time. A one-car garage sat right outside. The back yard was lined with the Weeping Willow and apricot or peach trees. I can't remember exactly what they were, but I know they leaked an amber resin that stuck all over me when I climbed them.

The corn rows started right at the edge of our backyard. Pappy built a cinder block fire pit to burn the trash. He took over at least 100 feet of lawn for his garden. The corn stood like the wall in *King Kong*, separating us from the outside world. There was our yard and beyond it was "out there." The fields.

Nanny warned me and wagged her finger. Her command was a scared bark: "Stay outta the corn! Jesus Christ, you get back in there we'll never find you. When we do find you, you'll be dead and all puffed up and black and the crows will have pecked your fucking eyes out."

She used a similar scare tactic to keep me out of the lake by their cabin in the Pocono Mountains. She couldn't swim. I think she felt the best way to keep me safe was to scare the shit out of me.

The incident that inspired *The Fields* started with a stick.

I don't know how long I was oblivious to the rustling in the corn around me in that backyard. I was playing "Ultraman, Johnny Sokko and His Flying Robot" or "The Space Giants," with the Weeping Willow branches, saving Tokyo once again. This was a lot better than thinking about the nightly news clips giving updates on the Manson Family.

"Mothers lock up your children because we're coming for them," one of Manson's whacked out girls told a TV camera. The media replayed the coverage of their spree and arrest to build-up hype for the new movie that chronicled the steps that brought Manson and his monsters behind bars. It was now 1976 and *Helter Skelter* was now a TV movie. It was a whole new kind of horror movie for me…because it was real.

I fought monsters in Nanny's backyard. Charles Manson was a real monster and I was sure he was going to get out of jail and hunt me down. The constant replays of interviews, telecasts and headlines terrified me. Images of bearded, crazy-eyed Manson with a swastika carved between his eyes were intercut with girls with shaved heads, singing together on city sidewalks and telling anyone who would listen how "Charlie" was innocent and how society was the one that was all messed up.

One afternoon I noticed something bigger than me moving in the cornrows that bordered Nanny's yard. I stopped playing and listened. If I fought my way to one end of the yard, it seemed like something followed me up and down as I fought Rodan, Ghidorah and a variety of "Ultraman" bad guys.

Whatever was in there was about six rows back. Anything past two was invisible.

"Hello?" I called into the corn. I didn't go into the rows and stayed at the edge of the grass as if held back by some kind of leash. "Hello?" I was answered with wind and rustling corn. Take that, Jamie Lee Curtis; I was calling into the darkness a good year before you.

"That sonofabitch was in the corn all those times," Nanny said later after it was all over. She talked about "The Man." I was convinced "The Man" was Charles Manson. That was going to be the original title for *The Fields*.

The real terror started a few nights later after I went to bed. I had my own bedroom in Nanny's house. She would tuck me in around 10:30 or later (depending on when her "shows" were over. She loved her detective shows: "Barnaby

Jones, Mannix, Columbo" or her comedies like "Carol Burnett, Bob Newhart or Mary Tyler Moore"). She would then head off to bed.

The house was quiet save for the occasional car that passed by on Kesslersville Road.

I slept in a giant bed that smelled like soap and lavender and listened to the crickets outside, replaying the funny skits from "Carol Burnett" in my mind or fantasize about Marsha Brady. She would hold my hand on our amusement park or beach excursions and we sat together at the giant family table as Alice served bad jokes.

One night, as I slipped into a pleasant, "Brady Bunch" induced sleep, a low pitched, rumbling hiss of air expelled through the screened window only four feet from my bed. It was a massive exhaled breath that seemed to go on for minutes.

"NANNNNNNYYYYY!"

Something on the other side of the window raked its fingers over the mesh screen in a manic spasm. The fingernails made the metal threads of the screen sing in bright, quick jabs racing wildly over the dark screen.

The real Gladys, my Nanny in the actual house that got terrorized.

I saw the red ember of Nanny's cigarette in the dark. The room lights clicked on and the scratching stopped. She stood in my doorway holding a small pistol.

"What the hell was that?" Her teeth bit down on her *Taryton* cigarette. Her golden hair was tight in pink plastic curlers. "Hiney! Some sonofabitch is outside the fuckin' house!"

Pap was behind her, loading his 12-gauge shotgun. What was left of his combed over hair stood up like tail feathers. He ran for the kitchen and the front door.

Pap returned a few minutes later without a shot fired. He found nothing outside.

"What do you wanna do?" he asked Nanny. "You want to call the cops or what?"

Nanny said she did and after the cops checked the place out, they too found no trace of anyone. They chalked it up to a peeping tom who got a bonus with a screaming kid to egg him on. They assured us it was most likely an isolated incident and wouldn't happen again.

"Was it Charles Manson?" I asked the one officer as I sat on Nanny's lap.

He told me no. Manson was in jail. This was someone who just wanted to scare us.

Nanny wanted me to play closer to the house after I told her I thought the Man might be in the cornfield. "You don't go into that cornfield." She would repeat lurid stories of kids taken in stores or locked in freezers to suffocate and that I didn't want to end up like that. "That crazy bastard could take you into that corn and we would never find you!" She would point her cigarette at me. "He could do all kinds of horrible things to you and your pappy and me would never be able to get to you in time!"

That was enough for me.

I played under a maple tree right in front of the house by the road and on the steps in front of her shanty porch. I replaced Weeping Willow monsters with a shopping bag full of plastic dinosaurs that Nanny bought on one of our Friday night jaunts to "the store."

I went into the corn. That's what people in horror movies do. They go into the place they're warned to avoid. Whether it's Jamie Lee Curtis going into a house of death or Kim Darby going into the basement or Danny Lloyd sneaking into The Overlook's Room 237, it's part of the horror formula.

I turned to use the Weeping Willow as my marker. It was tall enough but the deeper I went in, the taller the stalks seemed to grow, and they soon blocked out the back yard.

In *The Fields,* the directors opted for a more dramatic find. I did not discover a body. I did find a bloodstained mattress stuck with a bunch of spent hypodermic needles. There was a number of porn magazines scattered all around it. That was the first time I saw such hardcore images. I ran back the way I came and followed a straight line right into Nanny's back yard.

The Man returned a few nights later. This time he attacked the living room windows, scraping the screens like mad and banging on them with his fists so hard they rattled in their frames. We were watching the "CBS Late Night Movie" and one of the *Planet of the Apes* films. I went hysterical, running for the safety of the stairs. Pap went into his military vet mode and charged out into the night brandishing his gun and this time fired off several shots.

"Did he kill him?" I called to Nanny. She stood with concern in the doorway that led outside to the closed-in shanty porch. "Nanny, did pappy kill The Man?" I repeated.

She waved a quick hand for me to hush. She looked worried about Pap being out there in the darkness. After a while he came back into the house shaking his head.

"Sonofabitch ran into the cornfields. He's using them to move around." He laid the gun down on the table. If Pap couldn't get him, who could? After all, Pap killed Santa Claus.

Nanny heard a week or so later that a family a few miles up the road got a visit from The Man. He did the same thing: scratched their screens and pounded on their doors. Pap was right, he was moving through the cornfields.

I pictured this shadowy figure starting at sunset, slipping into the corn as he made trajectories for our house and the neighbor's. He did not come every night, and seemed to space out his visits. A few weeks he never showed at all. Then one night he scraped the screens or pounded on the front door until I screamed. Pap stopped toting his gun outside, and opted for turning on all the lights and waiting for me to calm down. The Man never returned after he got us up. One show per night. That was it.

Oscar winner, Cloris Leachman as my Nanny in *The Fields*.

I got up to pee one evening and to get a drink from one of the several green bottles of *7-Up* Nanny had in the fridge. The kitchen was lit by a single little fluorescent light over the stove. It lit up the whole kitchen in pale blue diffusion.

I grabbed the big green bottle of *7-Up*, took a swig and placed it back inside. Nanny used one of those little rubber bottle sealers that required strength and skill to use.

I turned to go back to my room and the front door caught my eye.

Did Nanny lock it?

Did she lock the big deadbolt that Pap had put on there?

What if she didn't?

I thought it was best that I checked. I shuffled to the door.

It occurred to me that The Man could be on the other side of the door. He could see me in the kitchen because of the stove light, but I couldn't see him. I was determined to make sure that the door was locked.

The floor was cold under my feet and my heart was beating in my throat as I stretched my hand out to the knob.

The door shook in a sudden spasm as something beat on it from the other side. BANG! BANG! BANG! BANG! My hand snapped back. I screamed.

My father decided to drop in on the house after his late shift from the bindery a few nights later. If the cops couldn't do anything, maybe he could. He drove a 1966 *GTO* and rumbled up the driveway sometime after two in the morning to check out the house.

Pap slept in his rocking chair with the shotgun over his lap. The shanty screen should have been locked. One night he forgot.

It took a lot to shock my father. If he was taken by surprise, he recovered fast. That's why he gunned the gas pedal, slamming it to the floor, to run down The Man who had leapt from inside the shanty porch and into his headlights. The fucker got inside and my grandfather was asleep just feet from him. What would have happened had my dad not pulled in?

A guy in jeans and a hooded jacket raced from the car's lights for his life as the tires kicked up gravel and bore the car down. He dashed beside the garage.

My father took the car into the yard, seeing that The Man was heading for the safety of the corn.

He ran into the rows and my father followed, the big muscle car divided the rows of corn like Moses parting the Red Sea.

"The bastard was running like a rabbit," my dad said later in Nanny's kitchen. He was laughing as he told the story. "He was zig-zagging back and forth, left and right, trying to ditch me."

Nanny fretted about being billed for the damaged corn. My father didn't run down the man, but I did believe him when he said he would have run-killed him.

"Next time, I'll shoot at that bastard as I run him down." He was serious.

It culminated about a week later. Nanny and I stayed up to watch *Island of Terror*, on "The CBS Late Night Movie." Peter Cushing battled some crazy looking monsters with long necks and turtle shells that could somehow climb into trees. They ate you from the inside, sucking your bones, I believe. Great, more death from the inside out.

Just as the film ended and the routine of shutting off lights got under way, the windows shattered. Large chunks of farm dirt, the clumps of wet earth that got baked in the sun after plowing, were like boulders landing in the living room. Nanny was really scared this time, screaming for Pap, who once again was up on command, gun in hand and out the door.

Shots rang out in the dark somewhere behind the house. He came back in, a hand to his chest. "Oh my God are you having a heart attack, Hiney?" I was more scared this time than ever as I could hear the panic in Nanny's voice. It wasn't just the attack on the house; she was facing the prospect of losing Pap, who did everything for her. She was pondering her fate as she did with Mrs. Bender's. How would she "make a go of things?"

He sat in the kitchen, breathing hard. Nanny picked up the phone to find it was dead. He motioned for her to stop. It wasn't a heart attack, he told her. He believed that the surest way to die was go to a hospital. "Once you go in, you seldom come out," he would say. "You wanna get sick, go to a hospital."

A week or so later, at the dairy farm behind our house, across the fields, a man took some rope into the cattle stalls. He strung it over a rafter and jumped from a stepladder, and hanged himself.

We never heard from The Man again.

"The sonofabitch killed himself at that damned dairy farm. That was the bastard coming down here to the house, I'll betcha." I heard Nanny repeat her hypothesis over and over again to her phone network.

She talked of a farmhand at the milk farm who was given the name Eugene in *The Fields*. I don't remember his real name, if I knew it at all. The film's directors took creative license and selected an actor that resembled Charles Manson. In real life, "Eugene" was kind of tall and fat with a shaved head. Like Manson, there were some weird hippy girls that hung around at the farm. I don't know if they were connected to "Eugene" or not. Pap once upset them when he told me not to talk to them. The girl pointed at him. Did she mark us?

"Eugene" was very interested in me. He found me every time Pap brought me to the milk farm. He'd kick the conversation off with the same question: "You still like Godzilla?" Pap would find me and politely get me to come with him and away from "Eugene."

It all stopped after he killed himself. Or did the girls kill him? We don't know.

Nanny might've been right. She read his name aloud in the paper, but I never remembered it. He was and still is The Man, faceless and nameless.

Horror became personal during that fall of 1973.

While I would have done things differently had I directed *The Fields*, it is the most personal of all my films to date. When you watch those family scenes, that's as close as you can get to experiencing the memories in my head. It's that accurate.

Another historical checkpoint: aside from the political and economic issues that plagued the nation, the genre returned to environmental issues. *It's Alive* tapped into chemical contamination of our food, our water, air and medicines. *Day of the Animals* would use the hole in the ozone layer. *Squirm* would blame electricity for whatever made those killer worms surface. *The Hills Have* Eyes circled back to radiation. The end of the decade would see John Frankenheimer's *Prophecy* go full mutant (One I will discuss at length). We had Satan, mutants, economic collapse, military defeat in Vietnam, inflation, the fuel crisis, racial strife, environmental degradation and just to make it interesting, corruption in our government.

You know…the good old days.

THE UNIVERSAL BIG BANG

Sequels and remakes are not new things. The *Godzilla* films were the first that I remember creating some sort of loose "extended universe." I'm not so sure I like the term "extended universe." It's just a slicker, more intelligent term for "franchise."

The *Godzilla* films seemed connected until about 1975. There were only a few that mentioned events from a previous film. Overall, it seemed the 1954 *Gojira* and its bastardized, re-edited 1955 counterpart, *Godzilla: King of the Monsters* stood alone. There was the rarely seen *Godzilla Raids Again*. If you were sharp as a kid, you might catch Doc Shock screening it. The problem was Godzilla died at the end of the 1954 and 1955 films. The monster in *Raids Again* was a new Godzilla. To complicate matters more, they renamed it *Gigantis, the Fire Monster* and that screwed up the timeline further. For some reason, Godzilla's trademark roar was replaced by a generic, weird monster sound that seemed shared by his opponent, Anguirus as well. It was a rushed sequel and the marketing was a mess.

Most of the *Godzilla* films were stand alone movies, needing no reliance on previous stories. A few of the 70s films with *MechaGodzilla* were loosely connected, but overall you could drop into any *Godzilla* film in the 1954-75 Showa series with no problems. It was about monsters fighting and that was about it.

The 1984 *Return of Godzilla*, re-edited and released again with a now severely corpulent Raymond Burr one year later as *Godzilla 1985*, ushered in the Heisei series of films that definitely relied on sequel continuity and connected to the original 1954 *Gojira* to create a "Monsterverse" if you will. The Heisei series ignored all of the events after *Gojira* through 1975's *Terror of MechaGodzilla* when the series went into a ten year hiatus.

I wanted things to connect. I wanted other worlds, anything that was different than the world I was born into. *Godzilla* didn't really give that to me, and by the time the Heisei series started, I was a senior in high school and pretty much past the kid fandom I had for *Godzilla*. It also didn't help that these new, post-1985 films found no release in the United States until the 2000s. The series also fractured into other timelines with 1998's American *Godzilla* which was considered an abomination by American and Japanese fans alike. Toho responded with *Godzilla 2000* aka *Godzilla Millennium* which started the *Millennium* series of films which performed fine enough but didn't ignite real excitement. The stand alone *Godzilla GMK (All Monsters Attack)* in 2003 attempted to resolve the 1998 American *Godzilla* film by dismissing the monster that attacked New York as Godzilla. It was another monster.

In 2004, the 50th anniversary of the original *Gojira, Toho* gave us *Godzilla: Final Wars,* a quasi-remake of *Destroy All Monsters* (They even pitted Godzilla against his 1998 American counterpart derisively nicknamed "Zilla" who was trounced by the Japanese Godzilla in less than 30 seconds) that set the handoff for a second American attempt to make *Godzilla* into a big budget Hollywood blockbuster.

This would give us Gareth Edwards' 2014 *Godzilla* which kicked off an official *Monsterverse* that has culminated at the time of this writing with the post COVID box office reviving *Godzilla vs. Kong.*

As a kid, the closest I came to finding an extended universe was in the DC and Marvel Comics universes or the *Planet of the Apes* series of films.

There was an exception. I found something close with the classic *Universal Monsters*. I might go as far as to say these films were the foundation of the eventual extended universes that *Disney* and other studios now desire.

It started with 1931's *Frankenstein*. I was maybe seven or eight when I saw it for the first time with Nanny. She served as my DVD commentary, and told me how this guy named Boris Karloff underwent hell with the makeup, suffered back injuries that would plague him all of his life. I'll talk more about the Jack Pierce makeup later.

I felt a kinship with the outcast monster, which was misunderstood. In the end he was bullied, harassed and hunted. All he wanted was to escape and be left alone. His demise by fire at the end in the burning windmill broke my heart. I knew, even at my young age, that I was watching something far better than the cheesy stuff Doc Shock threw at me on Saturday afternoons.

Nanny informed me there was a part two. There were MORE? Oh yes, she said. "They made a shitload of these." I fell in love with *The Bride of Frankenstein*. I was happy the monster lived and found a friend in the effete, weird Dr.

Pretorius. The best part was the Monster was getting a friend. Nanny told me how they created one of the most famous hairstyles in Hollywood history and how actress Elsa Lanchester suffered for her art. I also found out that Lanchester was later the Miss Marple-type detective in the comedy *Murder by Death* which made the film even funnier. Mind blown.

How could there be any more to the story when the Monster blew the castle up at the end, killing himself, his unrequited love and Dr. Pretorius who misled and used him?

Nanny told me there was another one! *Son of Frankenstein* picked up a few years later with the monster found in the ruins of the castle that blew up at the end of *Bride*.

I loved it! The worlds fit together! They MENTIONED the events of the previous films in each new installment. I was in this whole other world and I understood it! That's when Nanny took me further down the horror rabbit hole. The creepy criminal Ygor in *Son of Frankenstein* also played Dracula in that stand alone film! She told me that this guy, Bela Lugosi, was also supposed to be the original Frankenstein Monster but turned down the role because of all the makeup that would be on him. "The sonofabitch was worried no one would know who he was!" She laughed. "I'll bet he kicked himself in the ass after turning that role down."

I watched *Dracula* and sure enough it was the same guy, but there was no second *Dracula* movie. Nanny said they made one called *Dracula's Daughter*. Doctor Shock got around to showing it, but it turned out to be a letdown. There was no Lugosi Count Dracula and they didn't reference much from the first film. I loved that connectivity and was disappointed when it wasn't there.

Nanny introduced me to *The Wolf Man* when I was around eight and it scared the living hell out of me. The transformation of Lon Chaney, Jr. into the title character blew my mind. No blood, no gore, but the terror level for me was matched only by my sympathy for Chaney's Larry Talbot. He didn't want to hurt people and in the end he lost the woman he loved and his own father beat him to death with a cane topped by a silver grip.

Talbot's transformation scenes haunted me. The first few frames of the time lapse were fine, but once they added those teeth and that nose...all bets were off. I felt the fear climbing in me, and my hands were always ready to clap over my eyes.

The final step was when his eyes darted back and forth. When the transformation was done, Chaney would flick his eyes from side to side, his mouth would open showing those white canine teeth.

He would leap up, no longer the mild-mannered Larry Talbot. He was a monster and he would kill me if he had the chance.

My grandpa, Ronald Rewald, is the main reason I developed a love for horror. Before I was born my grandpa was sentenced to prison a federal correctional Institution on Terminal Island. My earliest memories of him were visiting him every Sunday and he had always been a massive fan of the Universal monster movies. During my time visiting him our routine was always getting food from the vending machine, sitting down at a table, and he would tell me stories he made up for me, usually involving one of the monsters from the movie.

The one that stuck out in my mind most of all was his particularly gruesome mash up of "Bambi" and "The Wolf Man." The first movie quote I ever memorized because I heard it so much (probably around age 5) was the line from "The Wolf Man:"

"Even a man who is pure in heart, and says his prayers by night, may become a wolf when the Wolfbane blooms and the autumn moon is bright"

I'll never forget everything he did to turn me into the horror lover that I am and will always think of him anytime I watch an original or remake of the old classic monster movies.

Whiskey Wasteland

There were more monster movies! While I watched *The Mummy*, that one didn't grab me as much as the others. Karloff was back and I was grasping the concept of actors playing different characters. *The Creature from the Black Lagoon* enthralled me, and while there were two sequels, I never enjoyed them as much as the original. They also did not play into the world of The Monster, The Wolf Man and Dracula.

Ghost of Frankenstein remained connected to the three previous films. It was not Karloff in the makeup and the performance was way different as Lon Chaney, Jr. played The Monster (He would briefly do it again as a pinch hitter in the lab scene for Glenn Strange in *Abbott and Costello Meet Frankenstein).* The film connected to something else coming up which really made the framework for eventual extended universes. I ate it up. This was popcorn horror.

Ghost of Frankenstein led into the mash up phase of *Universal's* classic monsters. Again, this is where historical context is important. By 1942, the Universal monsters were in decline. World War II was raging, the US was balls deep into multiple theaters of war. Movies took on a more escapist feel. The dark days of The Great Depression were fading from memory.

It is a fact that horror movies thrive during poor economic times. The basic reason for this is that people want to see others having a worse time than them. Seeing something horrible on screen provides context and perspective for one's own misfortunes.

The Second World War was won by the Allies in 1945 but by that time real-world horror was brought to the American doorstep. The classic *Universal Monsters* weren't scary any longer, and by the end of the war and the revelations of the atomic bomb, The Holocaust and the destructive toll on Europe and Japan, Dracula, Frankenstein's Monster and The Wolf Man paled in comparison.

There were now aliens and giant bugs and monsters created by very real atomic fallout. The Red Scare was upon us as Sen. Joe McCarthy terrorized Americans and upped our national paranoia. All of this was reflected in a new kind of horror in a country flush with victory after the most cataclysmic war in human history. Victory Culture horror had a very different texture and flavor than Great Depression pre-war horror.

The suits at Universal saw this too. They had these properties that, separately, were showing their threads at the box office. Someone had the great idea to mash them up. Combine them. Two for the price of one.

Frankenstein Meets the Wolf Man was born and so was the concept of "franchise" or more accurately, "extended universe." This hooked me. I was able to get more monster action with all new stories while sticking to the original canon that I loved and sucked me into the genre.

Picking up where *Ghost of Frankenstein* left off, Larry Talbot was somehow resurrected (How? Who cares?) and embarked on a search for Doctor

Frankenstein to cure him of his lycanthropic curse. This was weird because if being a werewolf was a curse, then that implied a supernatural cause. However, if you can "cure it" with medical processes, then wasn't that a physical ailment? It didn't matter. We will talk about the incessant need for minutia that the Internet will bring, later on.

Talbot had amnesia and this bothered me. He had a woman out there who still loved him. She could help, couldn't she? It was like when *The Bionic Woman*, Jamie Sommers, lost her memory of her love for Steve Austin, *The Six Million Dollar Man*. All of that happened around this age and THAT bothered me too. There was something about losing your life and everything you had but it was just out of reach. You could almost touch it.

The Wolf Man never met "Frankenstein." He meets Frankenstein's Monster (Now played by Lugosi in the role he declined years before). I've bristled since a boy when people called the monster Frankenstein. Frankenstein is the doctor who created The Monster. It's one of the oldest pet peeves of the genre.

Some of the storyline gets fucked up over the brain transplant thing from the last film (thanks to studio editing and interference), but in the end, The Wolf Man and Monster square off in another climactic ending where both seem to perish.

71

I delighted in this as a kid. This is what I wanted! Monster against monster! I found there now CROSSOVER films with *House of Dracula* and *House of Frankenstein*. They weren't really sequels from the original Universal storyline but some of the characters returned as well as the original actors. The problem was Lugosi still wasn't back as Dracula. John Carradine stepped in for the undead Count. It worked fine but it wasn't the same feel as the other films which had, for me, become a kind of horror soap opera.

Look at that lineup on the poster art. I love how they just list: "Hunchback" on the *House of Dracula* poster. However *House of Frankenstein* gives a "The" in front of their hunchback.

This leads me into *Abbott and Costello Meet Frankenstein* (again, a misnomer).

The comedy duo of Bud Abbott and Lou Costello graduated from radio to big screen films and helped carry audiences through World War II. Their teamups with The Andrews Sisters led them to meet some of Universal's other ghouls like Dr. Jekyll and Mr. Hyde as well as The Invisible Man. Nothing would approach the success of their "meeting" the Frankenstein Monster, the Wolf Man and Dracula in *Abbott and Costello Meet Frankenstein*.

Lon Chaney, Jr. returned to the role of the tragic Lawrence Talbot. Bela Lugosi donned the cape for the second and last time but Boris Karloff did not get back into makeup as The Monster. Glenn Strange stepped into the lead boots and did a creepy enough job.

Lou Costello felt the film would be a flop, and found the script to be unfunny and flat. The teaming of two diverse properties was just too alluring and the film was not just a hit, but became, for many, a gateway film into the horror genre.

By the time I saw *Abbott and Costello Meet Frankenstein*, I had a solid background on the monsters satirized, unlike my very young experience with *Mad Monster Party*.

Bud and Lou were on WPIX Channel 11 every Sunday afternoon at Nanny's. While a few of their films caught my attention, it was *Frankenstein* that I would always hope was that Sunday matinee movie of the week. I never found Doc Shock or any of the other creature features screening this film. I don't know if it was a rights thing or that because of its clear comedic tones, it didn't fit the format of matinee creature features.

The film had some genuine horror moments. Chaney's transformation into The Wolf Man still worked. The Monster hurled a beautiful doctor to her death through a giant window in the lab fight scene. It was just enough to let you know they weren't totally fucking around. And animation allowed us to see Count Dracula transform into a bat and back to his human form. It all worked and the film is considered to be the comedy duo's legacy. It is arguably their best-known (I am not counting their radio and TV versions of the *Who's on First* bit). When I chose young director Joe Raffa to helm my *6 Degrees of Hell*, he cited *Abbott and Costello Meet Frankenstein* as the movie that introduced him to horror and one of his all-time favorites.

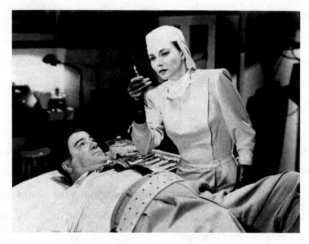

As I neared ten-years-old, heading to the fourth and fifth grade, I had a far better understanding of the genre and what inspired *Mad Monster Party*. The film was funnier as I got older because I was getting more and more of the inside horror jokes.

When *Bic* pens aired a commercial showing how tough their latest writing utensil was as The Monster freed himself from his ice coffin with a pen, I got the joke! The Monster was frozen in ice in *Frankenstein Meets the Wolf Man* and the narrator did a Boris Karloff impression and I got it!

This is why I emphasize the importance of more than just LOVING horror. One needs to understand its history and WHY things get made, WHY certain lines are important and WHY genres come and go, die out and circle back.

You need to know your U.S. and world history. You need to know your *film* history.

Bobby "Boris" Pickett's *Monster Mash* song made sense once I got what he was singing about. Pickett's Boris Karloff impression free-styled about mad scientist labs, Igor; and all the things that came with basic *Universal Monster* knowledge.

> *I always felt a sad kinship for Lawrence Talbot, the man who could never find a cure, who was always tormented by an aspect of himself that he couldn't control. He couldn't even die, even though he desperately wanted to. Dracula craves immortality. Frankenstein and The Mummy were indifferent to it. Lawrence Talbot, The Wolf Man, was doomed to be immortal. He just wandered through a black and white landscape, from film to film, just looking for peace. Even in a film like "Abbott & Costello Meet Frankenstein," the anguish just radiates from the character.*
>
> *Chris Caponigro*

The 1962 song, *Monster Mash* was featured on a novelty record of mine, along with other famous one-hit gag songs like "Purple People Eater, Itsy Bitsy Teenie Weenie Yellow Polka Dot Bikini" and others. The cover of the album no doubt evoked *Mad Monster Party* down to a chimp band instead of *MMP's* skeletal "Little Tibia and the Phibias."

All of this was far more than sitting down and saying: "Entertain me." Four chapters in and you have a pretty good personal background on me, my life and the times that shaped me.

My mother made me watch Nixon announce his resignation and then the news coverage of him walking out to Marine One and giving his famous "V" for Victory photo. The Kennedy's were dead. Martin Luther King was dead. Vietnam ended in 1975 when I was in third grade.

Manson was in jail and annually trotted out for a show's ratings boost. We went to the moon when I was almost two. I was three when *Apollo 13* had its trouble.

The economy was mired in inflation and OPEC had this country by the gas pump balls in 1976. The environment was in freefall and the Carter "Malaise Years" were upon us.

ABC scored a hit with its *Kolchak: The Night Stalker* in 1972. Based on two books called the *The Kolchak Papers* the intrepid reporter played by Darren McGavin, combined the Manson fallout with vampires. I was in kindergarten or first grade at the time and begged to stay up to watch it.

My mother relented. She wasn't Nanny, but she was also intrigued. I remember sitting in our East Bangor house while my father worked the late shift, and watched a Las Vegas serial killer exposed as a vampire by McGavin's pre-paranormal era investigator Carl Kolchak.

We watched on our 25-inch color console that needed those pliers to turn the channel. She popped popcorn. I sat with her on a large, black, plastic stuffed recliner after my brother was put to bed. Like Nanny, she would remind me it was all fake, but unlike Nanny, during the commercials, she would make light, fun talk and ask me how I was doing. There were no mental health checks with Nanny's horror viewings. She was hardcore and upped the ante by adding horrible stories of cancer eating neighbors from the inside out.

There was a quick *The Night Stalker* sequel called *The Night Strangler* and then someone thought it would be a good idea to turn it into a series and the whole thing vanished but not before creating a cult following. Chris Carter of the future series, "The X-Files" would take his inspiration from *Kolchak*. When McGavin was asked to guest star on the show, Carter wanted him to reprise the role, but the actor declined. A shame, it was a damned fine idea.

The original film and its sequel looked into the darker societal aspects where these monsters lurk. A few years later George Romero would explore these weird passages with his *Martin,* taking another askew look at vampirism combined with the serial killer motif. Martin was a little like Bobby looking for his liver.

CBS toyed with the idea of turning their hit 1979 mini-series *Salem's Lot* into a TV series but smarter heads prevailed. More on that later.

The original *The Night Stalker* TV film, was scary and fun even at my young age. It was just scary enough to make me come back for more. This vampire was not Bela Lugosi, and it opened my eyes to different interpretations of these monsters. *Hammer* would be the next step.

I couldn't wait to watch The Night Stalker because it was funny, terrifying and enjoyable. I developed a serious crush on Darren McGavin because I loved Kolchak so much. Nine-year-old year old me hoped that one day when I could write about the paranormal too. Hell, I even adopted a Kolchakism, Carl was a hero of sorts because he wasn't afraid to be different. He bucked the traditional reporting system and usually ended up ruffling the feathers of his peers, law enforcement and his stressed out boss, Tony Vincenzo. Here I am five decades later and I grew up to be an entertainment journalist who writes about the horror genre. So for every person out there made to feel weird for loving the offbeat and strange…embrace it. You never know where it will lead…

Susan Leighton

JUST THE SAME BUT DIFFERENT

Hammer Films was my introduction to the world of copyright and adaptation. The British studio came about around 1935 but it embraced the horror genre with 1955's science-fiction hit, *The Quatermass Experiment*, adapted from famed sci-fi/horror Nigel Kneale's (who would become one of John Carpenter's favorite writers and pen the original story for 1982's *Halloween III*) BBC serial. The film was a surprise hit and a sequel followed and the studio was on its way.

Think of it as the British *Blumhouse* with its own lineups and takes on the classic monsters. The studio was known for its lush, oversaturated color photography and embracement of the Gothic look for set and art design.

My horror diet was 100% American. I had yet to sample foreign horror. The closest was *Island of Terror*, which I mentioned before. That film stood out because it reminded me of my encounter with Mr. Bender. The monster movies and American 1950s big bug films were nothing like this stuff from *Hammer*.

There was a weird feeling of dread in watching *Hammer* films. They had a nastier edge or if they could smile, they had a shit-eating grin. While *Abbott and Costello* and the *Universal Monsters* and their spin-offs had some bite here and there, they were overall safe and not too scary.

Then I saw *Frankenstein Created Woman* from *Hammer* and wasn't just scared, I was *disturbed*. I never found Bela Lugosi's Dracula all that scary. Weird, yes, but the old film felt old even when watching it as a kid. The soundtrack was scratchy with pops and hisses and the special effects weren't all that special. It

was Lugosi who carried the show and he was the only Dracula I knew aside from Grandpa Munster or Alan Swift's Count from *Mad Monster Party*.

Christopher Lee's take on Dracula scared the hell out of me. The blood was vibrant red and there something terrifying when he went full Prince of Darkness in the climactic scenes. Lee was imposing as the calm, well-heeled Count but when he went batty: the teeth, the wild bloodshot eyes, and this fucking guy meant business.

"The CBS Late Night Movie" aired a number of Hammer *Dracula* films. That's where I caught most of them. The others came out of Philly syndicates like WPHL-17 and Channel 48. They seemed to focus more on the Edgar Allen Poe adaptations. I don't remember *Hammer* piping in from New York. They could have, I just don't remember.

I'll bring in the historical context of the *Hammer* era soon enough.

Hammer stands out because they took well-known properties and made them their own. I didn't understand copyrights, trademarks or the legal end of things. It was through school that I learned *Frankenstein* and *Dracula* were books. When I read them by fifth or sixth grade I found they were very different than the Hollywood film versions.

This was around the time I discovered *Jaws* the book was different from *Jaws* the movie and a whole other world was opening for me.

The Frankenstein Monster itself is not under trademark or copyright. The MAKEUP by original artist Jack Pierce is under legal protection. The image of *Universal's* Frankenstein Monster is protected. Mary Shelley's *Frankenstein* novel,

like Bram Stoker's *Dracula*, are in the public domain. You can make your own film; just don't create your monster or vampire in the image of flat top, bolts in neck Karloff or try to duplicate the distinct and unique visage of Lugosi. The same goes for any of the *Universal Monsters*.

Hammer tapped into the counter culture 1960s vibe. They adapted their own versions of Frankenstein's Monster and Count Dracula. I can't say they really scored on the Frankenstein front. Peter Cushing made a terrific Baron

Frankenstein, but the monster attempts were a mish mash of gross and kitsch. Christopher Lee played the monster in just one film with mixed results. Seven *Hammer* films featured variations of the monster and never came close to stealing

Karloff's thunder. The only monster to stand out for me was *Frankenstein and the Monster from Hell*, which featured a tripped out *Teenage Frankenstein*-ish mish mash of body parts in a gruesome creature. It's almost as if *Hammer* knew their monster wasn't working and tried to top things each time to get to the final incarnation. In some ways, this version was the most primitive and nightmarish of them all.

Hammer was known for its stylistic innovation. The filmmakers used over-saturated primary colors, grandiose sets with props that fit right into the color schemes. The studio took a turn at adapting and running with a number of Edgar Allen Poe properties.

Roger Corman's *American International Pictures* did similar, with *The Raven* being the standout for me. Boris Karloff, Peter Lorre and Vincent Price headlined a film shot in 15 days and was such a staple of Saturday creature feature afternoons, I mixed it in with *Hammer* films product as American studios tried to copy the *Hammer* formula for bright, red blood, gore and bizarre violence.

Corman's *The Raven* was so off the wall, that when it came time to tackle Poe's original poem in sixth grade, I found it a struggle. While Lenore is there in the poem, where were the dueling wizards? Where were any of the characters? I had Price, Karloff and Lorre stuck in my head and wondered just how the hell they got that film out of this poem?

I did go on to recite Poe's *The Raven* to my sixth grade reading class and that was no small feat. I memorized it on bus rides home from school with a friend who was tasked with her own poem recital. I was able to get through the entire thing but today can recite only the first several stanzas.

Back to *Hammer*. The cinematography was so good with these films that it betrayed their low budgets. While I said that Lee's Monster didn't connect with me, it did with many, making *The Curse of Frankenstein* a huge hit in England and eventually the United States.

It was Lee's turn as Count Dracula that terrified me. There was something so visceral in his performance. Even when he was the low-keyed Count, there was menace.

I sat up late to watch these films with Nanny who laughed out loud and chuckled. She enjoyed these films so much. Little did I know that watching all of this *Hammer* content would set the stage for the impact 1985's *Fright Night* would have on my life.

There was something so visceral about *Hammer's* take on *Dracula* that even when I saw Frank Langella's 1979 film portrayal (I never caught the Broadway production, which Lee apparently was offered by rejected) I still associated Lee with the role. This would go on to the *Star Wars* prequels. It wasn't Count Dooku (What a terrible, silly name) that I saw when Lee showed up in *Attack of the Clones*. It was Count Dracula and although I was an adult, the boy in me still saw Dracula's menace from those old *Hammer* films.

The stakings brought true horror and sexual stimulation. Cushing's Van Helsing or some other hero hunted down The Count's buxom female minions and aimed those wooden points between robust cleavages ensconced in white to bring forth a gusher of bright red *Technicolor* blood. Cushing made the Van Helsing role his own but his Baron Frankenstein overshadowed the monster. Cushing redefined the baron's image in horror to the point where Peter Cushing WAS *Hammer*.

The fangs, the eyes, the screams, *Hammer* eclipsed *Universal* for my monster movie fix and gave attention to my hormones. The women they got were beautiful - and hot. *Hammer* knew how to work it, giving you just enough, but leaving you wanting to see so much more. When Cushing positioned his stake, I always hoped he would have to pull the tops of the gowns apart, to expose the breasts and drive that wood home.

Lee's death scenes were show-stoppers. I compared them to Lugosi's death in the Browning film which occurred off screen no less. *Hammer* was giving you everything *Universal* hinted at. To be fair, the films were thirty years apart, but when it came to Dracula, no one did it like Christopher Lee.

The other *Hammer* horror monsters, like the Frankenstein's didn't do it for me. *Universal's The Mummy* with Karloff made little impression. *Hammer's* made less. Many disagree but I remember as a kid not being so vested into *Hammer* monsters unless it was "Dracula".

> *My parents took me to see "Bram Stoker's Dracula" on opening night. I wasn't sure what to really expect for the movie at the time.*
>
> *I remember sitting in the theater and I was hooked. When we left the movie theater, I left knowing that I wanted to tell stories. Especially vampire stories. I remember walking home that night and the ideas were already starting to come. I could feel the shadows watching me and my family and it just felt right. It was the first movie that actually spoke to something inside me.*
>
> *Frank Besser*

The clearest memory I have to sum up *Hammer's* impact was sitting up late on the couch, Nanny across from me in our house in the corn. The blue light of the TV filled the living room. Sometimes it was ice cream, other times a candy bar or popcorn, but a snack was always in reach.

Nanny smoked, munched and looked over to confirm I watched and enjoyed. She gave her commentary on how they did effects or asked me if I thought something was funny. Sometimes I told her I did just to placate her, but inside I was scared.

"That Chris Lee," she marveled, "he's a better Dracula than Lugosi. Yep."

She told me that Lugosi died from drugs and what a mess he'd become and how he died broke. He did a bunch of bad movies like *The Devil Bat*, (which I saw on Doc Shock) and *Bride of the Monster*. She brought up *Plan Nine from Outer Space* but informed me he died while they were making it and most of the film wasn't really Bela. They used someone else.

"What a fuckin' shame," she lamented.

Years later I found much of what she told me was pretty accurate. When I saw Tim Burton's *Ed Wood* my memories went back to Nanny. When Bela's funeral scene came, I wept as much for Nanny (she died in 1994 from cancer) and those memories as I did for the sad life of Bela Lugosi.

The real horror lesson from *Hammer* was adaptation and innovation. The studio's films showed me how there could be different takes on material and opened my eyes to variety in my horror consumption. It was okay to try something different.

Some will say Lugosi is the one true Count. Thanks to Christopher Lee, I was able to accept other incarnations of Dracula and other Counts and vampires into my life. They all didn't require Hungarian accents, slinking around decrepit castles. As much as I would not care for Coppola's *Bram Stoker's Dracula* when it hit theaters, I did appreciate Gary Oldman's take on the vampire. That's because of *Hammer*. The studio allowed me to enjoy Frank Langella's 1979 turn at the role as well.

Hammer made me fall in love with Tom Holland's *Fright Night* and also appreciate it. I knew every trope Holland was giving. Most of all, as I will point out later, I got the eulogy Holland wrote with his script. It was the end of an era, and at that time in my life, that context would be powerful.

Hammer allowed appreciation for *The Night Stalker* and eventually *Salem's Lot* because it was their Dracula that made me go back to find *Nosferatu,* the original Max Schreck silent vampire film which inspired *Salem's Lot's* Tobe Hooper to fashion his Mr. Barlow.

Hammer studios opened my eyes and taught me you could do so much more than just remake the same. You could take core material and run with it.

It was *Hammer* that introduced me to Nigel Kneale through their *Quatermass* films and this in turn would connect me with John Carpenter and *Halloween III* years and years later. *Hammer's* success inspired Roger Corman, who in turn inspired me with his low budget miracles and as a result, introduced me to Richard Matheson, one of the most gifted writers I've experienced. I discovered Roger Corman, I found William Castle, John Cassavettes, Jack Nicholson, George Romero, Dario Argento, Mario Bava, and bringing it full circle, John Carpenter.

Hammer led me to Corman which in turn led me to Doug McClure of *The Land That Time Forgot, Humanoids from the Deep, Warlords of Atlantis* and *At The Earth's Core.* I would meet Sid Haig, Robert Englund, Rick Baker; before they blew up: Alan Ormsby, Frank Hennenlotter, Lloyd Kaufman and *Troma Films*, Larry Cohen, Samuel Z. Arkoff and on in this "horror free association." That is *Hammer's* legacy to me.

The importance of historical context underscores the importance of these films and the times of their releases. *Hammer* was the counter culture studio—bucking the censor boards and "morality panels" that censored horror and called for "standards." They embraced full color blood red and gore. They wanted audience to be uncomfortable and they did it by stylizing their films, turning the stories on their ears and the level of their success was not just measured in box office, but in American imitation.

By the early 1960s, *The Beatles* changed music. Kennedy would be assassinated, touching off the real counter culture revolution. Civil rights would hit a boiling point. Vietnam was taking the U.S. down a rabbit hole and the entire world order seemed upside down.

Hammer tapped into all of this unrest and UNEASE. That's what I can say about their films: they made me uneasy because they tapped into the uncertainty of the times.

The studio was recently resurrected but in name only. Without the historical context that contributed to the original studio's success, the product has been flashy, well-produced but does little to evoke the unease and weirdness that the 1958 through early 70s product brought us.

Another cycle of technology and social change transpired since the last original *Hammer* studio film. A lot has happened and the new *Hammer* has not plugged into it. It's now well-made content and not much more.

This is why 1985's *Fright Night* will resonate so hard with me.

JAWS CHANGED EVERYTHING

1975 was The Summer of the Shark. *Jaws* changed everything. It invented the summer blockbuster, changed the benchmarks for financial success and how movies would be made, distributed and merchandised. The film would inspire an eight-year-old me to abandon all interest in dinosaur archaeology and want to be a filmmaker.

Jaws was the movie that made me want to make movies. The novel shot to the top of the bestseller list in 1974 and went into development as a major motion picture. This is not a book on the making of *Jaws*. You can find plenty of online resources chronicling the film's journey from book to movie.

Jaws was my first adult "chapter book," something that wasn't *Charlotte's Web*. I was eight and couldn't get through it but the cover scared me—the shark

shooting up like some monster phallic symbol for the naked woman. I got through a page or two and would get back to the book when I got older. The horror of not knowing what was coming from me below in that dark water was enough for me.

The commercials inundated TV. Look back at the *Jaws* trailer, it's terrible. We now have "trailer reviews" that pick apart every piece of minutia. Most trailers these days give away everything to the point where there is almost no need to watch the film…the entire movie is either encapsulated into one long trailer or over a series of trailers, the whole plot is revealed. Trailer "reviewers" like to analyze and comment (there is a big difference between a comment and a review) but they don't offer any type of intelligent critique. Instead it's fan gushing or snark that constitutes their "trailer reviews." The original 1975 trailer for *Jaws* was too long, badly paced and tells way too much. The nostalgia falls on "The Voice of *Jaws*" narrator, Percy Rodriguez (whose "James Earl Jones before he was Darth Vader and the voice of *CNN*"), narration went on to do all three trailers for the sequels. His voice haunted me as much as any of the images on my TV.

> "Jaws", is the movie I've seen more times than I can remember.
> **WoodsWalkerX**

I would try to imitate Rodriguez's voice in the shower. While others sang, I tried my hand at his narration, remembering so much of the dialogue and doing my best deep, baritone voice before puberty kicked in.

I told my mother I was going to ask Nanny to take me to *Jaws*. I'm not sure if she saw this as a threat (knowing Nanny rarely left the house save for her once a week Friday excursion to "The Store) but she relented. I was terrified of the water, not because of what could eat me, but because of drowning. I went unconscious at Monroe Lake up at the cabin. Whether I was thrown in by my father or I leapt in to impress some sunbathing girls (according to my father), but I technically drowned and never wanted to go near the water again.

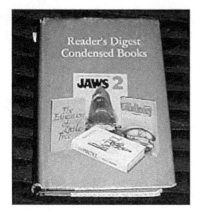

I would later get kicked out of Red Cross swimming lessons the summer between third and fourth grade for choking the swimming instructor after she tried to drag me off the pool ledge and into the water. She got black and blue marks around her neck for that move. She handed my mother her money back and told her to never return.

We went to East Stroudsburg to the single-screen *Grand* theater. It would become a porn house in the 1980s and then disappear altogether. The line went around the block. Little did I know we would be moving to this area in just three years and the *Grand* would become a major fixture of my mainstream theater fun.

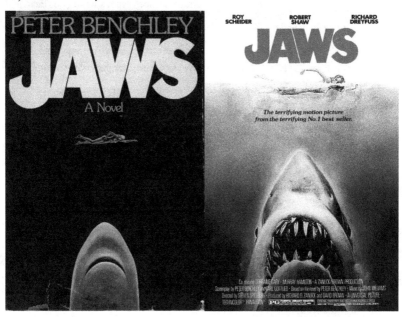

The poster dominated the outside Plexiglas frame and then another on the wall where I got the chance to stare at it with some dread and excitement as we waited in line. It was a literal blockbuster line.

"You sure you wanna see this?" My mom smoked a bunch of cigarettes as we waited for the first show to let out. I was sure. We drove 30 minutes to see this movie.

I don't remember much of the 1975 theatrical experience except the ending. The audience stood and applauded at the end. When Roy Scheider's Brody said his famous line before blowing up the air tank, the audience cheered as the fish exploded all over the screen, but when the end credits started to roll, they stood and applauded, cheered and whistled. I never saw this happen before.

When we got into the car, my mother asked my thoughts. I said, "I want to make movies." She went right along with it. If that's what I wanted to do, then that's what I was going to do. The movie scared her and she had plans to never watch it again. I heard years later that *Jaws* was X-rated for anyone over 30. Kids ate it up.

I wanted to make people laugh, scream and cheer. That's what the theatrical experience does for people. It is a culturally binding experience. We are all the same in that dark theater—politics, religion, none of it matters. When a film touches something in us, we react as group. There is nothing like hearing a full movie house scream or laugh or applaud in unison. It's an incredible experience and *Jaws* was the first film to bring that to me.

I tackled the book again in fifth grade as *Jaws 2* was released the summer

of '78. We didn't have *HBO* and VCRs were still a ways off for the average consumer, so my only memory of *Jaws* was from eight years of age. I dug out my mother's paperback novel because *Reader's Digest* was running a condensed version of the coming novel for *Jaws 2* by Hank Searls. Before I embarked on *Jaws 2*, I needed to read *Jaws*.

Hammer helped me with the pop culture shock of Benchley's novel compared to the movie. I saw the film first and the book was nothing like it. Aside from the basic premise of a shark terrorizing a New England town and the characters of Brody, Quint, Hooper, a mayor not wanting to shut the beaches, there was little about the book that connected with the film.

I was surprised, even on the cusp of my teens, at the sexual content of Benchley's story. There was a line about boys grinding their pelvises into the beach sand. Ellen Brody screwed around with Hooper. Brody and Hooper hated each other. Quint played the two against one another. There was a mafia subplot, with Brody's cat killed to send a message as the mayor was balls deep with mob connections. One scene went into great detail of Brody urinating that seemed to last forever, while another had Ellen changing in a gas station bathroom before a rendezvous with Hooper, dabbing perfume on her crotch.

It was more soap opera than horror. The shark attack imagery paid off, but at the end, the shark just died. It was harpooned to death and tired out from Quint's barrels. Brody watched the beast slip into the depths, Quint's body spinning alongside it, tethered to the shark like Ahab strapped to his white whale. The book was a letdown and the fifth grade literary critic that I was didn't feel it was all that good.

Jaws 2 was a different story. I made sure to re-read the condensed Searls' novel before seeing the film that June of 1978. It was the only thing I wanted to

see. I had *Jaws 2* fever. I stopped whatever I was doing when the ads played on TV. My heart raced as the fin broke the water behind the water skier and the ads promised action, a lot of shark, and some hot girls.

It was the summer of 1978 and on the heels of *Star Wars*, the previous year. The guy that abused me and my brother was now dead. Things were different. Maybe better.

I'm going to backtrack. At the end of 4th grade that guy's handgun went off in his holster at a local shooting range. While not fatal, the stress of the gunshot triggered another heart attack not long after. While my mother had us at Nanny's for a Fourth of July picnic, he dragged himself out of bed, down the stairs and made it to the kitchen phone where he called for an ambulance.

The heart attack was just another symptom of congestive heart failure. He was taken to Walter Reed veteran's hospital in Washington, DC where a second open heart surgery repaired what could be done. Aside from a heart transplant, he would die; they just didn't know how long he had.

I never said a word to my mother about the slaps, punches, broken tooth or dragging my brother up the steps by his hair. His verbal abuse was always there, but worse when she wasn't around. He never laid a hand on us when my mother was present.

Nanny was sharp and knew something was going on and she told my mother that this guy hit us. My mother dismissed it. She didn't want to know.

The summer of 1976 was a deathwatch. He came home. A hospital bed was put into our living room and my mother, with nursing training, dedicated herself to taking care of him.

He was helpless, rarely leaving the bed. He lost weight and slept most of the time. My brother and I paid him very little attention and we were told to play outside as much as possible and when we ate, the three of us ate quietly at the table to make sure he wasn't disturbed.

We drove around in a Volkswagen Beetle with no front brakes. My mother would have to pull the emergency brake and pump it to help bring us to a stop sign. His Duster sat idle, as she was forbidden to drive it. We had a perfectly good, safe car, but the asshole dying in the hospital bed in my mother's house made it off limits to the woman who nursed him.

The term "lung tap" entered my lexicon as he had to go to a local hospital to have his lungs "tapped" to drain the fluid building up in them and the sac around his failing heart.

The last argument I heard between him and my mother ended with her saying, "I think you've been hitting my kids," to which that defiant fucker, as sick as we he was, said, "You don't know shit."

He returned to Walter Reed Hospital that August. My mother went down to be with him. I heard, but to this day, never confirmed, that they got engaged on his deathbed.

He never came home and died before school started.

I would hear my mother weeping, the hardest I ever heard her, behind the bedroom door as she picked out his service uniform for burial. I never confirmed her suspicions of abuse. Hearing her mourning so hard, that kind of revelation might just kill her.

He was the first dead body I ever saw. Mr. Bender didn't count, as he was in the process of dying. I never attended his service after the cancer ate him from inside out.

My mother took our hands. My brother and I flanked her as we approached the coffin. She held her shit together as best she could and asked both of us if we were okay. While I am sure we did not answer in unison, I do remember saying we were fine.

We were. My mother's mom, Miriam, would have us say our prayers before bed, the "Now I lay me down to sleep" template. When she left the room I would ask God to kill the man who was in the coffin in front of me that summer. I felt nothing about his death, except relief. I felt bad for the pain my mother was going through, but for me, I couldn't have cared less.

My mother brought someone new a year later in the middle of my fifth grade year. He was a co-worker with her at the auto parts warehouse where they both were employed. He was also ten years her junior. She was 29 and he was 19. What the hell was he thinking? I was on the defensive, expecting the abuse to repeat, but it never did. He was quiet, gentle and respectful of my brother and me. He treated my mother kindly and he soon moved in with us.

He was interested in my love of movies and encouraged it. We walked about *Jaws* and he bought me this large issue of a *DC* or *Marvel* version of *Star Wars*.

It would take a lot to trust him, but he made a good impression. My mother's parents were wary of the age difference and asked up front why a 19-year-old boy would want a woman almost 30 with two kids and a mortgage. Trust me, I will bring this back to *Jaws 2*.

It didn't matter. His entry into our lives couldn't have come at a better time. Fifth grade was also the year where I was called to the nurse's office after home room to find a girl I had liked in fourth grade sitting in the waiting room. We were both sent to talk to some counselor to discuss growing up without a father.

No one asked permission from our parents and my mother flipped when I told her how my day went. Her parent-teacher conference brought her home in tears when my fifth grade teacher said he expected little from my future without a male figure to help raise me.

Maybe that's what motivated her to find someone.

Fifth grade was a turning point. I was stepping up my horror passion. Someone had a novelized version of *The Manitou*, the Tony Curtis horror about a woman possessed by a Native American shaman who physically births from her spine. The photos in the novel held me in horror seeing this lump grow out of this woman's back.

We were a year away from *Fangoria's* 1979 debut and printed stuff like *Famous Monsters* or even *The Monster Times* were soon gone or vanished. Movie novelizations and their "dozens of terrifying pictures inside" became a new source for scary movie images.

Carrie's TV spots disturbed me the year before. The 1976 film painted the movie out to be some Argento-style, oddly lit film, showing mostly the horror of the prom massacre. The title would float over the TV screen. I found myself hiding my eyes or sometimes just up and leaving the room when the previews came on.

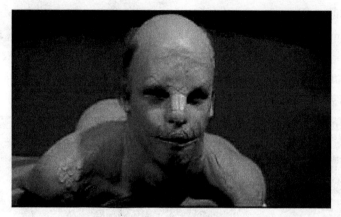

I would avoid the film for years until I finally got my hands on the book, which in turn would open a whole new door in the horror genre. I just remember a blood-drenched Sissy Spacek gliding through flames, out of the gym doors and Piper Laurie screaming, wielding a knife and at that time, that's all I needed to see.

I worked my way up the TV horror ranks after *The Night Stalker* with the cheesy *Sssss!* which featured character actor, Strother Martin as a mad scientist turning people into human-snake hybrids for carnival freak shows.

It had a bit of *Freaks* to it, especially the ending, and was important as it increased my horror tolerance. "Made for TV" was having a bit of a horror rediscovery. Steven Spielberg's *Duel* aired in 1974 and showed what could be done with little money and a creative director in the chair. It wasn't pure horror, but scary all the same and the folks at Universal were impressed enough to give the kid a crack at *Jaws*.

1972 gave me *Gargoyles*, a made for TV movie that was a lot scarier in the ads than as a full film. The afternoon monster matinee previews would show the scariest scene in the film as its preview to hook you. A barn housing skeletal remains of some horned, winged demonic thing comes under attack with a family caught inside. The preview hooked me and when I watched it, I was disappointed to spot the zippers up the backs (thanks to hours of Japanese monster movies and shows) of their suits. The gargoyles themselves were not all that threatening. It did introduce me to Bernie Casey who I wouldn't see again until 1984's *Revenge of the Nerds*.

1976's *Burnt Offerings* tapped into the whole demonic thing continued by *The Omen*. The Bette Davis theatrical flick premiered on *NBC* network television with horror stalwarts Oliver Reed, Karen Black. Nanny wouldn't miss it. I sat up with her one weekend night to watch it. We both agreed the creepy chauffeur guy was the scariest thing about it. The film had a flat, clean, TV movie look to it. It didn't chill me the way I had hoped.

My mother and I were watching "Burnt Offerings." My mother did not like horror movies, so I don't know why she decided to watch this with me. It was so out of character; maybe that's why I remember it so well.

The movie terrified me, especially the final scene, in which it is revealed that Karen Black's character has turned into the evil Mrs. Allardyce. The ending of the film, climaxed by Oliver Reed's character literally diving out of the attic of the house and landing on top of the family car, completely shocked and horrified me. To this day, it's one of the best conclusions to any horror movie I've watched.

A few moments later, I looked at my mother, who contorted her face into this strange, trance-like appearance and began to groan while saying over and over in haunting fashion, "I'm Mrs. Allardyce... I'm Mrs. Allardyce." I was about 12 or 13 at the time--old enough to know better; but my mother's performance scared me, even more than the scene we had just watched, to the point that I started to shake her in an effort to snap out of this trance. A few moments later, she returned to normalcy, smiled, and then started to laugh. Only then did I feel like I was "safe" again.

My mother died only a few years later from cancer, at too young an age. But I still have that memory, and it's a good one. Thank you, Mom, for that.

Bruce Markusen

Trilogy of Terror had Karen Black in a triple role that is best remembered for the Zuni Doll episode. Black is pursued about her apartment by a killer warrior doll that comes alive when the chain around its waist is broken. The pure energy of the scene held me as Karen fended off knife attacks before dispatching the little bastard in her oven with some unfortunate results. It made for a great and memorable last scene. It would become one of those movies years later that always came up with something like, "What was that movie where that doll was chasing that lady with the spear?" Few remember the other episodes, but the Zuni Doll is embedded in our collective unconscious. I have a replica in the window of my office as I write this.

TV was a stepping stone for horror in the 1970s. It allowed watered down clones of the scarier, bigger theatrical films. 1973's *Don't Be Afraid of the Dark* was another made for TV creeper that dug into my brain and had the balls to end with such a downer that seared deeper into my memories. The Kim Darby creature feature combined "the old haunted house" with monster movie as the sealed off fireplace was a gateway for these little walnut-headed humanoids to come forth and drive Kim batshit crazy.

This one got to me because of its ending with Kim kicking and screaming, dragged like some bagged big game to the hell hole in the basement. Her husband thought she was crazy, that whole 70s paranoia thing ran strong here. *Don't Be Afraid of the Dark* was a kind of low-rent *Rosemary's Baby* and the film that should've carried William Castle's name on the credits.

Sally wasn't pregnant in the movie, but the things wanted her soul. They wanted her to become one of them. It was this kind of assimilation horror that became the core of what would scare me. Monsters are one thing. Sharks aren't in lakes or pools or bathtubs. I know there aren't little creatures in my basement. Scary? Sure. A lot of it was, but the theme of "they want to make you like them," that shit was terrifying. It struck me on a level that other films did not. Monster horror, even supernatural horror was more visceral and didn't push the reality buttons with me. But when no one believes Sally in *Don't Be Afraid of the Dark*...that scared me.

By 1976 I had not seen *The Exorcist* or *The Omen*. Their time was coming, but The Devil didn't scare me like real-life paranoia. The best two episodes of the Rod Serling *Twilight Zone* that resonated with me and stayed with me as an adult were: *The Monsters Are Due On Maple Street* and *Eye of the Beholder*. Both segments had themes of conformity, and the consequences if one did not relent. It was the nebulous "Them." THEY were out there, and they didn't necessarily want to kill you…they wanted to absorb you. That's how I discovered the 1956 Kevin McCarthy *Invasion of the Body Snatchers* which took my paranoia to new heights because these sonsabitches got you while you slept.

> I was seven-years-old and the youngest of five kids. My brothers were watching a movie, and it sounded HORRIFYING. Not nearly as horrifying as some so I was not afraid but intrigued. I walked out of my room and stood in front of the TV. Either I was seen and taken back to bed, or I was not even noticed for a good period of time which allowed me to take in whatever it was that was happening.
>
> I saw Karen Black chased through her home by a savage little doll wielding his spear and slashing at her legs in "Trilogy of Terror." I was FASCINATED. I was seen immediately and taken back to bed and I was PISSED. I wasn't scared. I didn't lie there, like my mother thought I would, afraid to go to sleep because of what I saw. I was pissed because I wanted to see the rest.
>
> Mildred "Midi" Miller

The alien pods in *Invasion '56* didn't want to kill you. They made perfect replicas of you. Your smallest memories, the faintest scar or blemish on your body…your copy was indistinguishable from the real you. The only thing was different was that you had no emotions. This new entity sounded like you, looked like you, wore your clothes, even did your job, but it was merely an automaton—emotionless, devoid of joy, life, happiness, love…

This concept hit me at a young age. Maybe it had something to do with always being the "faggot" kid on the outside at school. I never quite fit in. No athletic skills, I wasn't a model— I didn't have money for the latest fashion trends (I wore my female cousin's bell bottom jeans and hand-me-down T-shirts to school). I didn't conform or assimilate.

Mad Monster Party solidified my dork/faggot image. My best friend association with Michael didn't help me either. We were the freaks and geeks.

Michael loved horror and the genre built a solid foundation for our friendship. We talked endlessly about horror movies like *Don't Be Afraid of the Dark*. By fifth grade Michael was the one who introduced me to *Rosemary's Baby*.

We made the commitment to see *Jaws 2* that coming summer of 1978.

In the meantime I did what I could to get through fifth grade. My marks were in the toilet, my mother was now dating this younger man. I still had zero trust for him. I dug deeper into horror, reading as much as I could about it and finding it on TV.

I got through maybe the first 20 minutes of *Race with the Devil*, which was not a made for TV horror but also tapped into the 70s paranoia that pervaded the genre at this time. I could barely watch the TV version. The terror of that group of motocross enthusiasts witnessing the human sacrifice and then pursued through the Texas (where else) countryside was too much. I knew the moment they met the sheriff that the guy had to be in on it. Then he drove out to the place in question without any directions and boom! He's one of THEM!

Trust no one. Not even the police. The anti-establishment movement still reverberating, through the country was clear in the horror genre.

Texas was for horror what Florida would become for the bizarre human freak show that would dominate Internet headlines. Bad shit happened in Texas in 70s horror movies. *The Texas Chainsaw Massacre* solidified this. The previews were terrifying and both my mother and Nanny let me know every time the TV spots came on that it was based on a true story. I still had no idea what that meant. It would take a few years to realize that "based on a true story" meant 70-95% bullshit. I won't rehash the Ed Gein story that it was very loosely based upon, but I can say that the TV ads prepped me for a hideous and gruesome film. When I finally saw it in on VHS in high school, I was more amazed at how TAME the movie was. It hardly lived up to the gruesome accounts I heard others tell. What I do know is those TV spots terrified me and gave me nightmares. One day I would sit across a dinner table with Leatherface and some of the cast as we prepped *Death House*.

Me with "Leatherface" Gunnar Hansen and some of the *TCM* crew at a party.

Think about the real horror of *The Omen*. Damien is the son of the Devil and bad things happened to the people who discovered this. Real horror is more pedestrian. It is the growing realization that a mother's child just might not be her own. Compound that horrific suspicion with the belief this changeling is trying to murder you, and you have great paranoia horror. Lee Remick's own husband gaslights her through the movie, all the way to her ending up in a body cast before Gregory Peck thinks it might be a good idea to come clean. Even then he doesn't with tragic results.

> *My mother took us to the drive in for a double feature of "Love Butcher" and "Texas Chainsaw Massacre." Scared the shit out of me. This was the late 70s or early 80s. I got jumped and beat up walking back from the mall after seeing one of the "Nightmare on Elm Street" films in the 80s. I was in middle school. We had to run on to some old ladies porch for protection.*
>
> **Bob Brydun**

Damien Omen II followed that same paranoid thread. William Holden's suspicions grow with every unfortunate death to culminate with a secondary horror—that his nephew is something inhuman and must be destroyed. How is Holden's character dispatched? His own wife is part of the Damien cult, and stabs him with the holy knives needed to kill the Son of the Devil.

> *I was 13 years old, the same age as Damien in "Omen II." Hell, we even looked similar, right down to our haircuts. Damien was undergoing an identity crisis, as was I. We were both shaking off the "innocence" of childhood and reckoning with who we were going to become. Like Damien, I was starting to get into trouble, although I never used supernatural powers to slice anyone in half with an elevator cable or crack the ice beneath their feet, but there were times when I wanted to. There was just something about the young teen Damien that I immediately recognized in myself. He didn't really want to be bad or evil, but maybe he couldn't help it. I didn't want that either, but at 13 years old, I was growing angrier and rebellious. I think I even checked to see if I had 666 growing in my scalp. Like Damien, I was changing as I entered my teenage years and, like Damien, I wasn't exactly sure what I was changing into.*
>
> **Chris Caponigro**

A standout example of 70s paranoia is *The Stepford Wives* but I am going to hold off here until the end of the 70s and my encounter with 1979's *Invasion of the Body Snatchers*. I think the context works better there.

Perhaps one of the best paranoia horror pieces that connects directly to *Jaws* is 1976's *Let's Scare Jessica to Death*. This quiet vampire film released quietly into theaters and quickly ended up on *The CBS Late Night Movie* where it creeped me out every time.

Directed by John Hancock, *Jessica* is fueled by the paranoia left over from the *Helter Skelter/* Manson era. Hancock would go on to be the first director on *Jaws 2* before being fired over behind the scenes politics.

Jessica puts a spin on the vampire legend, focusing on Zohra Lampert's Jessica, a leftover flower child heading to Massachusetts with her husband and a friend in a hippy hearse no less, to take over a creepy New England house on an old orchard. Somehow they're gonna make a go of it and help Jessica recover from a nervous breakdown (we never find out what caused it).

A pretty, red-headed drifter girl named Emily has been squatting in the house. Both men are attracted and Jessica is game to be kind, but we know there is something very wrong with this girl, and she has a stalker look in her eyes for Jessica.

Soon the whispers start, a bizarre blonde girl who may or may not be in Jessica's imagination appears in the damndest places around the farm, a half century old family photo found in the attic has a girl that uncannily resembles Emily.

No one believes Jessica. She's sick. We never really know what happened to her, it was just this mysterious "breakdown." This is what scared me. Hancock made it pretty clear this wasn't in her head. I felt awful for Jessica as she watched her husband fall under the seduction of the vagrant Emily. The girl pretended to befriend Jessica, but the whole time was working against her. She was stealing her husband. She was taking their friend. Soon they would all be against her.

This is how I felt in school. I got Jessica. I knew what she was feeling. My mother's boyfriend hurt me many times but I couldn't tell anyone. They wouldn't believe me. I knew what it was like to have the monster get into your house and invade your life.

The town's residents wear scarves around their necks, talk little and stare a lot. By the time it's all over, Jessica is on the verge of losing her mind again. A homoerotic encounter at the nearby lake reveals Emily to be a vampire and Jessica has to fight for her life to escape with her sanity and her life.

The first horror film I can recall seeing, at least in part, was "Let's Scare Jessica to Death." There was a drive-in not far from our home that played a lot of older films during the summer.

My mother hid me in the back of a VW 72 Beetle with a blanket over me while a few of her female friends came along. For nearly 40 years the images, just flashes of memory of the whole event stuck in my mind about that night.

The water scene was especially memorable, along with a mouse being killed were a few things that flashed in my mind when I thought back on it.

Just two years ago I was going through "Shudder" on a mission to find this lost film. I was pouring through 70s horror films in an effort to prove to myself it wasn't my imagination. After many weeks of trying my perseverance paid off and about thirty minutes into it I realized, "This is the movie!"

You know how a scent can give you that perfect memory recall? In this instance, this film did the reverse for me. As it reached the scene with the mouse, I immediately could smell the menthol cigarettes, that distinctive VW Beetle smell, a chili dog and the light aroma of cheap "Avon" perfume that one of my mother's friends wore.

In a way I wish I hadn't found it. While it proved what I remembered, and it did give me a lot of nostalgic memories of an era--seeing it as an adult decades later ruined the feeling it gave to me as a boy. It wasn't as scary or mysterious, but it did reveal something to me we tend to forget. A good horror isn't just what we see but what we imagine it to be when we see it.

Jack Taylor

The film is shot in a bluish, under-saturated picture with lots of mist, overcast skies and shadows. It is visually disturbing. The whispers and sounds get under your skin and Hancock shoots the entire climax without a note of horror music. He lets the images get you. And they did for me. *Let's Scare Jessica* was nightmare fuel. I would get sucked into it every damned time it was on, and most of all, took it to bed with me where that haunting image of Emily rising from the lake and gliding toward shore haunted me.

There is one scene in *Jaws 2* that was shot by John Hancock and saved by Spielberg who told the new director, Jeannot Szwarc, to use it in the final film. It's all of 30 seconds where the shark surfaces at night in Amity harbor. The fin breaks a slack water surface, slicing through the bluish night, not seen by a soul, but letting us know it's out there even if Brody doesn't know it yet. Those 30 seconds are a hint as to what kind of *Jaws 2* we would've had if Hancock stayed on board.

> *I first saw" Jaws" in my grandparent's basement when I was four years old, and it changed my life immediately. My creativity blossomed and I took an interest in drawing, writing and filmmaking at an early age.*
>
> *"Jaws" made me fall in love with sharks. So much that I donate to protect them. I consider it to be one of my first loves. Much like Godzilla and Spider-Man, Jaws influenced me at a young age. I owe everything I am today to this film.*
>
> **Anthony Baamonde**

Who's the real villain in *Jaws*? It's the mayor and his toadies. Mayor Larry Vaughn (Murray Hamilton) has gone on to become a movie cliché, a character no other film mayor wishes comparison. Former President Donald Trump found himself in an unwanted comparison for his inept handling of the Coronavirus pandemic outbreak, stating that the country, like Amity's beaches, would be open for business by Easter.

Chief Martin Brody was the one who went against the system. He was outnumbered on the Amity ferry at the opening of the film after declaring a shark attack as the cause of death of a young girl a few nights earlier. Brody was surrounded by selectman, the local paper editor and the coroner who made it very clear he's been absorbed by the Amity collective and sides with the "boating accident" story. "I'll stand by that," he told an incredulous Brody.

All Brody had to do was play the game. He was gaslit by the mayor and his gang into believing he's acting rashly from inexperience. In the end, perhaps the only shred of honesty to come from Vaughn's mouth laid it all out for Brody: "You yell shark, we got a panic on our hands on the Fourth of July."

Jaws is economic horror. The actions of the shark are just part of nature. It's not out to commit murder, it's not looking to ruin lives. The real villain is the mayor who knows the right thing is to shut down the beaches. He stands silent as Brody takes the smack in the face from Mrs. Kintner, not once speaking up to defend his police chief. Vaughn says more in that silence than any of his platitudes or press releases.

Brody's paranoid and he has every right to be. This will be explored further in *Jaws 2*. Benchley's original novel played on that paranoia further, with the Brody family having to fear retribution from the mob that kills the Brody family's cat to send a message. Larry Vaughn may be involved in the mob in the book, or at least beholden to them. Regardless...*Jaws* is paranoid in its inherent mistrust of government and its officials.

Why the paranoia? Eisenhower left office in 1960, not with a victory lap rehash of his two successful terms, but instead, as one of the greatest generals in US history; he left us with a warning about the very military industrial complex he helped to build. For the first time in U.S. history, the country had a centralized military machine to make weapons of war—whose interest was perpetuating conflict and Eisenhower warned us to watch for it everywhere, from the highest office in the land to our schools and local government buildings.

Three years later we saw the death of President John F. Kennedy and within 24 hours a shocked nation watched his alleged assassin killed before our eyes on live TV. Circumstances around the assassination left a number of Americans wondering just what the truth was. On the heels of this, Martin Luther King and Bobby Kennedy are gunned down by the same "lone assassins" and those official stories just weren't able to be told without massive holes.

Something was going on. The Manson murders showed our own children were turned against us. The Vietnam War was raging, triggered under dubious circumstances in what we now know was a false flag operation called The Gulf of Tonkin Incident. Stories of mind control and drug experimentation from the CIA proliferated and were spoken of in hushed circles and the dark corners of bars.

The nightly news brought Vietnam into our living rooms and the death count in those broadcasts kept going against the narrative that war was about to be won. The image of a victorious post-WW II United States was taking a beating.

Few knew what to believe and the country fractured. What was once a trusted source of information, the news was now seen as a partisan propaganda machine, not to be trusted as images of the civil unrest joined the fever burning up the country.

Richard Nixon was elected President in 1968 with the promise of bringing order back to America. With a successful first term that saw some change but no de-escalation of the war in Vietnam, the Administration was putting the icing on the paranoia cake.

Watergate tied together mistrust for "The Establishment" as a President stood before banks of reporters on live television and lied to the American people. Behind the scenes were dirty re-election tricks, break-ins, blackmail, extortion and abuse of power. By the time the scandal broke, the Nixon tapes revealed and calls for impeachment ringing from coast to coast, faith was lost in our government.

Watergate was part of a maelstrom of assassinations, political and military corruption, war, and abject lies to a public that was growing unable to process fact from fiction.

You couldn't trust your kids anymore, they dabbled in the occult. Satanism was on the rise according to the news and a new blackness was falling over the land as our kids died overseas, foreign governments fell in the name of democracy, but really oil, and then the rest of the world caught on.

Arab countries that held oil unionized into OPEC and turned off the cheap oil. We were betrayed by our own automobiles. The giant machines at the center of an American love affair were now our enemy, draining our wallets and purses.

Kids were questioning and they turned against the government that their parents grew up believing in and going to war for. Outside influences were to blame: Fluoridation of the water supply, drugs, Communism, Socialism, Television, Porn and then music and movies.

"They" wanted to get your kids. They were out there, in the shadows, the dark city alleys, and even next door. By the early 1970s news moved into a more exploitative format: the TV magazine and special shows looked at the growing focus on serial killers. They were like you and me. Often these were the people who lived next door, down the street and then one day a strange smell comes from their basements and crawlspaces.

As the 70s wore on, serial killers emerged as handsome, sometimes dressed as clowns, and TV was giving it unprecedented coverage, saturating our minds to the point where we started to believe this was a common part of our society.

See where I am going with this? Do you get a little better idea as to why historical context is so important to this genre?

The economy continued to sink as war-driven inflation coupled with spiked fuel costs to pummel a rotting American auto industry that was under attack from foreign imports.

Nixon resigned but his replacement, Gerald Ford, pardoned him not long after, prompting cries of deals made to keep the public from ever truly knowing what went on. In 1975 the US House of Representatives convened a special select committee to investigate the assassinations of JFK, and MLK, concluding there were "likely" conspiracies resulting in the deaths of both men. Nothing more came of it, fueling the paranoia and mistrust of official narratives.

Neighbor no longer trusted neighbor. TV shifted from simple sitcoms to social commentary in the form of "All in the Family, The Jeffersons and Maude." The miniseries was born, giving us *Roots* and *Holocaust*. America was in a dark, dark place by the mid-70s.

This brings us full circle back to *Jaws 2*.

I was in full *Jaws 2* mode by May, 1978. The ads were starting on TV. I read everything I could on the making of the film, which was found in tabloids like the *Star Magazine* and *National Enquirer*. This was before The Internet would leak every tidbit, plot detail and onset issue to ensure there was very little to surprise you once you got into the theater to see the film.

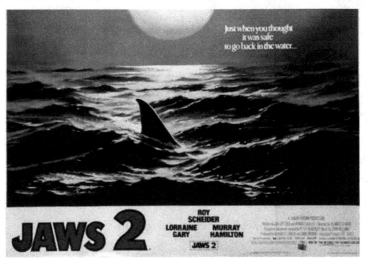

My favorite "coming soon" poster art was the lone shark fin in the sunset with the infamous tagline: "Just When You Thought It Was Safe To Go Back In The Water…" Nothing else was on my mind that spring of 1978.

Michael was hesitant. Despite loving the cheesy old horror films and even the campy made for TV stuff, he admitted that *Jaws* had scared him in a different way. He looked uncomfortable just talking about it and now wasn't so sure he wanted to see *Jaws 2*.

There was no way I could accept no for an answer. I badgered him until he relented, giving his word that he would come with me on opening weekend to see it. Keep in mind, no *Fandango* or any online ticket services. You could not get tickets in advance. You waited until opening night, got in line and took your chances.

My mother told me we were going to move to a town called Stroudsburg in The Poconos by the end of the summer. It was over thirty miles away and I  would be attending Stroudsburg Middle School in the fall. I put on an act, pretending I didn't want to move, but I was relieved. I had nothing in East Bangor and at Five Points Elementary. Other than Michael, I had no real friends at school. I concocted some stupid scenario that a girl in our class was bent on taking over the school. I got Michael and some fourth graders to buy into it. Why? I have no idea. It kept me preoccupied and away from the boys who hated me. That's what I was losing.

The *King Kong* "play" I did the year before in Mrs. Dean's class haunted me. I was still in the "gifted program," a series of enrichment classes that were offshoots of my second and third grade years. I spent second and third grade with nine other little "wunderkinds" as we were part of an experiment for children deemed intellectually gifted.

For two years I was with only nine other kids. I was insulated from much of the bullshit that would come in fourth and fifth grade after we were all released back into the wild. I would later call it Bangor's "catch and release" program. Then I was pulled from classes for "enrichment."

Jaws 2 and some Cub Scout overnight camping trip were going to be the last hurrahs of Bangor. Michael would be with me on both adventures.

My mom married Brian that Memorial Day Weekend. I had a new stepfather and he was only nine years older than me. My mother later told me that his agreement to marriage was changing school districts. Brian wanted my brother and me in a better school district and he was positive Stroudsburg was that better district. They started the house hunt and found a green bi-level five years old in a development called *Beaver Valley Acres*.

Jimmy Carter was still President and *Charlie's Angels* was the top-rated show on TV and there would be no bigger movie that summer than *Jaws 2*.

The film opened after school let out in mid-June. Michael was dropped off to my house around five in the evening. We would drive to the Eric Theater in Easton, PA, which was an hour drive.

"Do you like my house?" I think I asked him at least five times. My house was a dump and I knew it. Before my father left us, he had tried his hand at paneling the entire downstairs with a terrible black walnut wood. They weren't level and the paneling sloped up and down along the ceiling line. He planned to replace all the doors in the house and left us with doors with no doorknobs. I had to show Michael how to shove the towel in the top of the bathroom door to go to the bathroom with some privacy.

The carpeting was old and filled with holes and pulled threads. The old TV console still was missing the dial and the pliers sat on top. Our furniture was still from 1972 and with holes and black tape covering them and cigarette burns.

The township shut down one of the city dumps nearby that was once a slate quarry. They burned the place out, driving the dump's rats into town. We had a dirt floor in our basement and the rats dug under the foundation to come up into our basement. My grandfather (my mom's stepdad) was Chief of Police in East Bangor and he would come up and shoot the rats with his service revolver.

A few mornings I went for the breakfast cereal on the shelf inside the basement door with a broom to fend off any rats bold enough to come up the steps to check out the dry goods. It just became a matter of course. However, Michael lived on an estate. His grandfather was a wealthy developer and into road construction. The family had a barn of antique cars that were used in the *CBS* miniseries *The Dane Curse*. Michael's living room window looked out over huge grounds and a giant pond that held two magnificent, nasty swans: Henry and Lizzie.

My backyard was a swamp from a cracked and leaking cesspool that filled the flat backyard with shit and piss water. Wild ducks let alone swans wouldn't be caught dead there.

My brother pulled a fast one. He said he was going to see *Grease* with my parents but then at the last minute, with a shit grin announced he would be seeing *Jaws 2* with Michael and me. That little asshole was so pleased about it. I begged my mom to reconsider. *Jaws 2* wasn't for little kids. I was going with Michael. I am sure the popular guys at school would say I was treating it like a date.

My mother dismissed my protests. We were leaving and it was decided. The whole trip down I glared at my brother who seemed quite pleased with himself at this victory.

We knew nothing about the film going in, other than what we saw on the previews. There were no TV specials or "making of" extras. I had a basic idea the shark's face was burned, but we didn't know why. There was some stink that *Rona Barrett's Hollywood* entertainment gossip rag released a photo of the shark with its burnt face, but I never saw it.

It was a time when you went into a movie with only the basic information given by the studios. They still had full control of the medium with no pain in the ass "spoilers" leaked to the public. *Jaws 2* was going to be an experience.

We talked about the first film the whole way down. My mother helped refresh my memory since I was eight when *Jaws* played at the *Grand*. The other shark was dead. It was blown up. This was a new shark but it looked like the guy who played Brody was back and that mayor got re-elected somehow.

The *Eric Twin* was a big deal. It was a double screened theater unlike *The Bijou* on main street Bangor or *The State Theater* just up the hill from *The Eric* where I saw *King Kong* two years earlier.

The Eric was new, modern and cool. You could choose a movie and the choices were *Jaws 2* and *Grease*. We stood in line outside. I have no idea which movie held the most in waiting. We got our tickets. I bristled as my mother said, "Three children for *Jaws 2*."

Dammit.

She handed us tickets and my brother waved his at both of us with that smartass smile. We were now inside and waiting for the first show to end. The doors for the *Jaws 2* side had windows (a bad idea) and while we could see the first show ending, I did my best to not peek and ruin anything. I could see some kind of island, kids were screaming and then that fucking shark ripped up through some kind of canvass or cloth.

That's all my brother needed to see. He stepped back, his face white. He turned to my mother, shoving his ticket at her and in front of the crowd started crying, begging for her to take him into *Grease*. "Please don't make me see *Jaws 2!*" he wailed. "I wanna see *Grease*! Please!"

He slipped into *Grease* when the ushers opened the theater and he never looked back. He was humiliated. Michael and I rushed into our theater and found ourselves seats about ten rows back from the screen.

This was not my first "multi-plex" experience. My father sometimes took us on Sundays for the afternoon after my parents split. I saw *The Land That Time Forgot* there in 1974 and *Close Encounters of the Third Kind* in 1977 at the *Eric* twin. *Jaws 2* would be the last movie I saw there.

Some girls were seated to Michael's left. To a fifth grader, they seemed like college girls, but they were probably not much older than us. They were chatty and talked loudly about how scared they were for the film to start. If it were now, they would talk into phones, posting their "fears" on Tik Tok for the world to see.

The lights went down and again…people started to applaud when the Universal logo came on the screen. When the title *Jaws 2* appeared in glaring read, there were cheers and applause. This wasn't just watching a movie, it was a total immersive experience. Five years later *Jaws 3-D* would break this cheering streak. I can't wait to tell you the audience reaction to that opening sequence.

There was Quint's boat, The *Orca*, looking pretty good for sitting at the bottom of the ocean for almost four years. I discovered John Williams since the first *Jaws* and heard his original *Jaws* motif in the discovery of Quint's sunken lady by the divers. Then the music.

The audience cheered as the shark point of view shot moved toward the two unsuspecting scuba guys. A flash of a camera, the silhouette of a charging shark into the camera, underwater screams, hands gripping for the surface in a cloud of bubbles and then—FLASH! One last photo as the diving camera fired off one last shot.

From there the audience laughed at the wise ass remarks from wise ass teenagers and being on the edge of teen young adulthood, I found I could relate to this film a little better with all these kids. I wanted a boat gang like Amity's teens. I wanted to hang with all of them, making jokes, teasing each other and sailing as a troupe. Suddenly I wanted to live in Amity and knowing I was moving in a couple of months, hoped my new home would give me something like the Catamaran gang from *Jaws 2*.

I fell in love with Donna Wilkes and her Jackie Peters character. The hair, the doe-eyed bad girl looks—I even got a hint of her black bra through her wet T-shirt when the shark started its mayhem. I wanted to be Mike Brody, being propositioned in the Hog's Breath bar, giving in to her womanly wiles. Larry Vaughn, Jr. was the kind of guy that hated me in school, the one who wanted to steal the girl of your affections. But she only had eyes for me, I mean Mike Brody.

All these years later, she's known as "the screaming chick" that, in reality, had the proper response to a situation like that.

She would later show up in 1984's *Angel* but I wasn't

interested in seeing Donna play a hooker. I liked her as the wholesome, screaming, girl next door in *Jaws 2*. Even the temptation of seeing her nude in *Angel* wasn't enough of a lure to watch the whole film as an usher, standing for free in the back of the theater in Stroud Mall. Donna was Jackie, and Jackie was my ideal girl for awhile until Alexandra Paul's Leigh Cabot came along in *Christine*.

Jackie Peters in the movie differed from Jackie Peters in the Searls novel. I preferred movie Jackie over novel Jackie with the exception that novel Jackie was a tad more promiscuous and racy.

There were a few around me who complained for Jackie to calm the fuck down. I remember a few laughs and claps when Larry Vaughn, Jr. told her to shut up as they floated toward Cable Junction. For me, Donna Wilkes brought home the realistic terror someone expresses if put into the situation playing out on that screen.

As the shark made its final assault on the kids and Roy Scheider, one of the older girls leaned over to Michael, took his hand and said, "Hold my hand." He did it without question and I was pissed. Mike got the girl! Come on!

1970s paranoia returned in full force in *Jaws 2*. Chief Brody knew there was another shark out there. The evidence racked up but was circumstantial. Mayor Vaughn gas lit him again, and told him to not be crazy. Even the marine biologist, Dr. Elkins, told him that "sharks don't take things personally" (which we know to be bullshit in 1987's *Jaws the Revenge).* A great opportunity was missed in not pairing Brody and Dr. Elkins (Colin Wilcox) together to confront the shark. She was a great character and was in only one scene.

The audience cheered when the shark bit into the cable. I could feel some relief that it was over. The girl that still held Michael's hand asked aloud, "I wonder what they're gonna do with all that tuna fish?" He gave a polite chuckle and they broke their grip. No sparks (except from the shark onscreen), no love connection—just two movie strangers united by a fish.

I was hooked. *Jaws 2*, as blasphemous as it sounds, surpassed my love of *Jaws*. No other horror film mattered. I didn't care about The Devil, monsters, ghosts; it was that shark and those teenagers because I wanted that to be my reality. I wanted friends like the ones I saw on the screen: Andy, Doug, Timmy, Marge, Jackie, Mike, Polo, Lucy, Tina, Ed, Brooke and maybe even Larry, Jr. Maybe. I wanted both to be Chief Brody and also would have loved him as a dad. *Jaws 2* filled the personal need for family and belonging and it stayed that way for a few years. "The Addams Family" and "The Brady's" were replaced by The Brody's.

Michael left the theater quiet and remained that way the ride home. I grilled him: did he like it? What did he like best? Did he think Jackie was cute? What did he think of the shark? He returned with basic answers. I wore myself out in my excitement after rehashing the entire film to my mom and stepdad on the way home.

We both left for our weekend Scout overnight camping trip. I recounted the entire movie around the campfire because Michael and I were the only boys there to have seen *Jaws 2* opening night. There were a lot of questions: Was it the same shark? Was it bigger? Did it look real? Did it eat a helicopter? How many people died? Was it gross and bloody?

They were listening to me. I had something to say and people wanted to hear from me and a scout campfire was the perfect setting. I had the scoop. Michael was content to just sit next to me and nod once in awhile.

We slept in the same tent, and that night he confessed—he hated the movie. It scared him and bothered him more than the first film. Michael had a leg up on me when it came to viewings of the original *Jaws*. He had *HBO* and saw the film numerous times when it came to cable. Our VHF, one dial TV didn't get HBO. I saw *Jaws* once, back in 1975 and that was it.

It wasn't like him to get rattled over much. What bothered him? He said the deaths were worse this time and he cited Marge's death as the main attack that got to him. Marge (Martha Swatek) was the nice teen that allowed Sean

Brody to spoil Mike's day and ride along with her. She saved Sean from being eaten, unwittingly sacrificing herself in perhaps the film's most gruesome and eerie attack.

I knew what he was talking about: that nightmarish image of the shark surfacing as Marge tried to get Sean clear and up on the overturned boat.

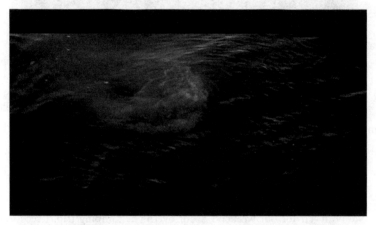

The fish surfaced and in a single chomp took brave Marge, leaving a red blood slick while both Sean and Jackie screamed. That was the moment where Jackie lost her mind.

Michael was haunted by Marge's death. He told me he was tired of talking about the movie. He understood I was excited, but he would rather not talk about it for the rest of the weekend. I honored his request and forced myself to shut up about *Jaws 2*.

An excursion to a lake later that summer inspired me to create a fake Styrofoam fin. I ran a belt through it and thought I was going to fool people into believing a Great White somehow got into fresh water. I was so pumped in its construction, I forgot that I couldn't swim and hated the water. I hid the fin and belt under my towel and when we got there, I left the whole thing in the backseat of the car.

The move to Stroudsburg was defining. I can't underestimate its power and impact on my life. Everything changed. I was now in sixth grade and had *Jaws* on the brain. There was still no ability to go back and rewatch the films. *Jaws 2* was still out in theaters August, 1978 but my mother felt once was enough. There was no need for me to pay to see it again.

"Move on," is pretty much what she was telling me.

I did yard work and household chores for an allowance. Just before we moved I bought my very first soundtrack album. Nanny got me the original *Jaws* LP but I saved up the whopping five dollars to get the soundtrack to *Jaws 2* on stunning vinyl.

I had some cheap, plastic sky blue record player. I transferred the vinyl to audio cassette so I could walk around the neighborhood playing the soundtrack. I was an ass-kicking waiting to happen as I strolled along the streets of East Bangor with *Jaws 2* blaring from my cassette tape recorder—the same one I recorded *Mad Monster Party* with. Why was I so proud of this and most of all thought anyone would want to hear the music from this movie?

We moved to Stroudsburg August 27th, 1978. The doors in the new house had knobs *and* locks. I thought we were rich when I saw our new house for the first time.

It was a non-descript, green aluminum sided bi-level on two acres inside this little development of 20 homes. It was named *Beaver Valley Acres*, tucked away in a hollow surrounded by rolling hills of forest. The humor of the name was lost on me, but I would get a lot of mileage with it throughout high school.

Moving in was a family experience as both sets of grandparents helped transport everything to Stroudsburg. Scott and I had our own rooms and we had a basement with real cement. My mother decorated my room in a *K-Mart Star Wars* theme.

Nanny helped clean while my mother's mom unpacked the kitchenware. We bought new furniture for the living room, a new table and chairs for the kitchen. The living room furniture was this funky New Age style. It looked like it was made out of cargo crates with dark futon-like cushions. The sides were marked in faux-sprayed stencil: "FRAGILE" or "NO HOOKS." It was new and in style and there wasn't any duct tape holding it together. I finally had a house I wasn't embarrassed of. I remembered being excited to bring Michael up so he could see that we were now rich too.

The neighborhood houses were neatly kept, landscaped ranchers and bi-levels on green lawns surrounded by woods. Our bay window let us look out over these new sights. People smiled and waved. It was opposite of East Bangor's post-World War II era row homes and rundown streets. Everything back there seemed washed out and grey. Up here the greens were *really* green, the sun was this rich golden yellow and the air didn't smell like shit as our backyard always did when that cesspool percolated.

School would be starting in a few weeks and the first thing on my list was to find out what other kids lived here with me. You didn't have to go looking for kids because they would find you.

MY *JAWS 3*

I need to make a pit stop to give you the historical context so the horror stuff makes more sense. All of this is important to understanding why "80s Horror" will become such a thing.

Stroudsburg Middle School was seen as one of those "last great educational experiments" of the 70s. Only several years old by the time I got to it, the place was legendary for not having walls or windows. It was a giant circle with an exterior siding that oxidized into a rust surface, giving the building the nickname of "The Tin Can" or "Tuna Can."

The middle school was divided into two sides or houses: Lake House and Mountain House. It had two of each grade, fifth to eighth. I was in Mountain House. The kids from Lake House said they were the smarter side. The kids in Mountain House assured everyone that Lake House was full of shit. Teachers got caught up in the "which side is better" competition. This would later prove a major problem in our high school years.

They put Lake and Mountain Houses together to compete against each other at pep assemblies and gym rallies. The administration and teachers encouraged the rivalry.

Some friendships transcended the Mountain-Lake barrier. It was not uncommon to be in a ninth grade class and know only a handful of your fellow classmates. You didn't know them for the past four years but would be graduating with them all in the next.

The ceiling of the middle school was ringed with fluorescent lights. It had wall-to-wall carpeting. Classrooms were separated into grade "areas" by primary colored closets, coat racks and bookshelves that were all on wheels. All of these were encased in color-coded blues, purples, greens and reds. If a teacher flipped out in eighth grade you could hear it all the way down in fifth grade. One teacher was so famous for his frequent tirades and trademark: "SHUT UP!" that fifth graders were well-groomed for him by the time they reached his eighth grade class. The school was never silent. Going back into it years later, it seemed like a hive with this constant drumming of noise. It's amazing we learned at all.

We didn't have lockers. Instead we got a large plastic tray housed with 30 other trays in these particle board cabinets on wheels. You stuffed a tray with your books, papers and anything else you didn't want to lug around with you. The weight would be too much for the wooden dowels that supported your tray on a piece of thin wafer board. Inevitably, the dowels would break and if you were one of those with a tray on the top row, your crap would spill down and into all of the other trays below. The poor bastard who had the last tray on the bottom got filled with everyone else's junk spilled from the top. It was a genius engineering move for kids by people who didn't have them.

Corrals were round stalls with a cushioned seat. They had a side entrance that you kind of slipped into and disappeared. Inside there was only a small table and nothing else. They were painted egg shell white inside and the lights made them vibrate on the eyes. You were cut off from the outside world inside these "tubs" as we called them. You went in there to make up tests or catch up on work. They served as "time out" chambers for unruly kids who were kicked out of class. Other kids could walk by the tub and peer down inside at you. You would look up like this trapped rat with big helpless eyes. Sometimes kids would drop notes to their imprisoned friends, but little could be done to alleviate the stir craziness that came with being sentenced to a tub.

There was a pool in the bowels of the building, below the gymnasium with the real rubber floor. It was this health club-sized in-ground swimming pool. Sometimes frogs got in there, but no one knew how. Before some classes, you would wait while the teacher skimmed dead Leopard frogs from the water.

Horror was having to get into the water or changing with my fellow class-mates. The swimming lockers were separated from the regular gym lockers. They had their own chambers with tall lockers to get air to wet towels and trunks. In Bangor, we never changed for gym. I never saw a single one of my male Bangor classmates in his *underwear,* let alone naked.

You got to see who was hitting puberty first. I don't think I had seen my own brother naked. I never saw more penises (peni?) in my life and, for the most part, no one cared until someone sprouted pubic hair. Some of us got the modest growth that didn't draw much attention. Then there were the guys that looked like they had *ZZ Top* in their crotch. I can't imagine what it was like for the girls over on their side. They not only had the hair issue, they had boobs and periods. This was real horror.

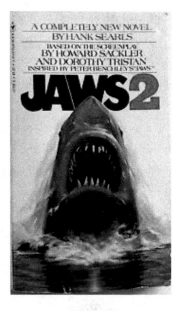

I had new neighborhood friends. I made them fast in school as well. The social climate was different than Bangor. My *Jaws 2* fixation was still going strong.

The first book I bought from the *Scholastic Book Club* was the full novel of *Jaws 2*. Think about that, they were selling *Jaws* AND *Jaws 2* in a middle school book service. *Jaws* described Mrs. Brody's public hair perfume, had a lesbian called a "dyke" named Daisy Wicker, Matt Hooper's empty sexual prowess as he banged Mrs. Brody in a cheap hotel room, boys grinding their pelvises into warm beach sand, a skinny dipper getting ripped apart after fucking on the beach at the start of the book. No way any of this would be found in a school book fair these days.

You got a book because you didn't want to be the only one who didn't when that box came in and the teacher handed shit out. I added *Jaws 2* to my growing collection of paperbacks. For some reason I toted them around in a tire chains box with a handle. It was this little cardboard carrying case. I had no idea why I thought this would help my image. One kid took to calling me "Tire Chains."

Thankfully it didn't stick.

I read the full *Jaws 2* novel since my only exposure was the *Readers Digest* condensed version. I was still thrown off by how different the novel was from the film I worshipped. A lot of it was the same, but there was that continued Mafia presence, a subplot with a seal named Sammy, but there was also a far better helicopter scene and this whole missing sonar ball storyline. The water skiier scene was way more terrifying than the movie. I found myself enjoying the full book so much, I decided I was going to be the guy, in sixth grade, that would write *Jaws 3*.

I used one of my back-to-school notebooks to handwrite this masterpiece. It was a green *Mead* spiral and I used a Number 2 peincil. I drew my poster art inside the cover: a full length Great White heading straight on for a power boat, the massive fin breaking the water on a collision course.

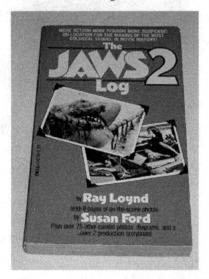 

It didn't take long for my class to find out what I was doing. I was allowed to read pieces of it to the group during reading/English class. My fellow sixth graders were in awe when I was permitted to say "hell" and "damn" aloud because, well, it was literature, right?

This did not make me legit. It took the official endorsement of perhaps the most popular girl in our class…Toni. She was a cheerleader, in the top academic learning level with me, and she was as beautiful as she was strong-willed. She argued with teachers. She called people out and she dictated who was cool and who was not.

I impressed her with my knoweldge of *Jaws* and *Jaws 2*. It was gleaned from the "making of" books, *The Jaws Log* and *The Jaws 2 Log*. I was going to make movies one day, I told her and anyone else who would listen. She believed me. We sat together in almost every class and one day she asked if she could read my *Jaws 3*. I let her take the note-

book home. I was stunned. THE Toni wanted to read MY novel. She returned it the following Monday and gave it a thumbs-up. The snickers and doubts given by others (mostly the popular athletic crowd) went away. That was it. Toni endorsed me. Making fun of my writing books was no longer acceptable. She was joking (or maybe she was half-joking) when she suggested I make her a character in my book.

My *Jaws 3* picked up two years after *Jaws 2*. I decided I would follow the timeline of the films and stick to those events rather than the Hank Sealres or Benchley novels. Chief Brody is on guard for another shark attack. Mayor Vaughn is still doing his mayor stuff (*How?*) and this time, a young, teenaged drifter makes her way onto Amity Island and is arrested by Chief Brody for shoplifting at the Amity Pharmacy. That drifter was, you guessed it, Toni. Brody took her in and Ellen was thrilled to have another girl in the house. Toni wasn't the only one to drift into Amity. Another shark inexplicably makes Amity its home again. It chomped on some actress and the film crew making a commercial on the open water. It took out wayward swimmers and, just like *Jaws 2*, did it all without definitive evidence. Mayor Vaughn was a little more prone to believing Brody this time around. Toni eventually dies, falling into the shark's mouth in a climactic death that leads Brody to avenge his quasi-adopted daughter by driving a speedboat full of explosives into the shark. He lept from the boat in the nick of time before he blew the fish to smitereens. "You have to kill me," Toni demanded. The shark had to get her. I oblilged with that finale. She nodded as she read her death scene. "Perfect." It was "Toni Approved." Many others approved as well and this girl put me on the path to being known as a writer in my class. I wrote the weird stuff. I read the weird stuff, but this time it was cool because I had the designer "Toni" label on all of it. The notebook with that handwritten mansuscript disappeared somewhere between sixth and seventh grade. I wish I had kept it.

In a weird way, Toni's character in my *Jaws 3* was much like Jamie Lee Curtis's character in *The Fog* which wouldn't come for two more years. Jamie's drifter girl brought the stigma that bad things followed her. That's what many in Amity felt with the arrival of Toni's homeless, drifter girl. Things were okay until she came along, and then not long after this girl arrives, another shark appears.

When I saw *The Fog* in the spring of 1980 on *HBO*, I told Toni she needed to see it because the Curtis character was a lot like hers from my *Jaws 3*.

Toni signed this at the end of our eighth grade year in my middle school year book:

Bruce,
well dear I'm honored to know my name is in your books. I'll laugh my ass off if I become famous and you don't! (ha! ha!) Good luck always

Toni

1979: HORROR'S GOLDEN SUMMER

A new house, a new school, a new life gave me *HBO* that fall. A little brown box wired to our TV with the plastic buttons would be my gateway to premium horror late nights. More on that later. This chapter is brought you buy the word: "Malaise."

First some history to put the Summer of 1979 into perspective. It was Carter's last full year in office. The election of 1980 was shaping up and it looked more and more that former actor and California governor Ronald Reagan was to be the Republican nominee. Before you roll your eyes and think you're stuck back in history class, as a horror fan, you need to know the impact of Reagan's election and two terms will have on the genre and will almost solely shape the face of 80s horror.

A nuclear reactor at Three Mile Island in Harrisburg, PA almost melted down giving more power to the "eco-horror" sub-genre. Films like 1976's *Squirm* gave us lots of wet, slimy creepy crawly real and rubber worms belching up from beneath some Southern town because of electricity from a downed power line (Who knew?).

The film was drive-in, nature-run-amok low budget cheese. The commercials exploited the few gross out effects the film carried (it's often just long and boring with bad acting) as did the poster. It worked. It was a theatrical and home video success. This was a time when these ultra cheap exploitation horrors had a chance at some kind of theatrical venue, even if it was just the drive-in.

> *My earliest memory of a horror movie is of "Frogs," from 1972, and "Ben" [The sequel to "Willard"], from the same year. The animated opening sequence of "Frogs," that played out against the still closed curtain, was like magic to my seven-year-old eyes. (Remember when big theaters still had curtains over the screen?) We watched "Ben" at a drive-in theater with "Willard" as the opener. I cried when they killed the rats. I had one of my own at the time—a white lab rat named Rosy. I loved those movies and rats so much, that later in the mid 70s, after moving back east, I was given the nickname, Ben (which became Benny), by the boyfriend of one of my oldest sisters. To this day, Bobby Hamilton still calls me "Benny" and it makes me smile.*
>
> **Noel Soul**

The "Blame The Bomb" giant bug era was eco-horror, but they were replaced by the more grindhouse feel of *Squirm* or the equally cheesy *Bug* which would see

its director, Jeannot Szwarc, replace John Hancock as director of *Jaws 2*. None of these were all that good, and *Bug* was no exception. Madagascar Hissing Cockroaches and other big bugs were used along with low end props to lead an invasion of prehistoric bugs capable of creating fire. Once again a small Southern town was ground zero for the monster mayhem.

HBO delivered this wonderful crap and I was up late on weekends, holiday breaks and summer nights to catch it all.

The schlock master himself, director, producer William Castle, was behind the marketing that promised such a horrific film it could mentally and/or physically harm the viewer. Castle was famous for this kind of sideshow promotion and Joe Dante would go on to make *Matinee* with John Goodman as a tribute to Castle.

I was too young to experience William Castle's theatrical shenanigans. This kind of carnival showmanship was fading by the mid-70s. He would hire fake nurses to take blood pressure at the door, issue fake "Fright Insurance" policies in the event one of his films scared you to death and even ensured electric buzzers affixed to theater seats jolted customers during the climactic theater escape of the titular

135

monster in Vincent Price's *The Tingler* (a personal creature feature Saturday after-noon favorite.).

Castle has *Rosemary's Baby* to his credits and even a cameo in that film, but he was and still is known for the cheap-o, goofy gimmicks with his low budget content. There is absolutely nothing wrong with that. He was one of film indus-try's last great showmen.

> *When I was around seven, living in Detroit, "The Tingler" came on one night while my mom was out of town. My dad and I watched it together and he said he had to go "get something." He left through one door and then snuck back in on hands and knees and hid behind my chair. When the Tingler attacked someone's spine, he shook the shit out of my chair!*
>
> *Scared the hell out of me and I became a horror addict from that day forward.*
>
> **Jeff Millenbach**

At the time of this writing there are only two left: Roger Corman and Lloyd Kaufman.

The closest I ever came to a William Castle gim-mick was during my time as a manager at our mall multiplex. *A Nightmare on Elm Street IV: The Dream Master* opened that fall 1988. Several frat assholes who attended the local university were on the floor that night. They were funny as hell and terrific after work drinking buddies. I told them about William

Castle and his fright insurance gag from back in the day. One of my frat asshole employees asked if we could try it. Sure, why not? Hot girls love horror movies, let's see how it went. Sure enough two college girls came up to the box office for the film. My guy asked if I would back him up if needed. Again...sure. I was single, too, maybe I could get a date out of this. I just wanted to see where it all went.

He was a big guy, his brother a pro ball player, so when he approached the two women they gave him some regard. "Excuse me ladies, can I see your tickets?" Confused, they showed him their ripped ticket stubs. I was over by the candy stand with a clipboard pretending to be busy but watching the entire time.

"Hey Laura," he asked the girl in the box office. "Did these two buy their fright insurance?"

Laura was as confused as the two girls. What the fuck was he talking about? One asked if this was a joke and with that he called for me to come over. I did, decked out in my manager's jacket and tie. "Manager" was monogrammed above my left breast pocket. I was legit as shit.

"Is there a problem?" I asked.

My employee told me these two girls were going to see "The Freddy Movie" as he called it and did not buy the fright insurance mandated by the studio. He was good in adding that little touch. It sounded almost believable. The girls looked to me. "Is he being serious?"

Yes, I told them with a grave, official voice. "The studio had some people have heart issues in the film's test screening. They feel it's so frightening they request an optional 25-cent surcharge on tickets so if you die during the viewing of this movie, you have burial coverage."

You could just tell they were on the edge of buying this or dismissing it. I expected them to wave their hands and dismiss us with a "fuck off you guys." Instead, my employee followed with the offer to waive the total of 50 cents if they answered a few questions.

137

I approved the suggestion and said that would be fine. I offered him my clipboard to make it look even more official. The two girls didn't leave. They stayed in their spots, and I recused myself from the matter. The show was all his. He licked the pencil tip and got to work.

The conversation went something like this:

THEATER GUY: Okay ladies, just a few questions. Your names?

[The girls gave their names.]

THEATER GUY: Addresses please?

[They weren't so sure, but they finally said, whether true or not, that they lived in one of the girls' dorms at the nearby university.]

THEATER GUY: Phone numbers?

[This was a day before cell phones. Now they were a little more edgy.]

GIRL 1: Do we have to give you that? Why?

THEATER GUY: Ladies, please, it's for the form.

ME: "Yes," I told them from across the lobby. "Phone numbers are required. Thank you."

They gave their numbers but weren't happy about it.

THEATER GUY: Color of underwear?

GIRL 2: Blu—HEY! Fuck you!

They had smiles on their faces and he joined their call out by tearing up the paper. I laughed and we let them know it was a joke. They bought their junk food and went in, giving us props for being so clever.

Thanks William Castle.

Back to the summer of 1979. Eco-horror came at us hard in 1977 with *Day of the Animals*, a "blame the ozone hole" horror movie where the planet's animals go nuts and turn on human beings in a wilderness uprising.

It would star Leslie Nielsen who three years later would be forgotten for his science fiction and horror roots when *Airplane!* made him an unlikely comic icon. He would solidify that image in the 80s with *Police Squad!*

I missed *Willard* in its limited theatrical run but it became a staple of late night TV horror shows. Not sure if *Willard* classifies as "eco-horror" but it tapped into the whole Manson-type counterculture fear and paranoia as Willard and his rat pal, Ben, dispatched anyone who crossed them. After the rat exodus from the East Bangor dump, with a number of them invading my former home, *Willard* was definitely personal.

1978's *Piranha* was the wonderful little *Jaws* rip-off that charmed Spielberg into not legally shutting it down. It brought attention to Joe Dante and focused on fucked-with piranhas from some US military science program. The TV spots sold it to me but my mind was distracted that year with *Jaws 2*. When I got around to catching it on cable, I could see why Spielberg enjoyed it so much.

Back to "Malaise." The United States was in one hell of a slump across the board. President Jimmy Carter, an outsider in the wake of Watergate, was hoped

139

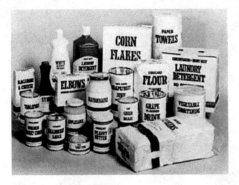

to be the guy to break politics as usual. Instead he was beaten up for not playing the game. Fuel prices were high at the pump and for home heating. Inflation raged. My house saw the emergence of "generic" groceries. My mom was buying foodstuffs that came in plain white bags with bold black print: COOKIES, FRUIT PUNCH, BREAD, CHICKEN SOUP, TUNA. No name brands, just the plain white packages screaming their contents. One time my brother and I polished off two full boxes of name brand *Count Chocula* in a single sitting. My mother was so upset as that was to last two weeks, she retaliated with what we called "Fuck You Cereal."

It was Puffed Rice or Puffed Wheat in plain plastic bags. The shit tasted like Styrofoam and the only way to get through a bowl was to dump a mound of sugar on it—so much that it pooled like silly sand on the bottom of the bowl.

A sweater-clad President Carter talked to the country from The Oval Office. News reports stated he turned down the thermostat in the White House to show solidarity with the American people as we weathered the cold and high fuel prices brought on by the Arab embargoes. Unemployment was at its highest since pre-World War II.

The car industry was stagnant with the *Chrysler Corporation* on the verge of bankruptcy and asking the federal government for a bailout loan. The entire city of New York only a few years earlier went broke and when former governor, then Vice-President Nelson Rockefeller was asked what he thought about New York's financial request, he flipped his middle finger to reporters. No doubt that didn't help at the election polls and boosted Carter's chances of winning.

The Soviet Union (That's now Russia for all of you under the age of 35) invaded Afghanistan and the US sat back, unable to do anything. Carter's only response was to boycott the 1980 summer Olympics. We were a laughing stock across the world. The United States was weak—a failed empire collapsing under its own weight.

The fall of 1979 would see the Iranian Hostage Crisis put the final nail in Carter's coffin. The U.S. watched helplessly as Iranian students and revolutionaries under the urging of their new Muslim leader, The Ayatollah Khomeini, breached the U.S. Embassy walls in Tehran, eventually holding 52 Americans for 444 days. Carter ordered a rescue attempt that literally crashed and burned in the Iranian desert leaving America looking like a limp dick on the world stage.

Carter took to the air July 15, 1979 to address the nation as things seemed to get worse on a daily basis. Known officially as "The Crisis of Confidence Speech" it became known derisively as "The Malaise Speech."

Speaker of the House Tip O'Neil is said to have called it perhaps the finest speech by an American President, but it was also political suicide. Carter told Americans he heard them. He knew of our disillusion since the deaths of JFK, RFK and MLK. Watergate demoralized us. The oil crisis, the Russians…he got it. He also said that we need to pick ourselves up and not expect the government to solve our problems. Americans need to find their own, individual senses of purpose. He went on to say we need to wake up, not be consumed by material things and look to improve this nation from the inside out.

It's not what Americans wanted to hear. It's said The White House was flooded in the hours after the speech with telegrams from citizens demanding Carter resign. He had given up on America. They wanted to hear good news, and Carter was seen as wringing his hands in frustration and helplessness as the Soviets ran all over the Middle East and Europe.

Ronald Reagan prepped backstage for the 1980 showdown.

Disco was still strong, although fading. *Saturday Night Live* was only four years old and Chevy Chase was one of the top stars in the world. John Belushi was still alive and Studio 54 was cranking as the national club of choice among the rich and famous.

Cocaine and pot were everywhere, shared generously backstage of *Saturday Night Live* by "The Not Ready for Prime Time Players." You had one section of the country waiting for the party good times 80s and another section stuck in the end of the 70s and looking for any distraction available. Moving through the shadows was AIDS.

With that mini-history lesson, do you see why horror reigned supreme at the box office not just that year but through 1980 and all throughout the next day?

Horror has done well and continues to do well in bad economic times. It is no coincidence that the top box office winners of the 1930s were *Frankenstein*, *Dracula*, *The Mummy* and *King Kong*. When the Corona Pandemic struck and studios shuttered and theaters closed, the genre to take the lead and continue to make money was horror.

People needed an escape valve, a release from real-world horror and the movies are it.

The big horror films on my radar that summer: *The Amityville Horror, Alien, Dawn of the Dead* and *Prophecy*. The only obstacle that stood in my way for a few of them was that damned letter "R" on the poster and marquee. For some reason the old Sherman Theater in downtown Stroudsburg usually got the good horror over the brand new mall *Music Makers Cinemas* multi-plex.

It was the summer *Fangoria Magazine* debuted and it was my first magazine subscription.

The Sherman Theater was one of "the old buildings" in downtown Stroudsburg. Once a live theater and music hall, it was turned into a single screen movie theater and then somewhere in the 70's's they split that giant auditorium for two screens. It's where I saw *Star Wars* in 1977 and where I caught a lot of my 70s theatrical horror.

Stained tiles pocked the ceiling. A giant stage jutted from under a screen flanked with old curtains. The place smelled like it looked: old, mildew with popcorn and butter mixed in for good measure. There was a balcony but it was mostly closed for safety reasons. The projector was from the 1960s. The Sherman had character. There was still the old style box office out front. Someone sat in a windowed enclosure with a cash box and that little silver, ridged speaker hole right in the center of the panel that usually blocked the face of the ticket seller. They had the tickets on a roll and peeled them off, slipping them under the glass.

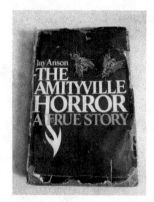

The concession stand was this long series of glass cabinets. The popcorn machine usually had a bulb missing and the soda machines were stained and spritzed from not being cleaned.

The red carpet leading from the front doors was long and beaten and probably installed when FDR was president. Everything was dark, dim sconces and track lights masked worse deterioration.

We were kids and didn't care. You went into that dark theater and you were hidden yet part of something. This was like the old *Bijou* theater in Bangor. It was nowhere near sterile like the multiplex black box theaters. No, The Sherman was all right in our books. Parking was the biggest pain in the ass.

The big summer movie that year, horror or not, was *The Amityville Horror*. Based on the best-selling book, it promised to be the *Jaws* of haunted house movies—the one, definitive film that all haunted house movies before and after would be judged.

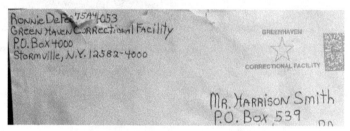

I got the book as a hand-me-down from my then-stepmother. She read it, was done with it and asked me if I was interested because "you like all that ghost and horror stuff." I took the hardback off her hands and started reading and was totally sucked in. First of all, it said "A True Story." That meant to a fifth grader that it 100% true. That shit happened. There was no Internet to verify, no sources other than what you had in the book. My mother did confirm that "a guy killed his family," just like the book said, but she didn't buy into the ghost stuff.

I did. I convinced Michael to read it. The voices, the "Get Out!" flies, Jodie the Pig, slime oozing from walls, marching bands in the living room…all real. Just like the book cover said.

Decades later I would write "that guy" (Ronald DeFeo) as he wasted away in an upstate New York prison. He wrote me back in 2010.

The news from the New York stations like WPIX Channel 11 and Channel 5 ran interviews with George and Kathy

Lutz. Marvin Scott of Channel 5 got roped into covering a séance that invariably attracted "ghost hunters" soon to be "demonologists" Ed and Lorraine Warren. They made their fame bones with Amityville, as the case propelled them into celebrity status and we know how that turned out with *The Conjuring* franchise.

I brought my hardcover *Amityville Horror* to one of the Warren's speaking events. The couple spoke at the same university where the two girls who didn't buy fright insurance hailed. I sat through almost two hours of slides with streaky images and possible dust particles said to be spirits and bad audio recordings. The Amityville pictures showed little more than what I saw on TV spots years earlier. Lorraine tried to show a connection between an image of Padre Pio and similar images of him showing up inside the Amityville house as well as elsewhere.

In the end, I stood in line for their autographs. Lorraine exclaimed her surprise to Ed at my original hardback, saying she hadn't seen one in a long time. They signed the chapter where they came into the story.

The entire country awaited the movie in 1979. "The Merv Griffin Show" kicked of "Amity-Mania" with a first-time in-depth interview with the owners of the alleged haunted house. They showed the infamous photo of the boy with no eyes (or glowing, depends on what you see) that was taken during The Warrens' examination of the Long Island home.

Talk shows and tabloids were major marketing outlets back then. That's how pre-awareness was made. You grabbed a scandal rag while waiting in line at the grocery store. Daytime TV trotted out their subjects to hock their book or movie. I had no idea I was learning about hype but I was buying right into it.

No movie had me more hyped summer 1979, than *The Amityville Horror*

I cut out every ad, read every single trash tabloid piece, mostly from *The National Enquirer* and *Star Magazine* that Nanny bought without fail. America was fixated on *The Amityville Horror* because the real horror of unemployment, inflation, high fuel and foreclosures was just too much to take.

The movie was coming to The Sherman. It was the perfect place because that old theater could've been haunted from the way it looked. I got a bunch of us psyched to go. The only thing that stood in our way was "R" on the poster.

My mother made it clear she had no interest to see the film and would not be the parent/guardian to "accompany those 17 and under." Heading into 7th grade, I thought the movie rating system was law. Years later after I became an usher up at the mall cineplex I discovered it was just a "guideline" and at that time the only state where the MPAA rating system was a law was the state of Florida. Not sure if that's still the case, but my manager told me it was so back in the 80s.

I didn't realize that *The Amityville Horror* was the Mt. Everest of haunted house bullshit stories. That summer I wanted to believe and a year later would make the haunting the subject of my eighth grade research project. I approached the middle school administration to approve a field trip for my eighth grade reading class to visit the actual house.

That request was declined. Fast.

My mom drove us up to town and let us off at the bottom of Main Street. The line was already down the block. If I pulled this off, it would be my first rated "R" movie. It was four of us, my kid brother and two friends. We were ready to be SCARED. I blabbed on and on about the book until my one friend told me to shut up about it because I was giving too much away.

We crossed the crowded street and got in line. Foot by foot we made our way up to the box office. I was the leader who was going to ask for the tickets. The box lady was smoking and chewing gum. She asked how many. I told her four. She nodded, told us the price and slid the tickets under the glass. That was it. Sonofabitch. That was it? It was that easy?

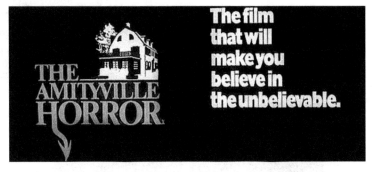

No alarms went off. No cops came. She took our money and gave us the tickets as if we were going to see some Disney movie. There had to be a catch. We'd walk in and some manager would come chasing yelling, "Hey! You kids!"

We sat down in a packed house. Somehow we managed to gets seats together. Aside from Lalo Schiffrin's creepy theme (I keep seeing the unconfirmed rumor Schiffrin's *Amityville* theme was the rejected score of *The Exorcist*) we got a few jump scares, a tacky, schlocky opening showing the murders of the unfortunate DeFeo family who still have to endure so much shit every time one of these lousy movies is released. I was surprised at how CHEAP the movie looked, sounded and felt. The lightning sound effects were out of a 50s Corman film. We got shitty special effects but…a puking nun. That's right. That nun pulled her car over and hurled into the street and we laughed like hell. I ended up in a coughing jag that made my brother re-enact the nun's puking which made me laugh even harder.

A little girl got her fingers smashed in a closing window and for some reason blood, not slime, oozed out of the walls. It looked like they just pumped it through holes behind the walls. The four of us annoyed the shit out of the people around us as we laughed, sometimes way too loud at the ridiculousness of the whole thing.

When the house goes into full self-destruct mode at the end, and the "eye" windows blow out of their frames, a lady behind us joined our *Mystery Science Theater*-style heckling and said she hoped the Lutz's had good home insurance. That was horror for her…the repair bills.

Jodie the Pig was purple with cheap red eyes and looked like some bad carnival animatronic in the brief moment we see it in a window. George Lutz goes crazy for some reason (the ghosts I guess) and goes on an axe rampage against his family. That wasn't in the book and even at my young age, questioned why it was needed. Weren't ghosts enough?

Rod Steiger's Father Delaney tied it all together with an over-the-top hammy performance that was rightly called out in the reviews that would come. I spotted Murray Hamilton who played Mayor Vaughn in *Jaws* embarrassed in this shitty movie as a priest who has to suffer through Steiger's over acting.

There were two moments, two hints that the film *could* have been good but they're so quick you can miss them through the laughter. One is in the opening of the film as the real estate lady, who just sold James Brolin and Margot Kidder their Hell House, is alone in the kitchen and has a simple, quiet ghostly incident. Just the papers blowing off the table and her spooked reaction was a good moment. The second was Brolin at wits wend looking for money that was lost in the house (we know those pesky ghosts took it). Having written a bad check he needs that money to cover it and he's already balls deep in debt from this ghost house. He discovers a money wrap, but no cash, like the ghosts are fucking with him. He let out this anguished wail: "Where is it?!" Right there, people sitting in the theater, unemployed, barely able to make ends meet. They got it. They knew where Brolin was coming from.

The horror was personal.

That's why the lady behind me wondered aloud about home insurance. I'll bet a lot of people across the country wondered that as well. Brolin's George Lutz just can't get warm in the new house. He becomes obsessed with chopping firewood (and foreshadows the coming axe rampage) but people at this time were having troubles of their own heating their houses. They got it. They got George.

That's it. Two moments, no more than two minutes out of a 90-minute film. This was the first horror movie that I paid to see, in a theater and my first R-rated movie. I spent almost the entire running time laughing at and heckling it. When the lights came up my one friend shook his head and gave it a thumb down. I assured them that the book was better. They didn't care. They'd never read it anyway.

I came home that night to find Jeffrey Lyons on *WPIX 11* ripping the movie apart on the late night New York City news. Listening to Lyons mock the film's terrible effects, over-the-topcheesy acting, especially from Rod Steiger, I felt like I wasted my "R"- rated virginity. It was my

Jeffrey Lyons of WPIX Channel 11

first taste of "not living up to the hype." The film would qualify as "so bad it's good entertainment," and later, as I read more and more of *Fangoria Magazine* I understood why. Samuel Z. Arkoff produced the movie. It was the last film for *American International Pictures*. Sam and his studio were the hallmarks of cheese movies. Once I connected the dots it all made sense. To this day I wonder how the big studios missed out on acquiring the book rights to *Amityville*. Did the studio execs dismiss it as a fluke bestseller and it wouldn't be a good movie? How did Arkoff, known for low budget content, get the rights to one of the biggest books in the country? I've searched the Internet and still don't have answer.

While I would hang on to believing the book, the terrible movie translation diminished my zeal for the overall story. It was my first whiff of bullshit.

The flipside is that it was one hell of a fun movie-going experience. The next time I would laugh that hard in a theater was during *Caddyshack* one year later. But the humor in that movie was intentional.

The Amityville Horror was the first summer horror movie out of the gate and it stunk. I placed my hopes on *Prophecy*, billed on TV and in huge ads in my parents' *Rolling Stone Magazine* as "The Monster Movie."

FANGORIA

I pilfered my mom's *Cosmopolitan* magazines to cut out the women's underwear ads. The *Sears* and *JC Penney* catalogues had underwear pictures but they weren't as hot as *Cosmo*. My mother got so fed up with finding stories missing because they were on the other side of a bra and panties ad, she stormed into my new bedroom and hurled a *Playboy* magazine at me. "Stop cutting up my goddamned *Cosmo!*" she yelled.

I asked for a subscription to *Fangoria* magazine for my 12th birthday. I was in the mall and saw that the first issue featured *Godzilla* and after reading as much of it as I could while standing in *Waldenbooks*, I was in awe of a magazine dedicated to horror.

This is where I learned much more about not just the movies and saw the pictures but HOW these movies were made. Articles on the old school filmmakers fleshed out more about William Castle while always focusing on the new up and comers like John Carpenter. Alan Ormsby, George Romero, Larry Cohen, Frank Hennenlotter, Lloyd Kaufman, Debra Hill, Roger Corman, Tom Savini and so many more filled those pages. I LEARNED about the genre. It helped to fill in the blanks at a time when that kind of information was hard to come by.

Now you just *Google* a name and take your pick from the thousands of articles, pages, websites and fan gushing. It's almost too much information. You wanted behind the scenes pictures—you went to *Fangoria*. I remember one article where Carpenter stressed the importance of finding good people for both in front and behind the camera and hanging on to them. That was his advice for indie filmmakers. Well, that and get the hell out and do it.

Fangoria wasn't for little kids like the old newspaper-format *The Monster Times*. It delivered more than *Famous Monsters of Filmland*. It didn't just focus on the old *Universal Monsters* or Japanese kaiju. *Fangoria* meant business, showing bloody stills from films, behind the scenes of graphic effects and sometimes the people interviewed dropped a "fuck" in for good measure. *Fangoria* made me feel more adult than porn because it educated me. I guess there are some who can say porn does that for them, but I think you know what I mean. It's also why I said

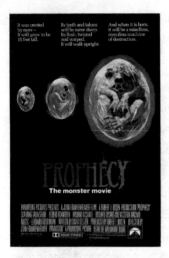

at the start of this book why horror and porn are the purest of all the genres.

The goal for both is to stimulate. Remember that?

The second issue couldn't get to me fast enough because the mutated bear of the coming 1979 summer monster movie *Prophecy* was on the cover. THIS was the one I wanted to see. The previews started early summer and whenever they popped up on TV I demanded anyone in the room watch it with me.

Fangoria was my DVD commentary throughout the 1980s. If I wanted to know more on a film I saw or to know what was coming, I went to my stack of horror magazines kept safely in my closet—not under my mattress.

I was really excited about the release of "Friday the 13th: The New Blood." I had recently bought the magazine w/ Jason's mask less face on the cover in my backpack for school. I had the issue with me when I was going to church school.

The church school teacher didn't like me and I didn't want to be there. So, rather than do church things I pulled out my "Fangoria." She was not happy and took my magazine. I was then told to leave the room and that I'd be picked up and taken back to regular school immediately. I of course protested about them taking my magazine and about why I should be allowed to read regardless of what they thought. The teacher went on and on about how vile and repulsive the cover and the content were and I told her it was far more interesting than anything she was presenting. She told me to get out! I said, "Gladly!"

Stephen LaRue

That's the poster that held my attention summer 1979. It was so "in your face" horror. They weren't pulling any punches. No shadowy beast with just eyes glaring at you. Fuck no, they went full monster, showing their creature in bright, creepy gestation art.

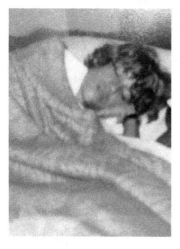

This was eco-horror to the max. Mother Nature was giving us a bitch slap. The poster told us that this would be *Jaws* on land. I could not wait to see this movie.

Once again, I gathered up a crew of friends. We walked from my house to the mall, which was a good seven miles one way and along some pretty treacherous highway. Again, no cell phones, no way to let our parents know if there was trouble. That would fall to the police.

The cold air conditioning of the mall fell over us and we made it in time for the first matinee show. It was tempting to detour to the *Time Out Arcade* tunnel for some video games, but no...I had to be strong. This was THE monster movie. We were still two years away from *Pac Man*, so the arcade had not become the major hot spot it would become in the wake of the *Pac Man* revolution.

Music Makers Theaters was decorated in garish red, white and blue tiles and stands. We got our summer matinee ticket for a whopping $2.50 and hit the candy stand. We bought popcorn, candy and these quart-sized soda containers that folded like milk cartons at the top and sealed with a plastic clip. We loaded up on shit to share and headed into the dark, black box theater in that triple-plex. The back row was free and then it hit me: most of the theater rows were open. Where the hell was everybody? It was summer and this was opening weekend for *Prophecy*. I thought for sure we'd be facing a line.

The theater was cold, the soda was gonna go right through you. Either drink it slow or pass it around, but I always had to piss right at the good part or a moment I didn't want to miss. It wasted no time. Bloodhounds broke through bushes in some Maine (*Fangoria* said they used Oregon for shooting but what did we know?) leading a search party over the side of a cliff. Something horrible down there killed the dogs and then the rescue workers who went after them. We were hooked because we didn't laugh. We didn't say a word and we had almost the whole theater to ourselves. It turned to the human interest story and "Rocky's" wife was up there on the screen and she looked like she could break into tears at any time. One of my friends couldn't resist and yelled "*Adrian!*" from the back row. The five other people in the theater didn't seem to mind. The human story was a good time for a bathroom break.

We got Robert Foxworth sounding like a pissed off dad or old man, grumping about injustice, pollution, pontificating to Armand Assante, Italian, playing a Native American. We got to see some great wilderness and then introduced to a camping family that you just knew was set up for a slaughter. We got a lot of environmental preaching and in hindsight it seems like Talia Shire cried through the whole movie. It was also a lesson on how Manifest Destiny really meant "stick it to the natives." We were almost 30 minutes in and still didn't see that Monster.

I lived through one of the most amazing periods of horror film history: 1979. That was the year that gave us (among others) DAWN OF THE DEAD, ALIEN, THE AMITYVILLE HORROR, and PROPHECY. I was twelve, so the only one I was allowed to see was John Frankenheimer's PG-rated PROPHECY.

What I really wanted to see was "Alien." The studio had done a great job of keeping the design of the title creature a secret, and the suspense of knowing what it looked like was killing me. Making things worse was the fact that my school offered a chaperoned weekend trip for its kids -- even kids as young as I was -- to go see the hit movie provided our parents signed a permission slip. When my parents found out the film was rated R, they tore up the already-signed slip, leaving me disappointed.

I alleviated my frustration by reading the novelizations of all of these movies. The movies might have been rated "R" but the books weren't age-restricted which was ironic, since there was a LOT more graphic sex and violence in the books than in the movies. Having read David Seltzer's novelization of the movie, I was particularly anxious to see "Prophecy." I put all my remaining hopes and dreams into seeing that film, begging my parents over and over again until, at last, my mom consented to drive me to the theater on opening weekend.

That was the plan, anyway.

If I'd had the chance to actually see the movie that summer weekend in 1979, I would have been even more frustrated, since the killer-bear-on-the-loose movie Frankenheimer made is considerably different from the story Seltzer's novel promised. But as it happened, I came down with strep throat the morning I was supposed to go, and I stayed sick long enough for the local theater to replace the underperforming "Prophecy" with something else. I didn't end up seeing it until 1993. I'm still mad about that.

Will T. Laughlin

We got a chainsaw fight, rabid raccoon, a giant salmon and tadpole and a family of campers hearing heavy breathing in the woods but it was starting to look like I overhyped this movie to my friends. I got those stares in the

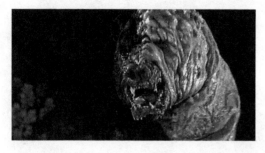

movie light. Those "Dude, this movie blows." Then the sleeping bag scene arrived and all was forgiven. From there on the movie became a fun, cheesy monster movie ride and never let up.

We laughed out loud and hard with that sleeping bag scene. The still I provided can't convey the unintentional hilarity of it. Holy shit, that big old rubber bear slapped that annoying *Brady Bunch* kid right into a rock after he tried to hop away, all zipped up in that ridiculous yellow bag.

The monster looked so silly. You knew it was a dude in a big bear suit. I was disappointed after seeing the stills in *Fangoria* compared to what was up on the screen, BUT there was another part of me elated with what we got. It was over-the-topcraziness.

Now THAT'S what I was talking about! The film kicked into high gear stupidity. A pair of creepy mutant bear cubs appeared and the whole ending was on a soundstage. It showed. I loved it–so much that I knew I would be back to see it again. My friends, not so much, but they laughed like hell when the helicopter pilot got his head crunched off like that owl finished that *Tootsie Pop* in those commercials. "Ah one! Ah two! A three!" CRUNCH! The monster moved out of the way of the camera to reveal a twitching, headless chopper pilot.

That monster mama bear was the best. The movie was meant to be a warning about environmental abuse and nature striking back. Instead, the story goes legendary director John Frankenheimer (*The Manchurian Candidate*) was half in the bag onset and David (*The Omen*) Seltzer's script was drunk-mangled as a result. Whatever the case, we got one enjoyable monster movie. I have also read the rating was to be "R" and a sizeable amount of gore and violence was cut from the final film in the fear of losing the "kids off of school" audience.

That mutant bear swatted and slung literal fake dummies into the air. We loved it. We laughed, shouted back to the screen and applauded.

That movie gave us the most fun two-and-a-half bucks could buy. To this day, it's one of the best in-theater movie viewings I ever enjoyed.

I walked out knowing damn well I was going to see it again. I did a few weeks later. I bought the novelization of David Seltzer which gave me more insight into the mutations and the fate of crying Talia Shire's possibly mutant baby. That could've dovetailed into an *It's Alive* sequel for sure. The last 30 seconds set things up for a sequel, but the movie bombed and it was just so bad it was terrific, but that doesn't get franchises jumpstarted.

If you haven't experienced something like this as a theatrical film, my heart breaks just a little bit. It was summer vacation. I was heading into seventh grade and we were without a care. Inflation, The USSR, Carter, the fuel crisis, none of it mattered as we sat in that dark theater watching that mutated bear crunch, stomp and swat people to their deaths. The movie proudly sits on my DVD shelf today. I still watch it from time to time and love it as much as when I sat in that mall theater. Treat yourself.

Prophecy was such a good time we tried to recreate it in our neighborhood. We were surrounded by woods.

"The Monster" was our most elaborate neighborhood prank. It also was the most infamous.

We stole the mutant bear story and set out to convince the little kids in our development that a monster had made its way into our valley. A car hit the monster. We would need blood. The scheme would need the neighborhood's coolest kid, Troy's approval. "What's the point in doing this?" he asked us. My pitch was simple: We would convince the kids that a monster is on the loose. We could terrify them with monster sightings and scare them by *creating* a monster!

Troy gave the nod and The Monster began its rampage. We needed to build an element of suspense. Naomi was a girl in our group, Troy's nemesis, and was credited with cultivating the art of suspense. The rest of us started to make a Monster costume and planned our strategy for running through the woods after any kid we could. "It would be over too fast," Naomi explained. We couldn't just CHASE them, we had to build this up, get them intrigued. Naomi had a plan.

The first step was to create physical evidence. We needed more than *Sears Weatherbeater* stain for blood. I met the physical evidence challenge by carving claw marks into the trees with a pocket knife. This Monster had to be big, taller than us at least. Troy put me on his shoulders and our monster grew to the amazing height of eight feet.

Footprints were needed. Naomi brought out an encyclopedia and we combined bear and wolf prints into our monster's spore. Leftover paint was dripped along the pathway near the prints to show the injured beast's retreat into the hills.

Naomi was the only one among us who respected the intellect of the kids we tortured. She had earned the kid's trust. They liked her, and while she showed a friendly, motherly exterior, she enjoyed the game underneath it all. "Kids are honest," she lectured us. She wanted us to understand our prey. She stood before us like Patton addressing his troops in front of that giant American flag. "If you're fat, they'll tell you. If you're ugly or you're wearing ugly clothes, they'll tell you that too."

We brought as many kids as we could round up to the site where the Monster had been "hit" by the car. Waiflike faces full of fear and curiosity stared at the dried "blood." Eddie's sister was our group's wildcard. You never knew what he would do. His little sister Kristin (nicknamed "Cornhusker") seemed the most scared. Her mouth was always ringed by some flavor of *Kool-aid* and her hair always looked as if she had just rolled out of bed. She got her nickname because it was her job to husk ears of corn for dinner.

"Why is the blood still there? It rained the other night," one of the kids said. It was Amy whose father looked like the villain King Tut from the *Batman* TV show.

"I took a sample of the blood before it dried," I offered. The kids thought I was smart. Plus I was in THE MIDDLE SCHOOL and we have places up there like BIOLOGY LABS and ENVIRONMENTAL STUDIES. This made me much more awesome and legitimate in their eyes. I dropped those terms a lot to make me sound legit. "I tested it in one of the BIOLOGY LABS."

Naomi nodded her head. She would never let us lie to them.

"I found some footprints," Troy said and their heads snapped to him. You could see them hitch a little breath as we went to the next level.

"Where?" Cornhusker gasped.

Troy was moving into the path that cut through a patch of weeds into the heart of the forest. "Back here," he motioned for them to follow.

They didn't. They waited for Naomi to take the lead. Once she followed they fell in line like lemmings.

Troy pointed out the prints, but he didn't point out the blood dripping along the ground or in the weeds. They found that. "It's still wet!" one of them exclaimed, rubbing it between their fingers and then on the side of a tree. We hoped they didn't smell it, or they might start thinking it smelled an awful lot like paint.

"Oh my God!" Amy yelled. Without turning, I knew what she saw and accepted Naomi's "Rules of Subtlety" as truths. "Look at those!" Vikki was pointing to the gouge marks eight feet above her in the sides of a tree. "What are they?"

"Claw marks," I said. I stole the mutant bear claws in the tree from *Prophecy*

The Monster costume was made with a raincoat, rubber electrician's gloves, black jeans, workman's boots and a cheap knock-off Darth Vader mask.

Troy and I entered the woods alongside my house after school and started hacking away at a large, dying tree. We were careful not to hack too far and stopped every so often to test how sturdy it was. Then, just when we felt that another hack would bring it down, we stopped. A picnic bench was brought out next to the tree. There was enough foliage left this late into fall for excellent cover.

Friday night was the big night.

Around ten kids assembled in my front yard. My mom and dad were inside, oblivious. Naomi helped entertain the kids while the guys beamed flashlights into the woods, awaiting the Monster. We said we put some bait out for it. Troy would yell at Naomi to be quiet, that we might scare the Monster away for a little touch of subtlety, falsely downplaying the "danger". Somewhere along the line, Scott disappeared into the house and a few minutes later came to the door. "Bruce," he called. "Mom wants you in here to do dishes."

I stomped and made a disgusted wheeze through my teeth. "Watch for it," I told Troy, Naomi, Eddie, my brother, and the others. "It could come at any time."

There was a shudder among the kids. Scott went out and I went in. I dashed up the stairs, through the kitchen (where my mom was doing dishes) and out the back door. I went down the back steps (painted that summer with a beautiful redwood finish) and into the woods where the Monster costume, placed there that afternoon, awaited me.

I stripped out of my blue jeans, donned the black pants and threw on the raincoat. The cheap mask cut into the backs of my ears and the hood went up. The rubber gloves were too big and stank of sweaty mold inside. I followed the path up toward the front of the house in my debut as The Monster.

I could hear the kids out there and Naomi's voice talking to them. I started breathing, and the mask helped to distort the sound of my breath. I broke branches and stomped hard as I closed in.

Like crickets in a summer field, they went quiet as danger approached. I could barely see them through the branches, lit by the streetlight out front. There were lots of "Shhh!" and "Didja hear that?!" from Eddie and Troy.

Silence.

Anticipation.

"There ain't nuthin' there!" one little kid yelled. He didn't sound so sure.

"Somebody get Bruce," a kid said. Scott squashed that idea by reminding them I was doing dishes.

I grunted and made a deep growl. My breath mixed with the growls to make something animal-like. This started the whining out in the yard. They were hooked.

"I'm scared," came a little voice. No tears yet.

"I can't see it. Where is it?"

Troy fired up his big *Ray-O-Vac* flashlight and beamed it my way. I roared now, angered by the light, and now there were full-fledged screams of terror out there. "I wanna go home! I'm scared! I want my daddy!" It was working. *Prophecy* provided the raw material.

I couldn't SEE anything out there. It sounded like it was going great, but I wish I could have seen them. To get too close would've been flirting with blowing my cover. There was the offhand chance that one of them would catch the Darth Vader mask.

Troy and the others did their best to stir up terror in the yard. They yelled to get back, even though no one had come close to the edge of the woods. He flashed the light wildly, trying to find me among the brush and trees while being careful not to reveal too much.

"That's no monster!" some kid yelled.

Years later John Carpenter's *They Live* had the perfect line for someone like this: "I've got one who can see!" That kid was just inches from being pushed over the line into believing but we were losing him. I stepped up onto the picnic bench, adding three feet to my height.

My head popped up above the brush. I heard a kid scream: "Oh my God there it is!" I could see that little arm pointing at an upward angle, conveying to everyone that whatever it was, it was BIG.

I pretended I was blinded or frightened by Troy's light and fled into the woods.

I did the quick change—dashed back into the house, through the kitchen, down the steps and out the front door.

"Troy!" I yelled. "Your mom's on the phone!"

I was rushed by a gaggle of kids who all wanted to tell me, at the same time, what just happened. My reappearance meant Troy's disappearance and he slipped by the throng of kids and into my house unnoticed.

He dashed up the steps, through the kitchen (while my mom did dishes), out the back door and into the woods where the costume was waiting.

Most of these little kids were crying. They huddled to Naomi who tended them like lambs. She'd flash me a glance of concern every so often, which said: "I think we've taken this as far as it should go."

The footsteps returned. The branches broke again.

It was coming. Now there were tears. Kids huddled together near Naomi. She looked like one of those fat German women with a brood of kids hanging on her apron. I flashed the light. "Where is Troy when you need him?" I tried to sound brave, but I made my voice tremble.

The Monster broke through the brush, its head coming up like some hideous periscope. It roared, waving its big rubber hands through the branches.

The light danced and Troy roared and breathed. Before I could say anything, there was a loud splintering CRACK! The tree we had chopped earlier came crashing down and crushed all of their doubts. Some kids ran for their lives, screaming as they fled my yard. Others grabbed tighter onto Naomi as if trying to climb her.

"Don't worry kids," she yelled aloud for Troy to hear. "I think it's friendly! It won't hurt us!" The picnic bench launched from the brush and sailed just inches over her head. She backed away, genuinely shaken. "Maybe not!" She backed away from the woods.

Kids ran from the yard and fled into the street for the safety of the streetlight. Troy vanished for good this time and emerged moments later pretending to be oblivious to what was going on.

It would be a great story if stopped there, but we had to take it one final step.

The time came to hunt The Monster and kill it. With sticks sharpened into spears and aluminum poles "borrowed" from a new house being built up the road, we formed a posse to go into the woods around the development. This time only a handful of kids would come with us. Word had spread since that night and some parents were becoming concerned. Not because they believed there was something out in the woods, but rather because their kids were afraid to go outside or be left alone for any length of time. Already there were four kids who could not sleep alone or without the light on.

We decided that it was for everyone's benefit to kill off the Monster and then things would go back to normal. One weekend afternoon I, Troy, Eddie, and Scott led six kids up the hill into the deep woods. Earlier that morning a can of *Sears Weatherbeater* redwood *stain* had been strategically placed in some bushes off the dirt road.

The kids held their spears to fight at a moment's notice. Plans had been arranged to "spot" the Monster, but this time the costume would not be used. We got lucky in the dark but there would be no way we could pull off a monster sighting in the day, let alone kill it. Ralph went ahead of us to scout for the beast.

He was the first to spot the Monster down by an old camping site we used from time to time. He let out a scream and we rushed down to find him lying against a tree breathing in gasps.

"I hit it. I think I got it good." He was overacting. In the tradition of great B-Movie dialogue he added: "We have to kill it."

I walked with Eddie and his little sister Cornhusker and one of her friends while Troy took a group of kids on his own. We had neared the spot where the redwood stain had been placed. Eddie stopped us all short and cocked his head, listening for something as if he were this African safari tracker. "You hear that?" Cornhusker started to whimper.

"Eddie," she glubbed. "I'm scared."

Eddie readied his aluminum pole and charged deep into a grove of thick bushes. There was a roar and the weed tops rocked as if they were caught in a violent storm. Eddie screamed.

Then it was quiet.

"Eddie?" Cornhusker called to the woods, her voice barely above a whisper.

"Ed?" I yelled. "Ed! Are you all right?" I turned to Cornhusker. "Stay here." Before she could protest I was into the weeds. No way in hell would she follow me.

Eddie was crouched down, his arms red all the way up to his elbows. "What the hell are you doing?" I asked, unable to keep my voice in whisper mode. "That's STAIN!"

The moron poured stain all over his arms. I mean ALL over, from shoulders to fingers. Only gasoline or turpentine would get it off. How was he going to go home and explain why his arms were redwood stained? Most of all, what were we going to tell his sister?

"I'll think of something," he said and motioned for me to get back out there. I left and ran back to the road. Cornhusker was standing there, spear pointed toward the woods. When I came through the brush she almost dropped it and ran. Her eyes were wide, mouth clamped tightly shut. "Where's Eddie?" she whimpered.

"Oh my God, Kristen, "I started. "Your brother's dead." It just rolled out. She dropped to her knees, crying and calling his name over and over again.

"My brother's not dead!" she yelled at me. "NO!"

Just before she went over the edge, Eddie emerged from the weeds, groaning, stunned. His arms were held out before him like a sleepwalker. "Ohh," he moaned.

"Eddie!" his little sister screamed. "You're alive!"

She ran to hug him and then saw his red arms.

"What happened?" I asked.

"It picked me up and it was crushing me so I stuck my arms into it. I killed it. There's no way it could have survived."

"*You stuck your arms into it?* You stabbed it with your *arms?*"

"Yeah," he said. "It's dead. Trust me."

Cornhusker didn't care what was dead as long as it wasn't Eddie. Troy and the others met up with us and we declared the Monster slain. The kids threw away their sticks and the development was once again safe for everyone. We sat behind Naomi's house for the rest of the afternoon trying to get the stain off Eddie's arms.

It caught up with us three months later during Eddie's 11th birthday party at *The Big Wheel* skating rink. Me, Troy and Scott sat in the area where you exchange your shoes for skates. Eddie's mother sat next to us as we laced up. She paid for all of us to get in as well as our skate rentals. She was taking us out to a movie afterwards and then ice cream.

"I just wanted you all to know what terrible kids you are," she said out of the blue. Stunned, we looked to each other. What did WE do? Was it because Troy farted in the car on the way up, igniting a fart war in the back seat?

"My daughter is terrified to be left alone. Did you know that?"

"Why?" I asked. I was always the one who broke the silence.

"Don't pretend you don't know what I'm talking about. You all know why. She has been in *therapy* for the last three months because of all of you and your *monster* bullshit." She was PISSED. She trapped us with the skating party as bait. "I can't leave her for one second, not even to walk away from the cart in the grocery store. You should all be ashamed." Her mouth was all pinched because she was biting her lip. "Maybe I should send your parents the bill for her therapy? How do you think that would go over?"

"Sorry," was all I could offer up.

"I expected better out of all of you. Especially you, Bruce." She got up, walked away and never mentioned it again. She never contacted our parents. We skated, went to the movies to see *Airplane!* We got ice cream and went home.

The night did not end the way we expected.

The Amityville Horror was a real bust. The promise of the most terrifying horror movie of the year gave us one of its funniest. *Prophecy* delivered entertainment but not in scares. To date, it was the most fun I had in watching a film in theaters. It still ranks up there in my top five best.

There were two more films to see before school started. *Fangoria* had a great article on George Romero's upcoming *Dawn of the Dead* and the issues the director faced with an "X" or "R" rating. The "X" rating was the kiss of death for commercial success. Audiences would not see the film as being too bloody or violent, but rather the "X" would brand it a porno. Porn was still in theaters at this time, although the transfer over to video cassette had begun a few years earlier.

Romero also knew an "X" rating would limit if not isolate the film to mainstream distributors. Many theaters just wouldn't play his movie.

The original *Night of the Living Dead* was a creature feature staple. I didn't understand copyright and film legalities back then, but Romero had an issue with the rights and his original film fell into a public domain hell. The word was this new film was going to be over-the-topgross and disgusting and would cause people to faint in their seats.

Aside from *Night of the Living Dead* which I never saw fully uncut in its many TV matinee showings; my only other experience with zombies was 1977's *Shockwaves* with Peter Cushing, John Carradine and Brooke Adams.

Shockwaves is one I wish I'd caught in the theater. Instead, it was another late night TV viewing, but once seen, stuck in my head ("rent free" as social media doofuses like to say these days).

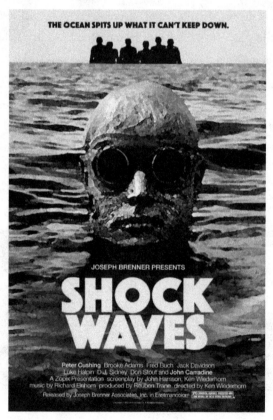

Shockwaves was another *Let's Scare Jessica to Death* horror mood piece that haunted my late night horror binges. Another gem found on "The CBS Late Night Movie," it has become a cult classic with its sunglass-clad Nazi zombies

hunting shipwrecked vacationers on Nazi fugitive Peter Cushing's Caribbean island.

With zero blood, *Shockwaves* managed to haunt my dreams with its almost sterile photography. The images of the zombies standing silhouetted against the stark ocean sunlight is still iconic. The paranoia and mistrust of the 70s runs heavy here. The stranded wasted no time turning against each other as the danger factor ramped up. Cushing had little more than an extended cameo but he gave the film gravitas right around the time he shot *Star Wars* and would become endeared to a whole new generation of filmgoers.

The Sherman announced it would get *Dawn of the Dead* for a very limited engagement. I don't remember there being any protests but I knew I had to see it. It was given an "R" rating after Romero made the required cuts.

It was just Troy and me. My brother and Eddie opted out, afraid by the TV spots and the advanced word on it being a total zombie gross out.

Fangoria let you know this was not going to be your run of the mill zombie movie.

Only a handful of people showed up for the afternoon matinee. Armed with popcorn, soda and candy we watched the film unfold before us. I was sucked in. It scared me, made me wince and one day I would get to sit down and tell Tom Savini in his own home how I sat with my mouth open watching his death scene.

It was not the theatrical experience I hoped for. The small group in the theater reacted with some groans at the makeup effects—the helicopter blades shearing the top of the zombie's head was a standout. You knew you were seeing something incredible and game changing even before the empty mall became the centerpiece for the action. I left wanting to know everything I could about George A. Romero and his films between *Night* and *Dawn*.

Dawn of the Dead was a REAL horror film. No camp or cheese. No men in rubber bear outfits with a drunken director trying to keep his shit together. It wasn't shot with cheap production values like boom shadows seen on Rod Steiger's head in *The Amityville Horror*. The humor of the zombies trying to walk up the down escalator to the awful, bland *Muzak* piped out from the mall speakers was Jonathan Swift social satire at its finest. I was too young to know that *Dawn of the Dead* was a brilliant swipe at American consumerism.

The audience was quiet. They watched. They absorbed the film.

We left the theater in quiet. A few people said aloud how good they thought it was. Troy and I would talk about it on our way home, but our exit was far more subdued than the party exit of *Prophecy*. Romero kicked our asses.

I heard more and more about this off-the-wall science fiction horror called *Alien*. The previews had a loud, in your face blaring signal sound, an egg cracking with quick, strobe cuts of scenes from the film. They never showed their monster but the TV ads were haunting. I can remember lying in bed down the hallway as it played on the TV out in the living room. I could see it in my head as that wailing siren blared.

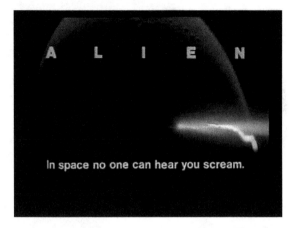

In space no one can hear you scream.

Alien was THE horror movie of that summer. My aunt and uncle saw it, and they told my mother with dire faces, "Oh no way should the kids see it!" They went on to describe scenes of how the thing changes shape and none of it made much sense to me. What was clear was they were disturbed by the film.

The poster was odd: green and black with this egg and some kind of nastiness coming out of it. The previews were scary but the word of mouth on the film was what hooked me. The way I heard people describe the alien almost always ended with, "Well you can't really describe it! You just gotta SEE it!"

I went to my mom. I begged. I pleaded. I made chores deals. There would be no way we would get into this film without her. They would never let us in. I reminded her that I got into *Dawn of the Dead* and that was so bloody and gory. It was rated "R" but (I pulled out the *Fangoria* data to back me up) it almost got an "X!" She admitted she was curious to see it and relented. Me, my younger brother, Troy and Eddie packed into our 1968 *Cadillac* and drove to a small single-screen theater in Mt. Pocono.

171

There was little to know except by word of mouth. My aunt and uncle said the alien shifted shape and that it started as this hand-thing and ended up over eight feet tall. They refused to describe a "kitchen scene" but repeated that the film was definitely not for kids. The Casino Theater had an ice cream parlor with its concession stand. The lady at this box office gave some shit. She looked at us kids, then at my mom and said something like, "You know this is a horror movie, right? It's not *Star Wars*." My mom got it and said she was going into the movie with us. She paid for the tickets and we dashed into a packed house. We sat maybe ten rows back from the screen, so it was going to be all up in our business.

You knew you were watching something cool just in the quiet opening of the film. It starts in silence and the sets, the lighting—it changed cinema forever. *Alien* allowed theatrical audiences to watch the mold broken right before them as the film played out.

I was scared enough when John Hurt's Kane got the face hugger leaping from the egg in the derelict ship. However, when he gave "birth," I was terrified.

No CGI, no computers, just practical effects and puppetry magic. I was repulsed and yet wanting more at the same time. The entire audience sat silent, as stunned as the crew of *The Nostromo* after that bloody chest-bursting scene. We all had a collective "what the fuck was that?" reaction.

My mom overplayed her hand. The film was scaring her, and she didn't like being scared. This was zero fun for her and she let these asshole kids sitting next her, munching on popcorn, talk her into it.

We were so scared there was no time to wonder, "How did they do that?" You just strapped in and went with it. The breaking point for me was Tom Skerritt's Captain Dallas going into the air shafts to drive the alien into an air lock and blow it out into space. The moments leading up to the reveal were nail biting. I didn't eat, I remember that. I knew something was coming and I didn't want to choke on my popcorn.

Veronica Cartwright (the last I saw her in a movie, she was screaming at Donald Sutherland in San Francisco) watched the alien heading for Dallas on a scanner, and urged him to run. He did, dropped down a ladder, turns and we got this—

That fucking thing lunged into the camera. I succumbed to a "fight or flight" response. My body rocketed from the chair. I ran past my mom for the aisle. She grabbed the back of my shirt and pants and pulled me back to her and into our row. It must've made a great silhouette for everyone behind us.

173

"Oh no!" she growled. "Sit down! You made me come to this, you're gonna sit through it!" I plopped back down in my seat, embarrassed as reality hit that I just ran like a pussy in front of my friends. My mom gave me the slap down in front of all of them.

You know you're scared when you're a horny 12-year-old boy and Sigourney Weaver strips down to almost nothing at the end of the film and the only thing that concerns you is "where's that fucking alien?"

Alien changed everything for me. The following spring I got two books: *The Illustrated Alien* by *Heavy Metal* and *Avon Books Alien Movie Novel*. The "Photo or Movie Novel" was a thing for a hot second in the early 80s. It was just a series of stills from the film in chronological order with some of the script dialogue thrown in. You got them for the pictures.

I enthralled my classmates after school started with the gratuitous stills of the "chest burster" and the various alien attacks in gory, bloody color. Once I had a chance to breathe and recover from the theatrical experience, I wanted to know, from a filmmaking point of view: "Just how did they do that?" It went beyond the special effects, it was the LOOK of the film and books were starting to catch on to readers wanting this kind of stuff thanks to *Star Wars* and the marketing power it tapped into. I grabbed a copy of *The Book of Alien* which showed story boards, concept art and, at the time I didn't know, but elements not used in the first film that would make their way into the subsequent ones. Who knew *Alien* would spawn a franchise?

I still have all three books. They allowed me to enter the gateway into the world of set and art design, storyboarding and the importance of vision to a film.

From there it introduced me to Carlo Rombaldi and his work in mechanical effects, HR Giger, and more. I researched and learned and studied their long creative histories. Their names meant more from reading *Fangoria* and filmmaking books...the dots were connecting. These were people that knew each other and were working against the system. The best horror seemed to be coming from people like this—using the same crews, a lot of the same cast. I was intrigued and wanted to know more.

I left that summer with a lesson in filmmaking and marketing. Hype was starting to become a factor in how I viewed trailers and what I got excited to see. All four films gave me a different big screen viewing experience but they educated me on the varying levels of quality and production value. The concept of "so bad it's good" entertainment was becoming a real concept.

Last on the horror list was Frank Langella in *Dracula*. It was back to The Sherman with my buddy Troy. The theater was packed and this time, with mostly women. Word had it Langella's Dracula did it for the ladies on Broadway and the big screen made him the Robert Redford of vampires. He had *Vidal Sassoon* hair, those dark, "come hither" eyes and a certain menace that did evoke Christopher Lee.

We got our jolts, especially with the cavern scene and Langella worked as "The guy who isn't Christopher Lee." The effects popped and, most of all, the audience screamed and the predominantly female audience LAUGHED a lot with scared amusement. They weren't laughing at the film *Amityville*-style but laughing with enjoyment. *Dracula* 1979 was a good time. It was the first time I realized that women can love horror too.

Summer '79 ended with *Dracula* and that was okay. September saw my arrival into seventh grade. No more tire chains box of paperbacks, I was now armed with my *Heavy Metal Alien* comic book and soon my photo novel to show everyone the most gruesome parts of the film. My image was changing from the nerdy new kid to the weird horror kid who wanted to make movies.

I found Toni on the first day back. I was filled with stories of my summer film adventures, ready to give my review to her and anyone who would listen or found themselves trapped. I was still a dork, but I felt I had *grown* as a dork with these theatrical experiences. I had two fun booby prizes with *The Amityville Horror* and *Prophecy* and two first place classics with *Alien* and *Dawn of the Dead*. *Dracula* got an honorable mention.

THE EDGE OF THE 80S

I had no idea *Carrie* was a book. The TV commercials for the film scared the hell out of me in fourth grade during its theatrical run. Sissy Spacek would always be that bloodied, demonic girl in those commercials, even when she was Oscar material for *Coal Miner's Daughter* a few years later. She could win all the awards out there and, for me, she's the blood-soaked girl drifting ethereally from a blazing gym with her name rippling on those previews.

I signed up for "SSR" which stood for "Sustained Silent Reading." Our middle school had "Exploratory" an end of the day class every other day where teachers created their own class based on their hobby or interest.

They were similar to the extracurricular classes in Bangor. A teacher would have a class for hobbies, crafts, whatever interested. Where one teacher in Bangor had "Rock Music" Stroudsburg offered: "Model Building", "Baseball" or one intriguing title: "What's in a Pond?" We got to hike out to the stream that ran behind the school to hunt for tadpoles, algae and crayfish. There were dozens of these exploratory classes. Grade barriers were dropped. An eighth grader could take an exploratory class with a fifth grade teacher and even have fifth graders mixed in as well.

Stroudsburg Middle School had that TV studio underneath the gym (I never understood building a sound studio beneath the thundering of a gym above). It had three big TV cameras, a control room with videotape editors, sound mixers and special effects switchboards. It was pretty state of the art for 1979: reel-to-reel videotape recorders, a *U-matic* video recorder (an oversized *Betamax*), and clip-on wired mikes that were more like leashes than anything else. However, to a 13-year-old boy with a film fetish, it was like Wonka's chocolate factory.

One exploratory class was titled "TV Production" and it jumped off the course-offering list in giant lettering. That memory will be more important for eighth grade.

I took a book reading exploratory because the teacher said they liked scary and mystery books. It wasn't going to enhance my social status, but I was curious and all I had to do was hear "horror." I was sold.

Aside from *Jaws* and *Jaws 2* and a few short stories here and there—the world of horror literature was largely unexplored. I was exposed to the *Tales from the Crypt, EC Comics* fare but nothing really in the form of legitimate literature. I checked Edgar Allen Poe out of our school library along with a collection of Alfred Hitchcock Presents short stories from famous authors like Daphne Du Marier, Robert Bloch, and HP Lovecraft. I discovered that *The Birds* started as a written story, and made my way through the growing weeds of horror writing.

My fifth-grade teacher back in Bangor voiced concern about my reading choices in a parent conference with my mother. She replied, "Well, the school library offers these books, correct?"

Aside from the classics (there was nothing wrong with that) my mainstream experience by sixth grade was Peter Benchley and Hank Searls. It wasn't like our school library stocked up on contemporary horror and the town library was in town and car-ride hassle. You got what you got.

Then I took that book reading exploratory and it all changed. A cute girl was reading *Carrie* by some guy named Stephen King.

Cute Girl was reading *Carrie*. The book sported a dull cover. No nightmarish bloody Sissy Spacek, instead it was this unremarkable artwork of a girl's face

and a shadowed profile. When I asked the cute girl what she was reading, she replied *"Carrie,"* holding up the book and its title like I was an idiot. She went on to say it was about this girl who can move things with her mind. I put it together right there. Holy shit—the movie was based on that book in her hands. I asked who wrote it and she let me see: Stephen King. I checked out the author's picture on the back.

I went home and asked my mom if we could go to the library or the mall to get a copy of *Carrie*. We didn't have to go anywhere as she had a paperback copy. Turned out my mother was a fan of King since *Carrie* and now she was happy to pass him on to me.

This chapter is not to review each of King's works. I am writing to lay out how horror changed the course of my life, influenced me as both a writer and filmmaker and most of all…allowed me to grow as a kid into a successful young adult.

Don't hear that much do you? Usually, the genre is a scapegoat for society's misfortunes and terrible acts. I am here to argue that horror made me more well-rounded, more understanding, and aware of the world around me. It gave me social skills and allowed me to flourish through high school and beyond.

I read *Carrie* and by the time *Salem's Lot* dropped as a miniseries that fall of 1979 I was all caught up. I wore out my copy of his *Night Shift* collection of short stories and must've read *The Boogeyman* fifty times before eighth grade. My math and history notebooks sported King novel covers (which counted as part of your grade). What *The Stand* had to do with eighth-grade algebra was not just beyond me, but also my teacher. She did give me five bonus points on my notebook check for the artistic effort I put into my cover. It helped. I was more interested in solving for "seX" than "X" with my blonde Farrah-haired girlfriend.

When King published *Danse Macabre* in 1981 it was satisfying to learn that I had seen most of the horror films on his back page list. I read some of the horror literature he loved. King checked off my boxes and he was my over-night, undisputed favorite horror author. By 1982 he was America's favorite and a global sensation.

King was the Spielberg of horror. He reinvented the format and changed forever how content would be made and released. All of this has been documented, listed, and footnoted. None of it is groundbreaking news. He was our modern Edgar Allen Poe.

  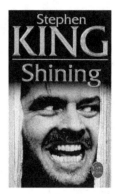

Before I get into how King influenced my life, summer 1980 gave us *The Shining* with Jack Nicholson and Shelly Duvall. Hollywood was waking up to the novelty that slapping King's name on a film meant dollars thrown at their work like some stripper on a stage.

I read the novel before seeing the film (a Christmas gift from a friend). While *Jaws 2* the novel was very different in tone and depth from the film, the movie was still a good time. I could not say the same for *The Shining*. We went to The Sherman Theater where *The Amityville Horror* nabbed my "R-rated" virginity and waited to be scared by *The Shining*.

I'm still waiting all these years later.

The Shining TV spots scared the B'Jesus out of me. That music with Jack Nicholson jeering into the camera, hobbling through the night snow with that axe and lots of wide-eyed shots of terror, yeah, you got me, Kubrick. I'm in. Take my lawn mowing money.

My teen posse asked "What the fuck was that?" a lot while we waited for one of our moms to get us after the movie. I was the only one who read the book so I had some perspective. For me it was a lot of "What about the...but where's this...they forgot that." The movie stripped away almost everything that made King's novel a personal nightmare. For my about-to-be-teen friends who didn't read the book, the film was slow, boring, and even confusing.

Without Jack you got jack. *The Shining*, for me, is one of the genre's most overrated films. It is hardly "terrifying" and does not deserve its high rankings on "Top Lists." Well-made, Jack Nicholson, well-produced, beautifully shot...yes. Weird, creepy imagery? Yes.

Terrifying? No. A whole cottage industry has risen in the digital age with fans claiming the film is deliberately esoteric, with some saying it's so high-concept and intellectual that its many mysteries laid in by Kubrick must be studied and understood to be truly appreciate the film.

Maybe. When I think about the film, it's like the whole movie was in slow motion. Another film, *The Keep* will evoke similar memories, a year later.

This is a perfect segue into my point about Stephen King. But one last shot at the Kubrick film...someone in marketing the subsequent paperback issues of *The Shining* got the idea to merge the movie's signature image of Nicholson's "Here's Johnny!" moment with the book. This is misleading. If you open this book with this artwork on the cover expecting it to be like the movie, you're in for one hell of a surprise.

Decades later, director Mike Flanagan would bring some kind of closure with Stephen King's help with the movie ending of King's *Shining* sequel, *Doctor Sleep*. There is a moment in that film involving the kidnapping of a boy baseball player that is more terrifying in its four-minutes than all two hours of *The Shining*. One single scene.

Back to King and why I connected to this guy's writing. Stephen King pulled the ultimate hat trick: he was able to bring back all of the old things, nostalgia–*the feels*, shall we say for horror, while packaging them up in a contemporary format with dialogue and characters that meant something to us. King personalized horror. That's his secret.

My mother was a casual horror reader. She preferred true crime. If you remember she declined our pleas to get us into *The Amityville Horror* because it meant sitting through it with us. She relented with *Alien* and regretted it. She said she hated being scared and meant it.

When I came home from that reading group from school, she revealed she was a closet horror fan and it was Stephen King who made her one with *Carrie*. Why?

My mother told stories of feeling like the misfit when she was a kid. She was the "chubby kid," the "fat kid." She took up smoking at the age of 13 and found that it also curbed appetite and she shed some weight. I have pictures of my mom as a kid and teen and have never seen evidence to support her "fat kid" stories. She was thin, but one's self-perception is very different than outside perspective. It didn't matter, it's what she thought and because of that, *Carrie* appealed to her.

Was my mom picked on as a kid? Did she want revenge against those who did? Was she rooting for Carrie White in the book's prom rampage ending? Did my mom want to burn down the entire town? *Carrie* was her first taste and she was hooked. She read every single King book until her death in 2007. Her bookshelf was dominated by his work and it was all in chronological order. He was the only fiction author that she invested into the hardback first before paperback.

Carrie appealed to me as well for similar reasons. The *Jaws* appeal was a monster shark swimming around eating people. Benchley's original novel got mired down in an adulterous affair between Ellen and Hooper. The mafia had Larry Vaughn by the balls and threatening Brody. In between, the shark showed up. The film rightfully got rid of all of that.

The underlying theme of this book connected to my early childhood in my oddball status as a kid. "Faggot" haunted me. I am not excusing the word, but it was the term lobbed by other kids who "belonged" against those who did not, and whether they really thought I was sexually attracted to other males, it was the preferred carpet bomb word–weaponized to hurt someone and shit all over their day.

I was a misfit like Carrie White. I knew way too much about horror movies and Godzilla. I couldn't play sports to save my life. I was into drawing, movies, and writing stories. I was "artsy." That translated into "gay."

There were many times in elementary school that I got off the bus crying. I was picked last in gym. Whispers went on behind cupped hands, with eyes looking at me in the classroom—followed by giggles and laughs I knew were directed at me.

I wanted to knock those kids out. Look, I love horror, but never once did I fantasize or think of bringing a gun to school to enact revenge upon my tormentors. However, I quietly cheered Carrie White on after the pig's blood prom humiliation. Stephen King allowed me to vent my hurt and anger through his characters.

Carrie was personal. I think it was to the people who responded so well to it. Brian DePalma's 1976 film became less of a horror movie to me. After reading King's book, and creeping closer to teenager territory, I wanted to see the film.

Carrie the film was less about supernatural horror and more about the horror of real-life. Spacek's performance transcended King's book character. We felt so badly for this girl and the private anguish she endured. Piper Laurie's crazy mother tied it all together and by the time the Bates High Bitches pulled their prom showstopper, we were ready for Carrie to fuck some shit up. She was the personified form of Columbine.

Anyone who was made fun of, tormented, picked on, verbally or physically abused could relate. I had too much of that in my life from home to school.

His characters weren't Arctic explorers or effete English gentlemen or scientists. They were everyday people. *The Dead Zone's* Johnny Smith (could you get any more bland of a name?) was a high school English teacher thrust into extraordinary events in *The Dead Zone* (which eerily predicted the rise of Donald Trump through crazy politician Greg Stillson).

The Stand played into one of my greatest fantasies...to be alone–to be the last living person on earth. My favorite part of King's book dealt with the rampant virus and returning the earth to a quiet planet. He wiped out the human race and I was fine with that. There were times I walked down rural roads in late summer, the insects the only soundtrack, no houses and I would imagine what it would be like to be one of the only people left on the planet like in *The Stand*. It was a wonderful dark fantasy.

His descriptions of the air smelling better, of Nick Andros and Stu Redman walking quiet roads with no cars passing, no factories, no human noise was bliss.

King did what good writers should, he transported us out of our regular lives into the ones of his characters. Even if those worlds were as mundane as ours because we knew something unbelievable was going to happen to them. We lived their experiences in his writing. We identified. Donna Trent's marital unhappiness in *Cujo* came through to us. While we may not agree with her choices, we understood and feared for her when they led her to the lair of a rabid Saint Bernard. *Pet Sematary's* Louis Creed was a campus doctor faced with a new home whose land has evil resurrection properties. Ben Mears was a writer, widower and before you can say *Salem's Lot* he and a school teacher and country doctor are battling vampires in his home town.

Stephen King understood that horror was personal. *The Shining* is less about supernatural things in a hotel than it is about the real horror of the dissolution of the family unit from alcoholism and abuse. Only later did we find out that King himself was haunted by these very things and writing was quasi-exorcism of these demons. He admitted once he remembered nothing of the writing process for *Cujo*—steeped into his addictions of alcohol and cocaine – and even consuming mouthwash, and living a *Lost Weekend* type of existence. Test my hypothesis. Find any King story and look at the main characters. They are usually like you and me: middle class, workday people who turn a corner, and BAM! The world ends, a hotel claims their soul, a monster, alien clown-thing rises from the sewers to ruin summer vacation…regular people dropped into incredible circumstances. The formula works.

Even in his first hands-on film, *Creepshow*, King's characters are all normal people. From Ed Harris's bewildered newcomer to the Grantham family, King's simpleton Jordy Verrill whose life has been the same since a kid (until that is he dares to expose his hands to "meteor shit."), to Hal Holbrook's *Walter Mitty* cuckhold college professor, the common person thread is clear. This holds true in all of his "Bachman Books" as well.

Real horror can come to us at any time. From anywhere—a call that brings the death of a loved one. A doctor visit that was considered routine turns into discussions of Stage Four cancer. The first time our kid gets behind the wheel by themselves and every fucking time your phone rings afterward…

186

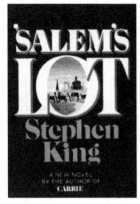  

This brings me to three personal connections to King's work: *Salem's Lot*, *Pet Sematary* and *IT*.

I grew up in a small town like Salem's Lot. We had the main street dotted with cafes, book stories, a cobbler, local hardware, and bank. We had streets lined with large maples and oaks. We had sidewalks and Victorian homes on postcard streets. It was a vacation town where everyone knew everyone. Our town even had the town Chrysler dealer and you went to school with his kids whose last name went above that Chrysler name over the dealership display window.

Shit, we even had milkmen for awhile.

Small towns breed contempt. King knew they also have a dark side to their picture-perfect façade (consider *Kings Row* and the later popular film and soap opera *Peyton Place*). In *Salem's Lot,* it was vampires that came for the town. They would destroy it, change it forever. By the end of the book, Salem's Lot is a ghost town of the undead, the exact opposite of how it started for the reader.

The evil in *Salem's Lot* was invited to the town in the form of Hubie Marsten, a wealthy rum-running hood in the 1920s and 30s whose mansion overlooked the entire town and held unspeakable things behind its walls.

Things were changing in my little town around 1980. Being a vacation town bordering New Jersey and a honeymoon and second home capital for New York City, Stroudsbug started to see a population increase from the outlying urban centers.

New York and New Jersey were moving in. Over a slow period of time more and more kids with those Jersey and Brooklyn accents popped into class, moved into houses around us…reproducing almost exponentially as New York TV commercials urged city folk to "come to the Poconos."

> *I saw "Salem's Lot" when I was eight years old. My brother being four years older, knew I would be scared shitless and took it upon himself to go outside my bedroom window that night and knock on it saying he was the kid from the movie. I ran screaming down the hall…he still to this day laughs at how bad he scared me and also made me a horror fan.*
>
> **Michelle Stanley**

New Yorkers and New Jerseyites moved into our beautiful little town, carving out new developments, cutting down the forests, and filling in the ponds for new homes and resorts. It was like King's vampire invasion in *Salem's Lot.*

They were invited. The Chamber of Commerce and Vacation Bureau marketed the shit out of The Poconos to lure tourists. The builders advertised on billboards along Route 80 and on the New York bridges to come to the Poconos. TV real estate showed small schools, low taxes, and the good life. "Beautiful Mt. Airy Lodge!" was one of many commercials pushed by vacation bureaus that fortified the images of heart-shaped and champagne tower Jacuzzis to the relocating undead.

The soul of our little town was drained. When I return there now, the mountainsides are dotted with water parks and new resorts. The highways are now clogged and places where we once camped and hiked are bulldozed under. Main Street now hosts a condom shop. Chain stores replaced the private owner restaurants. It's now a college town dotted with bars and nightclubs.

King's *It*, much like his novella, *The Body* (turned into the acclaimed Rob Reiner film *Stand by Me*) summed up my childhood as well as the kids from the 1950s, now our parents. Hiking, fishing, camping, biking, long summer afternoons tubing down cow creek, are now memories. I identified with The Losers from *IT*. My friends in middle school were much like the misfit kids in both stories.

I was the boy who wrote stories like Bill Denbrough in *IT* or Gordie LaChance in *The Body/Stand by Me*. I was the kid telling the stories as we walked the train tracks, the woods, the back roads, while we fished or sat around the campfire. I would one day go on to make real Hollywood films, the small-town kid done good and that's who I wanted to be when I read King's books. I wanted to be THAT kid...the kid that overcame the monster...the horror...to do right and people would see it.

King spoke to ME in his writing. He reached out to invite me into his worlds. I found they were not much different than mine because mine had monsters too.

It was *Pet Sematary* that drove home my personal point. I told you about our class celebrity and iconic hot girl, Toni. I loved Toni from afar and pursued her to be the celebrity name in my first feature film, a live-action middle school remake of *Mad Monster Party*. She declined but it made us closer and by high school, she was one of my closest friends.

It was Toni that gave me the confidence to run for class president, urging me to do it because I was just as good as anyone else—even though I saw myself as unpopular. Toni supervised my image remake and positioned me to take charge of my destiny. My wild times and great memories of high school are a large part thanks to her.

She gave me the confidence to aim higher.

Toni was killed in a car crash October 8th, 1983, at the start of our junior year. That was the fall of my new class presidency. I had a new image: longer hair, mustache, a safari bush jacket, and a true "Cali Filmmaker" look that she helped design.

Then she was gone.

My junior year was to be a celebration of accomplishment. The horror came six weeks in. It was the first time I lost someone so close to me that was my age. Friday she was there after Driver's Ed Behind the Wheel class and Saturday she was dead. By the middle of the following week, I was standing over her coffin at her viewing before her burial the next day.

My mourning took me to dark places. I was not suicidal, but I went to the places where heavy grieving will drag you. Suddenly my mind thought in Pre-Toni terms. This movie was shot or released while Toni was alive. I was doing this when Toni was alive. Overnight life became divided into "Pre-Toni" and "Post-Toni" categories.

Spandau Ballet's True was on a playlist from our local radio station and seemed to be on the car radio every time she and I had Behind the Wheel. Whenever it came on, I saw her, heard her, and smelled her. My heart truly hurt. My chest ached. I would break into spontaneous crying jags. I let my schoolwork slide. I flirted with impeachment as class president.

I gave up. Nothing mattered anymore. Something in me died with Toni.

Pet Sematary tapped into this grief. When Louis Creed lost Gage in that horrid trucking accident. I got it. I was with him as he ventured out to do the unthinkable, digging up his boy for the shot to have him back. I asked myself while I read…would I do the same for Toni if I knew there was a chance to have her back?

Let me make this clear, I did not give any thought to re-creating Louis's actions in *Pet Sematary*. This was grief, not insanity, delusion or the influence of an evil graveyard. I *identified* with that father's grief. King also made it very clear through the Greek Chorus that was next door neighbor Judd Crandall, that what comes back is evil and while it may fill the hole, what festers beneath that wound will kill you.

King's lesson was very clear: sometimes dead is better.

The book helped me manage my grief. Horror served as a sounding board for my dark thoughts and brought me back up to the surface. A close friend gave me a verbal ass-kicking to head off impeachment. I returned to my grades and presidential duties full force.

It wasn't overnight, but King's book was a factor in managing the pain in my soul.

King's ability to tap into the most basic of human emotions is coupled with his mastery of finding horror in the ordinary. He knows where real horror comes from. His horror always begins quietly…it seeps out of the woodwork. He doesn't start with grandiose alien invasions or supernatural perfect storms.

Instead, he knows what scares you, because he knows it's personal.

Stephen King is able to cut through the pretense of the genre and give us what we need and sometimes what we don't want. Since we were kids, horror came from the closet, under the bed…in the darkness. That common thing unites us all and then as we age, it networks outward like tendrils and King knows how to navigate that network. I am not scared of the dark anymore, but I am scared of going into it once I die and winking out of existence. King tapped into that with *Doctor Sleep*. The hospice patient that tells Danny Torrence his greatest fear of death is that there could be…nothing. What if we just disappear into the void, losing all that defined us? That is horror. Maybe not to a 15-year old kid, because at that age most kids think they will live forever and are indestructible. King knew how to pluck every one of those tendrils—from the child-like fear of the dark through the fear of going into it as adults…the man plugged into the ether and has stayed that way. *Carrie*, *The Shining*, *Salem's Lot* inspired me to write more—to work harder and improve my writing. I studied King's dialogue and what made it so fucking good. His writing improved my vocabulary…I searched out definitions and kept a thesaurus by my bedside when I read his work.

I wrote *Jaws 3* in sixth grade (with Toni a character) but that was "fuck around writing." By eighth grade I started new work, imitating King's style and attempting to ape to his dialogue. I wrote a supernatural witch/demon movie with teen characters that proved a hit among friends and warranted a sequel.

I wrote these on notebook paper by hand with my trusty *Eraser Mate* pen. I cranked out a monster story and also an *Orca* knockoff that never finished.

It didn't matter, Stephen King's books fueled my desire to do better, to work harder, and forge my own path.

All of these were done by the end of eighth grade with my beloved reading teacher, Mrs. Haddon spending her free time to review and critique and provide guidance to help me grow as a writer. High school gave me several great writing teachers: Mrs. Patricia Schneider, Mr. Edward Burnett, and Mr. Michael Steen who read my work and gave fantastic feedback.

I dedicated *Camp Dread* to them as these three high school teachers gave me their time, their insight and were not afraid to give the hard criticism which made me work even harder to impress them. I was truly blessed with them in my life and high school career.

Horror led me to Stephen King.

His writing inspired me. It made me appreciate the small things in life and to love the moments. There are so many wonderfully beautiful moments in all of his books. Horror teaches us to appreciate them because they are fleeting as the monsters are always chasing us, even when they are out of sight and out of mind.

I was more than a "fan" (I hate that word. It is short for "fanatic" which implies mental instability). I was a student. I listened to King. I did more than read him; I tried to understand him and what he was telling me.

I wish he taught writing. I would drive to Maine to sit in one of his classes.

Stephen King doesn't write about death, he teaches about life. Every single one of his books conveys that message. I wouldn't react to a horror author so strongly until my freshman year in high school when I was introduced to Peter Straub and *Ghost Story*.

I need to get us into 80s territory and my first filmmaking adventure in remaking a beloved horror classic.

MAD MONSTER PARTY REVISTED

Donna Haddon (an Angela Lansbury-esque reading teacher with a background in radio production) started a TV and film production class at the end of the day for extra-curricular "exploratories." Mrs. Haddon was that teacher that you would thank one day after accomplishing something great or becoming famous.

I met Mrs. Haddon in seventh grade, 1979, when she launched her TV Production exploratory. She tried to do an edgy adaptation of Evan Hunter's gang story, *On the Sidewalk Bleeding*. She got permission from our very open-minded principal to use adult language and even a prop knife. No way would that shit happen now in a middle school. Regardless, it never got completed save for a few scenes but I was hooked and knew I wanted to work with Mrs. Haddon again when I got her the next year for eighth grade.

I gathered my friends to make a movie. It was going to be a remake of *Mad Monster Party*. I originally thought of it as a play, but it was Mrs. Haddon who saw the possibilities of making it into a film in our downstairs TV studio. I even looked her up in the phone book right after the start of our eighth grade year and the teachers went on strike for six weeks. I called her at home and told her the movie was on Channel 9 that afternoon and she should watch it. She did.

We had a three-camera setup in the studio. The video cameras were connected to a booth where a reel to reel video recorder preserved it all. A long switchboard allowed sound and video fades and wipes and that was about it. I think your basic movie app can do all of that and more.

196

A close friend and classmate who lived four houses down transcribed my old audio cassettes I made of the film into a shooting script. We planned to use my comic strips as storyboards.

The next step was casting. You need marquee value. You need names.

I would play Boris Karloff's Dr. Frankenstein. My friend who slaved over the tape transcriptions would be Phyllis Diller's Monster's Mate, but I needed star power for Francesca. We did have a girl who was an almost perfect real-life double of Francesca right down to the red hair and beauty mark, but she passed before I could finish the pitch.

"I don't remember Bruce wanting it to be Toni," my one friend who wanted to be Francesca recalled. "I know he wanted Connie because she looked like the real Francesca or the fake puppet Francesca from the movie. Whatever, she looked like the character from the movie but her boobs weren't footballs stuffed down her shirt. That was the only difference."

I moved on to my next choice: Toni. Toni was STARPOWER. She was a badass in *Jordache*. She was "Toni," a single name like Cher or the soon to be known Madonna. If Toni played Francesca, it would make me legit. All those who doubted me, all those who thought I was "the weird kid" would pick me up on their shoulders and parade me throughout the school as tickertape and confetti fell from the ceiling.

Toni passed. "You want me to get my dress ripped off?"

"Yeah," I told her. I waved it off like it was nothing.

"In my underwear? Like real UNDERWEAR? On camera?" She had a deadpan face, not believing what she was hearing. "Everyone in the school sees me in my bra and panties?"

I explained that it happens in the real movie and kicks off the big monster bash. Toni laughed and declined. It wasn't just the dress ripping that got the "no" but also acting wasn't her thing. She was proud of me. I should find someone better than her.

We held auditions. I cast my then-best friend as Felix Flanken as he had that "aww shucks" kind of goofiness that would remind me of Tom Hanks. I rounded out the cast with other friends and we went forth to make our movie.

We shot it on black and white, reel to reel video tape (I still have the original video tape reel) and Mrs. Haddon supervised in that "executive producer" title. She taught us blocking, camera angles and she guided me in directing. The impact this woman had on my life can't be overstated.

I paraded through the middle school hallway to the gym stairs that led to the lockers and TV studio, in Mrs. Haddon's white wig, a white lab coat and spectacles to the embarrassment of a girl I was dating at the time. "Why are you doing this?" she asked once. "You are on the verge of popularity."

She didn't get it. Film was my life, and *MMP* was my long-time mistress. However... "On the verge of popularity..." Really? She saw that?

It took all year to make a film with a less than 30-minute running time. Halfway through the year our original Francesca got sick and replaced with her understudy. Then the original Francesca got better, came back to school and we swapped out the understudy and kept right on filming. Literally halfway through the film Francesca is played by an all-new girl, AND THEN changes BACK in the last ten minutes to the original actress who went on sick leave.

The island was supposed to blow up at the end. We made this scale island out of mud and moss with a toy castle stuck on it like a cake decoration. A kid promised he could deliver the explosion with cherry bombs. Mrs. Haddon met with the principal and secured permission to bring in the explosives. They would be kept in the office until the day of the shoot and would be supervised with an additional teacher to Mrs. Haddon.

He never brought the cherry bombs after all his hype and bravado. I had to settle for sinking the island by placing it on a paddle and lowering into the creek. A Maple leaf floated by that was bigger than the whole damned island.

There was some nominal "editing" and the final cut ran about 25 minutes, not exactly a full length feature.

No one noticed or cared. The teachers wheeled out these 25-inch *Magnavox* TVs on rolling carts into each eight grade learning area on the last day of school, June 1981 and my year-long project debuted. The 80s were revving up.

It was a hit and my then-girlfriend sat astounded at the positive reaction. I

199

wonder today if she's seen any of my professional films. My friends presented me with a homemade Academy Award which sits on my desk to this day. It followed me to college, then to Los Angeles after failing out of Penn State and to where I am now.

A kid's movie followed me all through school, introduced me to the horror genre and stayed with me to this day. On my desktop sits a big budget, live-action remake of *Mad Monster Party* that updates everything and does not just feature the classic Universal Monsters, but also some more current and familiar faces.

It will never get made.

MORNING AGAIN IN AMERICA

You can't discuss 80s horror without the 80s historical context. That applies to any era of film. Art is a reflection of life and this is where we run into the ever ongoing issue with remakes, reboots and re-imaginings.

The end of the 60s and all of the 70s sucked. The start of the downslide could arguably be the assassination of JFK. It got worse from there. Vietnam officially ended in 1975 with the humiliating images of American helicopters lifting off the Saigon embassy as thousands tried to flee (anyone hear of Afghanistan?) and were left behind as South Vietnam fell to the North.

Watergate, the oil crisis, war in the Middle East, the economy in freefall, unemployment, Russians in Afghanistan, the auto industry rusted away, social unrest, the rising poverty gap, American education falling further behind the rest of the world, Iran's Islamic revolution saw the taking of our American embassy in Iran. It was not a good time for America.

President Jimmy Carter saw his fate after he took to the TV to tell America and the world that he took full responsibility for a failed rescue mission to get our hostages. The planes and choppers crashed into each other and to the desert floor under Operation Eagle Claw. The next day Iranian TV broadcast the burned wreckage and American soldiers' bodies and told the world that America couldn't even save its own people.

The Republican Party nominated Ronald Wilson Reagan as its 1980 nominee. The Democrats had doubts Carter could win re-election and toyed with the idea of Ted Kennedy's nomination as they held their breath hoping NY Governor Mario Cuomo took a shot at The White House. When Chappaquiddick and other Kennedy family scandals proved to be too much, the Democrats backed their Georgia horse and hoped Carter could do it.

Reagan promised an American renewal. He believed in capitalism and embraced "Trickle Down Economics," which basically translated into the wealthy will get even more wealthy and their spending will expand the economy, benefitting all of us as it worked its way down from the top. Or scraps from the table. It depends on your point of view.

Reagan was a former B-movie actor, known for his low grade Westerns with a few stand out roles such as football player George Gipp in *Knute Rockne, All-American*, which gave Reagan the nickname of "The Gipper" as in "Win One For the Gipper." *Google* it.[2]

There was fear in the Reagan camp that Carter would pull an "October Surprise," a negotiated release of the 52 American hostages and thus become a hero, giving him a last minute boost in popularity and possible win in the 1980 election.

Even before Reagan drummed his patriotic mantra, America was working toward some kind of comeback all on its own through pop culture. *The Charlie Daniels Band* followed up their over-played *The Devil Went Down to Georgia* with *In America*, where Daniels told the Russians they could go straight to hell and America was more united than ever before.

The 1980 Winter Olympics saw the US Hockey team beat their Soviet opponents 1-0 and while it had no impact on Soviet Russia moving all over

---

2   https://www.reference.com/history/did-call-ronald-reagan-gipper-b90200e9baff314

Afghanistan and throughout Eastern Europe, it was a needed shot in the arm for all of us.

Carter held his own in pre-election polling. Later we found out that the Reagan team literally stole Carter's debate briefing book that held a number of debate points and responses. The national debates between Reagan and Carter turned into a spectacle as Carter would deliver clear, fact-based information only to have Reagan laugh, shake his head and respond with quips like: "There you go again." Carter came across as sullen, angry and defeated. America was tired of him. They wanted a change.

The final debate sealed it. Carter gave a closing speech that appealed to America's better senses. It was eloquent, steady, but in the end, not uplifting and for many it was too little too late. Reagan however gave his closing remarks and then asked one of the most famous questions in American electoral history. He looked right at the camera—to the guy in the bar that just lost his job, to the family sitting around the table or in the living room wondering how to make the bills, heat the house or pay the mortgage and said: "Next Tuesday is Election Day. Next Tuesday, all of you will go to the polls and make a decision. I think

when you make that decision, it might be well if you would ask yourself: Are you better off than you were four years ago? Is it easier for you to go and buy things in the stores than it was four years ago? Is there more, or less, unemployment in the country than there was four years ago? Is America as respected throughout the world as it was? If you answered all of those questions 'yes,' why then, I think your choice is very obvious as to who you'll vote for. If you don't agree, if you don't think that this course we've been on for the last four years is what you would like to see us follow for the next four, then, I could suggest another choice that you have."

Reagan won by a landslide. Carter didn't just lose; he was kicked to the curb.

On Inauguration Day Reagan told the country that government was the problem. He promised to restore our respect and economic might and he was going to get Big Government off our backs and out of our lives (He didn't).

I sat in eighth grade at my desk watching the inauguration with the rest of my class—TVs all over the learning areas. The entire school watched the oldest President to date in US history sworn in. The TVs went off, classes resumed and then less than an hour later our principal took the announcements and urgently told all teachers to stop what they were doing and to turn the TVs back on.

Did someone shoot Reagan? Did he die because he was so old? Heart attack? Did he declare war on Russia like some feared? The 25-inch consoles on the carts powered up and *ABC News* told us Reagan was about to make an important announcement.

The new President came on the screen and told us and the world that less than an hour ago, just after he was sworn in, a plane with all 52 American hostages, left Iranian airspace. After 444 days, our hostages were coming home.

America was back.

Reagan did in one hour what Carter couldn't do in a year. He turned his attention to inflation and unemployment. There was a new sheriff in town.

A renewed militarism arose. Reagan promised to stand firm against the USSR and called them out as an Evil Empire. He even joked about the death of several leaders in succession before Mikhail Gorbachev took office. "I keep trying to deal with them, but they keep dying on me!" he told the press.

The new President's sense of humor, his ability to control the media and light up the camera gave him another nickname: "The Great Communicator."

America was moving into a welcome home party mode.

New wave music and new electronic bands were springing up, reflecting a shift from the Disco 70s and *MTV* showed up in 1982 and changed the way we would hear and now see music forever.

Movies reflected this odd optimism. Action and comedies rose to the surface and they were fast and loose with upbeat endings. It's almost like The Reagan Administration went to Ronnie's old Hollywood stomping grounds and told the studios that this was how it was gonna be.

"Saturday Night Live" had a new cast but a 19-year old kid would turn it into "The Eddie Murphy Show" and become the decade's top star. Reagan sent military advisors and covert op teams with a message for the communists in Central America: Get the fuck out.

The Soviets found themselves in their own Vietnam in the hills of Afghanistan. Reagan started his long-term plan of bleeding the Russians dry by financing Afghan rebels. One of them was a Saudi ex-patriate named Osama bin Laden. Osama wasn't bin Laden at the time. He was just an operative for the US, approved by the Foreign Relations Committee.

Music was back. Movies were back. Military was back. America was back. With a kickass President who wasn't going to take shit like Carter did.

When the nation's air traffic controllers threatened to strike, possibly crippling US air travel and commerce, Reagan took to the TV airwaves and made it clear: Almost 12,000 air traffic controllers had 24 hours to return to work. If they didn't they have forfeited their jobs and will be terminated.

On August 3, 1981, during a press
conference regarding the PATCO strike,
President Reagan stated: "They are in
violation of the law and if they do not
report for work within 48 hours they
have forfeited their jobs and will be
terminated."

Those 11,395 strikers called Reagan's bluff and The Gipper shit-canned every one of them and replaced them with military until replacements could be hired.

The March after his inauguration a deranged fan of actress Jodie Foster, who had watched *Taxi Driver* a few times too many, decided to impress the future Oscar-winner by shooting Reagan outside a hotel in Washington, DC. Two bullets struck him and his press secretary was hit in the head and errone- ously reported killed.

Reagan was rushed to the hospital and as First Lady Nancy Reagan greeted him as he was wheeled into the building he quipped, "I forgot to duck." The media ran with that. A few minutes later, before being knocked out for surgery, Reagan is said to have looked up at the surgeon team and joked, "I hope you guys are all Republicans."

America ate it up. It couldn't have been scripted any better.

None of us knew just how badly the old man was hurt. Nancy was his gatekeeper and she hid much of his injury from the press. The media cropped his hospital photos to hide extensive tubes and wires to show the country a smil- ing president in good health and spirits. We now know that was not the case. Hinkley almost achieved his goal.

Within a month Reagan was back in the saddle, giving a triumphant, bright and upbeat address to Congress where he read a few fan letters from kids and made the Congress and nation laugh. We needed these light hearted moments after the malaise of the Carter years and the darkness in the wake of Vietnam and Watergate.

Does this outline the contrast between the 70s and 80s succinctly for you? Do you have a picture from this very oversimplified description of the 80s? Ronald Reagan was the 80s. The 80s were Reagan. That's why to this day I call them "The Reagan 80s."

Horror's transformation wasn't overnight, but it seemed like it.

The best place to start is 1980 and a little rip-off movie shot only 30 minutes from my house in nearby Blairstown, New Jersey. It was supposed to be called *A Night at Camp Blood,* but was re-titled to *Friday The 13*ᵗʰ.

Remember what we discussed earlier? Sequel was still a dirty Hollywood word and "franchise" had yet to be born? As of 1980 we had two *Jaws* movies, almost two *Star Wars*, one *Halloween*, one *Texas Chainsaw*, you get my point.

Jaws was re-released in theaters summer 1980, the summer before eighth grade. When my friend down the road said she and her family were going to the drive-in over at East Stroudsburg I about had a breakdown. I begged. I literally got down on my knees in the street and begged her to ask if we could go.

She went to bat and got permission. We packed into her family's 1973 Chrysler station wagon with wood paneling and headed off to the drive-in to catch my second viewing of *Jaws* in five years.

We sat on blankets atop the roof. A large speaker was attached to the passenger window, tilted up so we could see it as well. The field was packed. Dozens of cars parked in a half circle, pointed to a giant white rectangle.

The sun dipped and at that magic hour when it's just dark enough, the projector light hit the screen. You could feel the anticipation around us. The welcome reel played, a few previews and the screen went dark. The *Universal* logo came up and it was now dark.

I saw "Friday the 13th Part VI: Jason Lives" for the first time when I was eight or nine. I was with my mom at one of her friend's houses and she and her friend were hanging out in one room. I was watching TV with her friend's husband.

He did not have kids so probably did not realize what was or wasn't age appropriate (I believe it was probably on HBO or something). The scene that stood out to me was the one where the couple is driving the yellow bug that breaks down and Jason uses the fence post to pop their tires and then murders them in glorious fashion.

Even though we lived in a suburb/city, our house at the time was down a long driveway, probably 100 feet long, and it went in between the property of two neighbors so there were no street lights and it was dark as can be. Well as you can imagine on the way home from my mom's friend's house later that night, we turned into the driveway and I pretty much lost it. I was 100% convinced Jason was going to be waiting down the way to pop our tires and kill us. I was hysterical!

No matter how many times my mom tried to tell me it wasn't going to happen and Jason wasn't even real I didn't believe her and anytime we drove down the driveway at night I burst into tears because I knew one of these times Jason was going to be there waiting to kill us.

You would think that would traumatize me and make me hate horror movies but somehow it did the opposite and I love them. It's the fear of the unknown and what might be around the next corner that terrifies me and make for an awesome horror movie experience for me. It's probably where my love for the original "Halloween" comes from.

Liz G.

When the first groan of that shark theme bass rumbled over the speakers the whole place went nuts. Car headlights flashed. The horns blared—a hundred car horns exploded across that field. It was pure elation, mechanized applause. I loved it and now I realize most people will never experience anything like that ever again.

Back to *Jaws 2* for a moment. Roger Ebert once said that *Jaws 2* just might be the first "slasher" film of the "dead teenager" sub-genre. The shark is the psycho killer, picking off arrogant teens one by one, mostly because of their sexual hubris. When do Tina and Ed get attacked? Right before they're about to screw in Tina's boat. Why were the kids sailing? To party, drink and fuck. The shark was sent as their punisher.

When Sean S. Cunningham and Steve Miner set out to make a quick rip-off of *Halloween* they had no idea they would unleash one of the most enduring horror franchises ever. Even its star and only real celebrity name, former model and TV personality Betsy Palmer, dismissed the film as trash until its overwhelming success gave her more fame than all of her previous film and television work. Palmer took the role as the now iconic mother of Jason Voorhees because she needed money for a new car. It wasn't because she believed in the material. Palmer also gets credit with the filmmakers for turning the genre a bit on its ear and making the killer a woman as well. "Nobody is going to come to see this shit," she quipped.

The film got away with a number of cheats and because of its clever manufacture. To understand why the original did so well, and why fans turned an indifferent shoulder to its much more expensive and slicker 2008 remake—the horror viewer needs to look at the time surrounding the release of the film.

I just outlined the difference between the 70s and 80s in that thumbnail roadmap. With slashers like *Halloween* and *Friday the 13th,* fear is the killer. Sex is the fuel of the killing engine. The formula was boiled down like raw Maple syrup into bottled deliciousness.

I was 12 years old when "Friday the 13th" came to my local big screen at the mall. My older sister was 19 and tormented me every day. One night she told my parents she was going out to see "Friday the 13th" knowing I would annoy the hell out of her (and be a spy). My dad said "not without your brother." I got in and loved it!

The blood, the gore, the boobs and that lake scene at the end scared the hell outta me! All the way home my sister kept telling me Jason was gonna get me. I hid under my sister's bed for what felt like forever. She finally came into her room and went to bed. I waited a few minutes and reached up from under her bed and slapped my hand on her forehead like she was Kevin Bacon! I scared the shit outta her, I got my revenge! But, when I went to bed, all I could hear was "Ki ki ki ma ma ma."

I couldn't sleep for a week.

Kyle Fish

It was the big weekend before Halloween so I had spent the day with my mom and brother at my school's fall festival. I can't recall where my family disappeared to when we got home but I remember being alone when I turned on our living room television set. It was a giant beastly Zenith with wood paneling and a remote control that was as thick as a brick.

I flipped channels a few times until I struck gold: John Carpenter's "Halloween" was airing on some channel like TNT or USA. I had no idea what I was seeing. It was the opening shot where young Michael was making his way to his sister's room. Up until this point in my life I hadn't seen something so creepy or heard music that was so ominous and eerie. It wasn't long before I witnessed a brutal onscreen stabbing (edited for television, of course) and realized that the killer was around my age.

While that surprising reveal had already blown my little pea brain wide open, the film was nowhere near finished with me yet.

At the time I can remember thinking it was the perfect title because the film felt like Halloween in all the right ways. I sat there in the dark watching the daytime scenes as I ate the candy and caramel apple I brought home from the fall festival. To this day, certain sounds and images from the movie take me back to that night and I can still taste the treats. Hell, I can still hear the wind rustling outside the living room window. Eventually the film abandoned the safety of the daytime scenes and began to go to work on my poor mind.

The movie wasn't telling a story as much as it was providing a full-on visceral experience for the viewer. As the suspense began to build I started watching through the cracks of my fingers. I then began to use those hands to cover my ears when I felt I was sure the boogeyman would come out. At that point in my life I had seen a lot of movies, but nothing like Halloween. That was the most terrified I had ever been watching anything on TV and yet I could not get enough.

When I finally got a good look at Michael Myers' mask I could feel my soul leave my body. To this day I wonder how something so simple could be so sinister. Whatever chemicals my seven-year-old brain was releasing while watching that film had forever changed me. How could I go back to watching movies like "Home Alone" or "Back to the Future"?

After that one experience I had fallen in love with horror, with the spooky season in general, and most importantly: quality cinema.

Robert Shaw

The heavy-handed horror of the 1970s would change into something that allowed them to weave through the new social climate. Nostalgia for the 50s was coming around as the Baby Boomers approached their 40s. The late 70s and early 80s saw a revival in entertainment of all things 1950s. Our TV shows reflected this with *"Happy Days, Laverne and Shirley"* and a number of sitcoms that were throwbacks to the 1950s family sitcom style. *"Family Ties"* was the new *"Leave It to Beaver"* (they did an updated TV *Beaver* movie). Its breakout star, Michael J. Fox, would achieve stardom in a 1950s valentine, *Back to the Future* in 1985. Throw in *Grease, Animal House* (okay, early 60s), *The Wanderers, Hollywood Knights, Porky's* and you had the 50s fused with the 80s.

America went through the 60s "Decade of Love" that gave us The Pill, women's liberation and sexual abandon. It's futile to put the genie back in the bottle on something like that. Our music changed, our films changed and, like it or not, sex had moved to the forefront after decades of repression and cinematic dick teasing since film first hit screens.

The 60s also gave us the "opposite reaction" to the 50s with the death of JFK, King, and Bobby. Add to it the Civil Rights issue that had been simmering since the first African slave was brought to American shores and you had quite a contrast.

While Americans wanted a return to 50s "family values" they also wanted titillation but didn't want to be open about it. It's kind of like a wedding. The parents of the bride are so happy to see their daughter so beautiful on "her day." What they don't want to think about is "her night." They know what's going to happen but they just don't want to talk about it. So everyone pretends and dresses up the wedding as really one big, expensive opening act for the romp that usually follows after the bride and groom say goodbye to the guests. This is the way horror weaved through the conservative vs. liberal obstacle course of the 1980s.

Horror's nemesis, the "X" rating, was worse than any religious agenda. Religious zealots have no clue that studios love the press and boycotts drive more people to the film out of curiosity. A perfect example is *Silent Night, Deadly Night,* a total slasher rip-off that used the gimmick of a psycho in a Santa costume to drum up its business. It's not a good film but thanks to the pious religious right pawns, it became a success at the box office and spawned several sequels. The film would have come and gone with nary a blip on the box office radar if it had been left alone. I sometimes wonder if studios set these people up to be their own little marketing machines.

Today the "X" has been replaced by the classier "NC-17" rating, but it's really the same thing. The "X" rating was so powerful that you may remember the earlier chapter where George A. Romero backed off his stance with *Dawn of the Dead* and made the necessary cuts to bring it down to an "R". The same was done for Dario Argento's *Suspiria, The Exorcist* and the original 1979 classic, *Alien.* All made cuts to avoid the "X" rating, and are considered some of the most important films of the horror genre.

Halloween got away with almost no blood and while the nudity by today's standards is nothing, it was considered just a tad racy at the time. Likely the original 1978 film would receive a PG-13 rating today. *Friday the 13th* wanted to give what *Halloween* did not. While terror was its driving force, the filmmakers wanted to sex and blood up their movie because they felt that audiences were craving and demanding more. Their first smart move was to hire make-up artist legend Tom Savini to render the effects and that alone allowed a home run.

Savini is a modern day Jack Pierce—an inventive artist with a wild imagination that set the standard for trauma and violent effects. Perhaps it's no coincidence that he served in Vietnam and honed his craft there. The meat grinder war diminished "the good fight" mentality of the previous generation. Savini came from a generation caught fighting a war few could make any sense of. The cynicism that rose up from this time was already buoyed by the senseless deaths of JFK, MLK and RFK.

Savini's work on the original *Dawn of the Dead* is one studied to this day and he is one of the few artists, along with Rob Botin and Rick Baker, whose work bears its own signature. Savini not only created all of the kill effects but designed the iconic image of the young hydrocephalic Jason Voorhees in *Friday the 13th*.

The formula worked and avoided the X-rating by embracing the genre. The kills are almost designer label. They're a "Savini." Where Herschel Gordon Lewis and other gore films focused on entrails splayed everywhere, severe torture and

215

rape (the precursor to the slick torture porn films of late), *Friday the 13th* gives you its violence in quick, slick flashes and never goes down the torture porn route. It also manages to embrace the conservative moral attitude toward sex in the 1980s: immorality will deliver bad things. So the theme becomes almost righteous in a way: have wild, uninhibited sex without marriage…die a gruesome and deserved death because it's the Lord's way of sending you a message: Have sex and die.

The plot is almost always the same--a group of horny, obnoxious teens gather in the woods, try to reopen Camp Crystal Lake and somehow cross paths with the film's eventual killer. They do drugs, drink, get naked, have sex and pay the price with double-coitus impalings or a machete to head. The formula tapped into the sexually frustrated subconscious of teen America and made it okay to explore that sexual appetite safely onscreen because there was that underlying message that sex was bad. There is almost always a "final girl," usually the virgin or socially awkward female of the group who is the lone survivor.

The late Wes Craven will run wild in his *Scream* series, taking all of the horror conventions (which mostly were established in the 1980s) and build his own franchise. The 80s were a total contrast. The decade likes to be known for its wild, party atmosphere and yet at the same time the political right touted its fiscal and moral conservative values and a return to 1950s morality.

Friday the 13th works on a simple format: boobs and blood with a moral message. Throw in a good killer people can get behind and you've got yourself a franchise. It's kind of like a fucked up Hay's Code, the set of film standards before the present day rating system. You can show sex as long as the perverts get what's coming to them…that kinda thing.

The problem for the original *Friday the 13th* was they killed their psycho at the end. This shows the filmmakers never intended a series of sequels. This was to be a "hit and run" rip-off. Make a few quick bucks and decent return on investment.

The film was a smash and a sequel was ordered. By the time *Friday the 13th Part II* hit screens, the new "slasher genre" was ramping up. I saw both on *HBO*, missing their theatrical runs.

Before I go into the late night cable world of horror, it is important to touch back on why the remake of *Friday the 13th* was greeted with indifference. Something happened in the middle of the 80s…something horrible that would impact Ronald Reagan and the entire planet.

The horror of AIDS emerged and showed its face in the thousands of people afflicted. However, it was the face of legendary movie star and man's man, Rock Hudson, who made it hit home to the United States and his close friend, President Reagan.

Since the reveal of AIDS, a disease that literally meant have sex and die, the horny teenager movies faded by the end of the decade. New technologies rose up and by the mid-90s The Internet was in full swing. Cell phones were heading toward smart phones and teenagers became more insulated and withdrawn.

The concept of going away to summer camp was antiquated. They didn't do that anymore. A new generation, the millennials or *Generation Z* were seen as pussies. They were coddled, anxiety-ridden pussies who feared social situations and wanted nothing more than the digital world of chat rooms and online banter and eventually sex online and "sexting." Some sociologists worried that populations could drop because these new generations just didn't want to have physical sex.

These were kids that saw 911, Columbine, AIDS and domestic terrorism. Some hockey-masked hulking killer lumbering through a summer camp killing naked chicks was silly. They didn't get it. It was old school and it didn't age well.

On the flipside, these same technologies gave power to Generation X to revisit everything they loved about the 80s. The time was coming round to rediscover that decade like the Boomers did with the 1950s. The Internet allowed fans to gather, talk, organize, post information, post pictures, and interviews and more. It was like the JJ Abrams reboot of *Star Trek*. You could do it all over again, only better.

Generation X would take the millennials and *Generation Z* to see what they grew up with. They would drag them to conventions and pass on the memories of seeing these 80s horror films. Some of their kids would get it. Others didn't. This translated to "meh" at the box office for the *Halloween, Friday the 13*[th] and *A Nightmare on Elm Street* remakes.

Technology changed everything as well. Going to the movies for these new generations was not only a chore, because you have to drive or find a ride, but public shootings in theaters had become a reality. It was not beyond the norm to enter a theater and now pick a seat closest to the exit in case an active shooter starts firing. There was now the ability to stay home, watch it on a phone, tablet. You could stream it on a TV or…as many horror fans like to do…find a pirated copy and "torrent" the film and watch it at home while it played in theaters.

Cable TV shifted toward high quality series and original content to lure viewers against streaming giants. Content was everywhere. There just might be too much content.

The issue for horror is that it was no longer being EXPERIENCED the way it was decades before. Parents retelling their old drive-in, theatrical, late night cable or VHS war stories could not convey the spirit of these memories. They were just stories. There just was no context.

Everything had changed in just twenty years.

Not only did these new kids not understand the experience of enjoying old school horror, they didn't *want* to. What *Generation X* or even *Boomers* saw as awesome, these kids saw as lame. Bad effects, worse acting and tropes that did not connect with them.

The closest these "new generation kids" got to embracing older horror was the *Scream* franchise. Even then, they didn't really know or understand what they were watching.

When I was a teacher, a moment came up where I said, "We all go a little mad sometimes." A senior boy snapped his fingers and named that quote: "*Scream!*" he shouted, all proud of himself. He looked for props around the room.

I corrected him. "No, that quote is from *Psycho*." He went on to debate me until I called up the video online in front of the whole class. He saw the movie and yet he had no clue as to the origins of one of the most famous quotes in horror history.

> When Janet Leigh was knifed in the shower it terrified me and I knew this was a film I would never forget. Then came the second act…! But the feeling I had when the movie was over was strange to me. I was very sad because I knew I would never get to experience the sheer horror of seeing it for the first time ever again.
>
> **Jacki Kipe**

I suspected a lot of other kids in my class and around the country shared a similar dilemma. There was no context and they did not know what they were watching. They got the basics—there were trope-ish rules in horror and kids were acting them out with deadly results. This would go on for a number of sequels and at the time of this writing a new one is on its way.

Who are these films for? There's now a whole new generation of kids who never saw the original film in theaters, many more who never saw anything of the old 80s horrors to understand the underlying premise.

Scream just becomes content to be consumed with few memories of seeing it in theaters, with friends or a group. There is often no understanding of all the movies that went into its story construction and why it makes it a fun watch. Many will stream it or torrent it and watch it on a phone screen, never going to even a video store to rent something for the weekend.

Nostalgia is a powerful thing.

Let's step off the path for a moment (I'll get back to memories of *Friday the 13th* and *Halloween*, don't worry) to look at some of the horror memories late night cable gave before we get back to 80s big screen horror.

Right this way…

CABLE HORROR

There was a time when you had three networks and several pay-cable channels. It was late-night *HBO* where I got my fix of blood, boobs, babes and horror. My parents splurged in 1978 and brought *Home Box Office* into the house. It had been around awhile and my cousins had it and *Jaws* showed on there, but they lived too far away to go watch it and you were also beholden by the scheduled times. You had to watch it when *HBO* scheduled it. Not like today where you just turn on the TV and find your shit and hit 'play'.

Horror was *Scary Cinemax*. You could almost always count on nudity. In fact, you did count on nudity. There were some films where I hoped like hell certain actresses would get undressed…and didn't. That was a late night letdown.

Summer late nights, Christmas breaks from school; all allowed you to watch after hours. The parents went to bed and you got to tune into the movies you missed in theaters, due to the "R" rating, limited release or maybe you just didn't have the guts to watch on the big screen.

The Dark, Wolfen, Halloween II, Friday the 13th, Friday the 13th II, The Evictors, Homebodies, The Fog, The Legacy, Humanoids From the Deep, Dead and Buried, When a Stranger Calls, The Changeling, The Sentinel, Dressed To Kill, Dead Of Night, Mausoleum, The Burning, The Boogeyman, Motel Hell, Phantasm, The Howling, Up From the Depths, Piranha.

The list can go on.

A quiet house, dark living room and a 25-inch color TV and you were set. No VCR. Not yet. I would go to *Hess's*, a local department store, and find my way to the TVs and electronics to fantasize about owning one of the expensive suitcase-sized *Beta* machines lined up on shelves. The price tags made my mother scoff out loud when I asked if she could at the least THINK about us getting one. "Wish on one hand, shit in the other. Which do you get first?" was one of her idioms.

> *A staple of HBO's line-up at that time was "Humanoids from the Deep." Along with Peter Benchley's "The Island," with Michael Caine, "Humanoids" was the movie I sort-of, kind-of, almost-watched the most. It's hard to describe how exhilarating that was--catching a fuzzy, static glimpse of the forbidden! At a time when my older, cooler friends had figured out ways to get into the theaters to see these "mature" films for themselves. This method allowed me to keep up with them -- a little. And if the reception, bad as it was, got even worse to the point I couldn't finish watching, that was OK: it would be on again, and again...*
>
> Will T. Laughlin

April, 1981. Our middle school had its spring dance. I was dating this tall, Farrah Fawcett-haired blonde and the only thing I could do was slow dance to the *Moody Blues Nights in White Satin* or Boz Scaggs' *Look What You've Done To Me*. "Dancing" was defined as slow swaying, hands around the waists, mine dropping to Farrah's ass, then back up before a teacher caught me. Made out and swayed, played grab ass–that was 80s dancing for me.

With Adrienne Barbeau in Hollywood

I got a white rotary phone that Christmas, 1980 and spent hours tying up the single land line with this girl. My mother would pick up the phone and in a flat, restrained voice grumble: "I need the phone."

I was in love but…that night of the spring dance, John Carpenter's *The Fog* debuted on *HBO* and I was missing the debut. It would re-air at midnight (The Witching Hour as Stevie Wayne would say). My younger brother was home watching the first showing. I was making out with the cute blonde in the middle school gym.

I collected *HBO Guides*, those little six or seven page booklets that came a few weeks ahead of a new month to tell you what was coming to you on cable. *The Fog* was in April, 1981's guide but didn't even make the cover. I didn't see it the year before in theaters so *HBO* was my second chance and I couldn't wait. I remember waiting for my mom to pick me up, attention now focused on getting home to hear my brother's review of *The Fog* while my girlfriend knew something else was on my mind. She thought it was another girl, but in fact it was John Carpenter. I still did not see *Halloween* but I HEARD all about it.

The air was warm, it had rained. Spring smells were in the air. I was high on teen hormones and when I got home my brother said, "Just wait until you see it." We called our friend Troy, he walked up and we stayed up to catch the next showing. It was everything we hoped. *The Fog* was GOOD horror, but there was a lot of shit and cheese to sift through on late-night cable.

Onset of *Death House* with the late Sid Haig

My brother and I sat for back to back showings of *The Fog* that night, held in awe of Adrienne Barbeau's breathy radio DJ, Stevie Wayne. "This is KAB Antonio Bay," her words were a verbal sexual assault on my burgeoning hormones. Barbeau holds the movie together and gives it the gravitas that elevated it into an Edgar Allen Poe or even Lovecraftian kind of film. When that block of stone fell from the church ceiling onto the table, my brother and I jumped both times, knowing it was coming in the second viewing. All of this made us wish we got to see this one on the big screen.

It's where I devoured Doug McClure films, especially *Humanoids from the Deep* with a score from the yet-to-blow-up James Horner. I knew McClure from seeing *The Land That Time* Forgot at The Eric Twin in Easton back in 1974. He popped up again at the Eagle Valley Drive-in with 1979's *At the Earth's* Core. He was on *HBO* with *Warlords of Atlantis*. I continued discovering the wonders of Roger Corman with *Up from the Depths, Terror in Paradise* and *Galaxy of Terror.* The worm-rape scene still bothers me to this day and I often just zip past on DVD viewings. Little did I know then that one day I would work with Sid Haig

and have a drink with Robert Englund, discussing his coming aboard my movie *Death House.* *Galaxy of Terror* is hands down my favorite *Alien* rip-off and it sits on my DVD shelf.

It was late night *HBO* where I discovered *Homebodies*, a dark, nasty little horror film with senior citizens as the killers. Think *Harold and Maude* or *Cocoon* as a slasher. A city senior apartment complex is threatened with eviction and the old folks decide to defend their homes with deadly force. The humor was dark, but there was this scene where a female social worker came to meet with the kindly old folks, only to be impaled with a Banzai sword and her death was so traumatic it is burned into my brain to this day. The way she screamed and walked about with that sword through her torso, agonizing as she dropped to the floor while the senior citizens stand around just waiting for her to expire...it's on *You Tube* and I watched it once again and I am good for another 30 years.

HBO gave me *The Changeling*, the George C. Scott haunted house horror flick and it scared the shit out of me so much I went to bed with the lights on. That wouldn't happen again until 2010 after I watched *Lake Mungo*.

We heckled *The Dark*, that mess of a film that somehow was turned from a crime thriller into some alien, sci-fi horror film. It featured a headless walking body, somehow able to moan even without its head and Cathy Lee Crosby of TV's *That's Incredible!*

I watched Katherine Ross and Sam Elliott in *The Legacy*, and marveled at Roger Daltry's tracheotomy scene and for some reason liking this end of the 70s haunted house meets the devil movie. It had some moments, like the pool drown-ing that made me squirm a bit, but these kinds of films were better because I watched them after midnight. That made it perfect.

Good old *Prophecy* hit *HBO* during the fall of 1980 as the six-week strike groaned on. I can't remember how many times I watched my mutant bear movie, but we invited kids up to spend the night to watch it with us.

My brother and I found the bad stuff, the two in the morning stuff you found just by flicking through. We would heckle it, lowering the volume of the TV and adding our own commentary a good ten years before the folks at "Mystery Science Theater" made it cool. We had a blast with *Jaws 3-D* one night for old time's sake when it dropped on cable after its 1983 run.

Friday the 13th Part II and *Halloween II* ensured a steady stream of undressed girls for your late night horror pleasure. Many nights I went to bed, unable to sleep not from the horrors I just watched but the fine asses, hot lingerie and promiscuous teenage sex horror brought with it. *HBO* offered you a second chance at stuff you missed in theaters or the stuff you weren't keen on dropping the ticket price and going through the hassle of a hike to the mall. *Without Warning* amazed me with Larry Storch—Corporal Agarn from "F-Troop" killed by that silent, big-headed alien throwing *It Conquered the* World-type flappy parasites. Cable would start to fade for me by the time I reached the end of ninth grade, but it gave so many terrific late night memories.

To recap, network TV tried to step up their game. Before 1979, networks tried their hand at horror, but the Prime Time censors were the moral gatekeepers and often original network TV fare was tepid at best. *Sssss!* the Dr. Moreau-type turning people into reptiles movie with Strother Martin that I mentioned earlier was an example of TV trying to be

edgy. You had the offbeat *Burnt Offerings* with the stunt casting of Bette Davis, still in the creepy old lady casting left over from *Whatever Happened to Baby Jane*? That might come as close to high concept as it got for network TV and, like a film I am about to list, starred Karen Black.

There were films like the *Carrie* rip-off *The Initiation of Sarah* on ABC with Shelley Winters, various werewolf movies and even *Rankin-Bass* got into it with their weird giant sea turtle horror, *The Bermuda Depths*. *Devil Dog* tried to meet *The Omen* with a future *Cujo* but you got mediocrity trying to cash in on the waning devil movement. The 1980s would change all of that over to slashers.

You had some good stuff like the Kim Darby *Don't Be Afraid of the Dark* I cited with the paranoia of the 70s or the aforementioned Karen Black *Trilogy of Terror* which was famous for the Zuni doll installment (I have a Zuni doll in my office today), and if you want to argue Spielberg's *Duel* was horror, then that would be at the top of the list. Otherwise, horror movie pickings were slim on network TV.

I talked about the Bernie Casey-led *Gargoyles*, a TV favorite, often hitting Channel 5 out of New York on Saturday afternoons. Like shitty candy, I ate it up. Most of these films were that hard *Brach's* candy your grandmother had in a dish in her living room. It sat there for God knows how long, but she had nothing else sweet in the house, so after staring at it, deliberating, you then put your hand in that dish and took a few pieces.

You took whatever you could get. Bad horror was better than none and this new TV stuff was better than watching the same old thing over and over again.

CBS rolled the dice and turned the red-hot horror author Stephen King's vampire novel, *Salem's Lot* into an unprecedented horror mini-series. It was kind of like *Superman: The Movie*. Hollywood was taking the genre seriously like they did with Superman. *Superman: The Movie* legitimized big studio superhero movies and paved the way for *Batman*, DC and the Marvel universes.

227

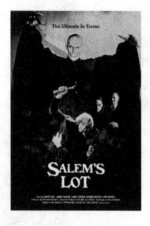

I will offer that *Salem's Lot* paved the way for the likes of "American Horror Story, Bates Motel and The Walking Dead" by showing serious horror could be played on network TV. Stephen King's work would get treated to a number of TV adaptations over the next two decades.

I was now a full year into reading King's work. I will go into greater depth on the written influence of Stephen King later, but when this miniseries was announced, I got my hands on a *Salem's Lot* paperback and read it in three days.

King's novel is one of the finest examinations in the death of small town America with the exception of Peter Straub's *Ghost Story*. The novel handles a wide list of characters and weaves their stories into coherent and interesting plot lines. Both *Salem's Lot*

and *Ghost Story* are great examples to new writers on how to handle large numbers of characters.

Salem's Lot: The Movie is a quirky and mild adaptation of the book, yet, it works. You know what? The vampires are really vampires—not angst-ridden *Abercrombie*, *Nair*-chested underwear model undead. There are some creepy and solid moments. Director Tobe Hooper efficiently moved the film through the rough seas of network television. So when *CBS* announced it was adapting Stephen King's bestselling vampire novel into a two night mini-series, there were groans and low expectations. And some of them were well founded. *Salem's Lot* is not a perfect horror film, but is one fun as hell ride. King has a warm spot for it and an admiration for Paul Monash's streamlined script. The script handles the numerous characters of Jerusalem's Lot and weaves them into a coherent and constantly advancing plot line.

I stayed up late to watch each installment. I went to bed with Danny and Ralphie Glick floating in through the windows with a practical, in camera effect that still holds it original impact.

I went to school to see who else watched it. Kids were talking about it, their parents were talking about. The TEACHERS were talking about it. *Salem's Lot* was THE mini-series to close out the 70s.

We got vampires. Lots of them. The reliable character actor Geoffrey Lewis has a good cemetery scene where he feels compelled to unearth the body of Danny Glick only to find Danny awaiting his arrival. Lewis does a haunting turn as a vampire against the solid Van Helsing-type Lew Ayres. Lewis's "Look at me, teacher!" is still a show stopper.

The real conundrum was Barlow, the lead vampire. The 2004 remake (and they still didn't get it right) was more faithful to Barlow's portrayal in the book. In King's novel, Kurt Barlow is a refined gentleman, an eloquent talker and master strategist. In the 1979 TV miniseries he is reduced to a squealing, grunting Max Schreck from *Nosferatu*. Played by Reggie Nalder, the *CBS* Barlow is bluish with buck tooth incisor fangs and blazing yellow eyes. It works. By going so far to the other extreme the series made Barlow into a true monster and doesn't mess around with trying to give him dialogue. James Mason takes up the chores and speaks for his master and provides the cool elegance that came

through in the book. Barlow's first appearance in the town jail is downright startling and his death at the hands of David Soul is one of the best vampire killings
ever committed to film.

The ensemble cast was what made this delicious cheese. TV names most
under the age of 40 today never heard of fleshed out the ensemble. Fred Willard,
Ed Flanders, Bonnie Bedelia worked alongside George Dzunzda, Geoffrey
Lewis, Lew Ayres, Julie Cobb and character actors Kenneth McMillen (Baron
Harkonen from 1984's *Dune*), Elisha Cook Jr. and noir queen Marie Windsor.
Add in some superb no-name actors and the teen heartthrob (turned religious
purveyor) Lance Kerwin (fresh off "James at 16" the brief hit teen angst show)
and you got yourself a nifty horror flick that pushed the boundaries of network
TV.

The series also introduced me to Tobe Hooper. I know, how can I call
myself a horror fan when at the age of 12 I still had not seen *The Texas Chainsaw
Massacre*? *TCM* was taboo even by the 1980s. It was considered even more

horrific than *The Exorcist* (which I had not yet seen by 1979). Both of these films were like Britain's "Video Nasties" and not available. Home video had not yet become widespread and content was almost zero.

Knowing Hooper did *TCM* made me want to watch *Salem's Lot* all the more. It would be horrifying, gory and gross and scary as fuck. I just watched the original *Psycho* in sixth grade and the shower scene scared the piss out of me. *TCM* and *The Exorcist* still eluded me and I don't remember them hitting *HBO* during this time. If so, I would have watched.

Something happened, the dots that *Fangoria* helped me to connect with horror faces, filmmakers and the industry formed a neural network. I was putting things together and despite being a kid and terrified of seeing *TCM* I searched it out and looked up as much as I could find on Hooper's previous work.

Paul Monash's script handled a lot of characters and after reading the book I respected the script even more. Monash combined some characters, eliminated others and was able to keep the building foreboding high while avoiding the deep-rooted sexual implications of the novel. The Nosferatu look works, and while Barlow is stripped of the chess-playing strategist of King's book, the visceral impact that Nalder's Barlow elicits makes it all worthwhile.

Salem's Lot confirmed my fandom for Stephen King. My friend got me *Salem's Lot* in paperback that Christmas and I still have it, all worn and beaten with its "eight terrifying pages" of photos from the miniseries in the middle. I used my allowances and birthday money to get every book King wrote to that point. *Fangoria* started mentioning his name more and more as King became a growing influence on the horror movie industry.

CBS pulled off a hat trick in prime time horror. The high ratings sent a message back to Hollywood…stop treating horror like the family's crazy uncle. The genre had a place at the "good folks" table.

I carried a Stephen King book with me in school. The covers caught other kids' attention and then after *Salem's Lot*, King's name was far more recognizable. He was becoming a household name like another Steven (Spielberg) was about to become.

Sporting a Gilligan hat and *Starsky & Hutch* shirt. I shoulda kicked my own ass.

This photo of me in seventh grade says: "Ass Kicking Waiting To Happen."

I was in "The Horror Kid" zone.

In my previous school, in fourth grade—my copy of Dick Smith's DIY makeup effects book got "faggot" lobbed at me quite a bit. Classes always had

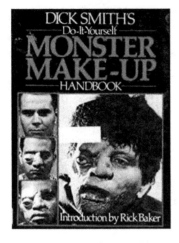

a number of "those kids—the dirty kid, the fat kid" or the "Horse Girl." Horse Girl was a quiet girl, often withdrawn who worshipped horses—they were on her notebook, on her T-shirts, necklaces, charms, barrettes….books on horses made up of by the James Herriot *All Creatures Great and Small* series. She almost always owned a horse. She liked horses better than people, and now as an adult, I can say—Horse Girl was on to something.

I was "The Weird Kid" who, by seventh grade, morphed into "The Movie Kid" and landed at "The Horror Kid." After all, I wrote *Jaws 3* in sixth grade and dropped Class Babe Toni into it as a character. Before these specific labels most of the guys just called me "faggot." That's why my blonde, Farrah-haired girlfriend said in eighth grade, "You're on the verge of popularity."

ABC had nothing original to respond to *Salem's Lot* or even *NBC's* Burnt *Offerings* which only *looked* like a TV movie. There was *The Last Dinosaur*, a Richard Boone, Joan Van Ark cheese-fest that I still adore but didn't really classify as horror.

ABC did have *Jaws* and in seventh grade, they debuted the blockbuster in glorious "edited for television" color and the following year they dropped *Jaws 2*. "Edited for TV" was cultural vandalism to me.

233

"The Horror Kid" discovered that free access to big horror films was a mixed bag. Not only were they interrupted by commercials, the networks could do something else besides "editing for television." They could ADD scenes. The deleted scenes the director felt should not make the theatrical cut were put back into the film to make up for lost time due to commercials. Often the scenes took you out of the moment, perhaps laying the foundation for the eventual Internet bullshit of "The Mandela Effect."

The film was not what I remembered and "deleted scenes" were new at the time. There was no "special version" or "behind the scenes" footage available like today. Many were unaware that deleted footage even existed. *ABC* gave us Quint tormenting a clarinet-playing kid and other small bits while *Jaws 2* gave us Brody giving parking tickets and an extended attack on the helicopter that showed how limited the mechanical shark was, and rightly excised from the theatrical print.

We also got vocal dubbing to change lines as "She's got tits like a sparrow," to "She's got a BODY like a sparrow." It was an eye-opener on how films were released and the fine line between "edited for TV" and censorship.

The cover of the summer 1980 *HBO* guide and its section on *Jaws 2*

Jaws 2 added similar mediocre stuff. The shark attack on the helicopter was extended to show the fish going after the pilot underwater. You saw why it was cut as it looked like a giant pool and the shark's limited movement couldn't be hidden by careful editing.

There was some other exciting footage of Brody giving Len Peterson a parking ticket. Thrilling. The only thing added of interest was a scene that showed the actual council vote to fire Brody with Larry showing his support for Brody and not voting to fire him. I think the theatrical version was better.

I made it clear to my blonde Farrah-hair girlfriend that I would take no calls during *Jaws 2*. We spent many evenings tying up the house phone lines with that white phone I got in my room. " I remember my girlfriend saying, "You love horror movies and that stupid shark more than you do me!" She was probably right. Who's still in my life?

I flipped out in summer 1980 when *Jaws 2* came to *HBO*. It was on the cover of the guide and I kept it to this day in a scrapbook. I also tape-recorded *Jaws 2* and by tenth grade would draw the whole thing out, making it my second quasi-storyboard.

My hand drawn comic adaptation of *Jaws 2* after recording the
audio from TV.

CBS pulled the biggest broadcast boner and a shining example of "Just
because you can, doesn't mean you should," with its 1980 network airing of

1973's *The Exorcist*. You can just
hear the suits around the network
table, "Take that, *ABC!*" We will
see your *Jaws* and *Jaws 2* and raise
you *The Exorcist* in Idiot Poker.

Take a film that skirted an "X"
rating with its signatures being the
foul language, sexual and religious

perversion that caused some to faint in theaters and put it on a general audience platform for the whole family. Gut it of all its horror subtext and religious meaning and somehow that translated as a good idea to the powers that be at *CBS*.

"Your mother sews socks that smell, Karras!" That was a "Saturday Night Live" line (they just cut it) from a satire *Exorcist* skit, *CBS* might as well have done something similar. The whole thing was a terrible programming idea. The cynical attempt to cash in on ratings over art was so apparent no one seemed to try hiding it. The film was gutted of everything that made it legendary as well as its powerful message of good versus evil.   A friend had a *Betmax* and one of the first films they purchased on tape was *The Exorcist* and I got to see it, uncut, in its theatrical version, before seeing the *CBS* abortion. At age 13 I knew a screwing when I got one, and the network premiere of this film was it. This opened my eyes further to the cynical machine behind the "movie magic."

Cable and network TV helped to widen the horror network. Cable allowed me to find new films, some that would have been overlooked, denied theatrical screenings or never saw the light of day on free TV. The home video revolution would expand the menu, but combined with *Fangoria* and a widening resource of books to buy, my understanding of the industry was growing fast.

It's one thing to love film. It's another to KNOW and understand it. Today's film critic qualifications have lowered to being a "fan" or an ultra-fan. There are plenty who attend horror conventions dressed as characters from horror films (cosplay) who never saw the actual film, or couldn't tell you anything about the making of their object of hero worship or the long, rich history of the genre. By eighth grade I could talk about horror, its history and formulate informed opinions on the stuff we were watching. Things were changing…a small independent slasher, *Halloween* had dropped and became the talk of everything. I remember family friends, adults, talking about how terrifying, violent and bloody *Halloween* was. I heard the same for *Texas Chainsaw*. I wouldn't see the original *Halloween*, like *Texas Chainsaw*, in the theaters. I would catch them eventually on late night *HBO* and home video. What surprised me was the hype behind them. After watching *Halloween* and then not much later the taboo *TCM*, I found them to be scary enough. Well made. But terrifying? Bloody? Disgusting? Faint-inducing?

I was learning about a whole new world: the world of hype.

My first experience with horror movies was at a Halloween sleepover party. They rented 2 horror movies, being "House" and "Halloween."

I was 10. "House" was up first and I thought it was hilarious. I remember loving the special effects, but it did not prepare me for the next movie at all.

I got a faceful of Michael Myers. I couldn't sleep for three weeks, hearing noises and seeing moving shadows. We moved to North America soon after and I discovered that those funny cupboard/closet things with white slatted doors really exist. I never spent too long near ours.

I've been inexorably drawn to horror because of that experience, but you'll never ever catch me in a room with "Halloween" itself (or any of them) on again. I suspect it's also because I don't want to let go of, or dilute, the raw impact it had on me. This first viewing has to be its last for me.

Interestingly, I don't mind William Shatner at all.

Suzy

NAVIGATING THE 80S ON CABLE

Reagan recovered and America continued with its own recovery and image rehab. Middle school came to a close in June 1981 and capped out with my screening of my *Mad Monster Party* remake.

We'd have off for a curtailed summer as the almost six weeks off had to be paid back. Summer, Christmas and spring breaks would all be shaved for the next several years to get that time back. Summer was just dragging out the start of school because now I was heading into the high school.

Middle school became this cocoon where I felt safe in the image I crafted. Then I was thrown back down to the bottom as a lowly freshman on a giant campus, and everything I did to make an identity would be gone. It was going to be a bad year. I could feel it.

1981 was an odd year for horror. There was this big burst of horror, thanks to Stephen King and Amityville, and by 1980 we had a slew of some fun, off-the-wall entries. Corman was still at it with *Humanoids from the Deep,* and *Alien* changed the entire game for horror and science fiction. The slasher movement was on the move and growing, and horror would become dominated by it for awhile.

It was also a year of change for me, personally.

I was a freshman on a giant, sprawling campus, very different from the win-dowless circle that was the middle school. Learning areas were traded for separate classrooms all over the campus. Lunchtime was now with kids three to four years older and we were the shit freshmen on their upperclassmen shoe heels.

No one up at the high school cared about my middle school movie. I contin-ued to write my horror stories and craft my writing thanks to Stephen King. My ninth-grade English teacher, Mrs. Schneider, encouraged my writing and gave detailed notes, and did what good teachers do: furthered growth and pushed limits. The word "faggot" resurfaced as it was clear I still didn't fit in despite the middle school delusion. I wanted to go back. This high school nonsense wasn't for me.

page :

Two square dance crazed students take a promenade break enroute to their next classes.
(photo by Ellen Michkapik)

This photo sums up everything I hated about myself in ninth grade. This dweeb square dancing for the school newspaper in gym class. I would get a new image the following year and never revisit this one.

A new horror film opened at the mall, December 1981. Some guy named Peter Straub wrote a book called *Ghost Story* and the weird, offbeat previews started around Christmas. A horror movie out at Christmas time? Sounded fun. I had a friend who had read the book. A friend and I ventured to the mall after Christmas break, January 1982 to see what it was all about.

It was the first horror movie, since watching Price, Cushing, and those guys that featured "old men" as the main characters. We were just starting down the slasher road, a lot of films that had casts of young, naked unknowns as their stars. I hoped none of the old people in *Ghost Story* got naked and engaged in wild sex. That would be a whole new type of horror like *Homebodies*.

Ghost Story jolted me. It had a New England, snowy setting. It would be the last film for almost every one of the old veteran legends. Dick Smith's Eva Galli apparitions jolted me so hard at one point, my popcorn cup spilled in my hands. There was a lot of sex. Almost too much. I came to be scared to watch some soft-core porn.

In the end, I loved the film, putting aside the very slow moments of the second act. You had Alice Krige as the vengeful ghost, long before she would become known as *Star Trek's* Borg Queen. Craig Wasson did his perpetually confused and surprised burn throughout the film and John Houseman offered the gravitas needed.

It was a refreshing change from the slasher spew coming steadily since *Halloween* in 1978. I went to see *Halloween II* in theaters and walked out feeling ripped off by the silly sibling plotline and lackluster direction. *Halloween II,* for me, was the bad version of *Halloween.* More on this later and hold off on your outrage.

*Friday the 13*th gave us a bunch of slasher rip-offs from that Halloween rip-off. My eighth-grade year saw one slasher film after another come out,

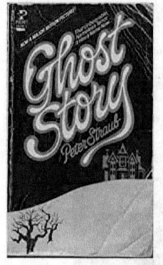

and it was now a sub-genre cottage industry. When *Ghost Story* came along, it looked like a nice change of pace. There aren't many modern films with old men as the main characters.

The theater was mostly empty, which added to the eeriness. The sound was loud, so when the ghost appeared, punctuated with the blast of score, it startled me all the more. At one point I jolted and spilled popcorn on my lap and the floor.

My friend left disappointed. She read the book and said the film had little of what made the book so great. She started talking about Fred Astaire's wife Stella, played by Patricia Neal. In the book, Stella was an older female gigolo, hooking up with younger men, making a mockery of her marriage, and in the end found redemption with her husband.

I picked up the paperback at the mall's *Waldenbooks* a few days after viewing the film to see what my friend was talking about. Straub's book was much like King's *Salem's Lot*. Unlike the film, it had a huge palette of small-town characters. Everyone had a role and Straub was able to handle this huge cast much like King handled the residents of Salem's Lot.

For example, the plow driver, Omar Norris, barely has two minutes of screen time in the film. In the novel, he is a major witness to the town's dissem-

bling. The entire town of Milburn, New York is damned—the target of an avenging and spiteful supernatural force that didn't get a lot of press at that time.

The villains in Straub's book were different than King's vampires. Both wanted their respective town's souls, but we had a more playful and perhaps even more dangerous villain in Straub's shape-shifting creatures. They played long-term games and hid under the guise of humanity and civility. They could walk the day and entrenched themselves into human lives for years, even decades before springing their traps. The vampires in *Salem's Lot* were unrefined cretins compared to Straub's Eva Galli, Florence DePeyser, and Gregory Bate.

Ghost Story gave me a new outlook and the novel became my favorite. It did not supplant King as my favorite author, but *Ghost Story* was so different than the monsters of King's works. It caught my attention. I found myself wanting to write something on the scale and gothic backdrop of *Ghost Story*.

Halloween II did what *Friday the 13th* did. Both films personalized their killers. While the killer in *Friday the 13th* was Pamela Voorhees, giving us a female serial killer (until Felissa Rose came along in another few years), Pammy did it all for her little boy, Jason.

Jason. Michael. Simple names. Boys next door. The killers were in neighborhoods. The banal summer camp. The normal places where horror can emerge. We would have a Freddy by 1984. It would take *Friday the 13th Part 2* to roll out and bring Jason to the lore as the main killer. Somehow, Jason revived or survived the drowning his mother painstakingly laid out in the first film. The afterlife or Hell must have a great gym because when we last saw Jason, he was a skinny, frail, mentally impaired boy leaping from the water for Adrienne King.

"Halloween" had a particular effect that no other has had-- which growing older I now can understand it was the thrill of being scared. I remember being nervous and my imagination took over on looking at a clothes line because of that one particular scene.

George Thompson

Jason got fit for the sequel. One film ahead of the iconic hockey mask, he looked more like a crazed Elephant Man with his burlap sack stuck over his deformed cranium. The word is Tom Savini thought the whole idea of Jason

returning as the killer was stupid at best, and he made himself unavailable for the next two installments.

Regardless, Jason was now our killer. He became Jason. He was familiar. We all knew a Jason. Let's face it; few of us grew up knowing a Damien, despite the notoriety *The Omen* gave the name. Almost everyone knew a Jason. Just like everyone knew a Michael.

Halloween II introduced the silly subplot of Michael and Laurie Strode inexplicably being siblings. What made the original *Halloween* so fucking scary was the RANDOMNESS of the murders. Michael came home and picked his victims randomly, or at least to us they seemed random.

Michael was like a tornado—he just touched down in Haddonfield. He could hit your house but leave your neighbor's untouched. He was a force of nature. You had no way to predict what he would do. Even good 'ole Dr. Loomis, who knew Michael the best, was relegated to hoping the guy would return to his childhood home, a pattern in otherwise chaotic randomness.

I have said over the years that *Halloween II*'s script was paper-thin. In fact, when I got to know *Halloween III: Season of the Witch*'s director, Tommy Lee

Wallace, he told me he was given dibs on the *Halloween* sequel. He said when he read the script, his heart fell. The script was everything they tried to avoid with the original 1978 classic.

The first film relied on terror, good directing, and storytelling to scare the audience. The sequel gave a hammer to the head, a hypodermic needle to the eye, and lots of blood. Tommy called it the "anti-Halloween." However, for better or worse, times changed with the advent of the much bloodier rip-off, *Friday the 13th* and audiences demanded graphic violence, not just suspense.

I felt ripped off as a boy sitting in that theater watching the sequel play out. I felt we got hosed but not everyone thought so. *Halloween II* was like McDonald's—people just wanted to shove more shit into their mouths because it tasted good going down. A number of people walked out expressing their approval of the film. I couldn't understand it.

This film got a **very** large free pass from blind fandom because it's the most loyal of the sequels. It took place on the same night. Curtis, Pleasance and Cyphers return along with Michael. The problem was, the film wasn't all that good.

Halloween II lacked the terror and suspense of Carpenter's original and substituted cheap scares and gore. It's a flat, one-note film that did what it had to in paint by numbers fashion.

"When the [Halloween II] script came in I thought it was…the anti-Halloween. All the things that Halloween did so well…had been tossed out the window…I understood that in the intervening time between the first movie and what was going to be the second movie that times had changed, audiences had changed…and maybe the dynamics of the movie and the amount of violence might be impacted by all that. I felt that John was betraying his own legacy. I held my breath and said "no." A director really needs to believe deeply in the material." – Tommy Lee Wallace on turning down directing Halloween II

Halloween II is a sequel for sequel's sake that duped its fan base into thinking it was getting something good for its devotion to the first film. I knew this as a kid. It was one of the first times I consciously realized I was being ripped off.

John Carpenter, The Horror Master, frowned on *Halloween II*, as did producer Debra Hill, but they knew there would be a sequel regardless of their feelings. Tommy Lee Wallace declined the sequel even though all associated knew it would be a guaranteed box office success. When Wallace vocalized creative concerns while considering directing *Halloween II*, he was told by the powers that be to back off. Any director would be a gun for hire.

The 1981 train was leaving the station. I didn't like the track I was on. Many of my middle school friends moved on to find their places in band or other activities. I tried drama club and that did zero for breaking the "fag" image. The people I did hang around were curmudgeons or nerds and we spent most of our social time bitching about high school, hating this kid, couldn't stand that kid. She's a bitch. He's a dick.

I felt like Jerry Seinfeld in that *Seinfeld* episode where he has had enough of George's complaining and says, "What are we doing?" From there he knew there had to be a change.

So did I.

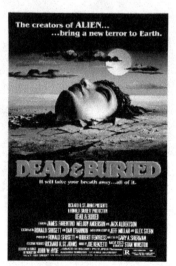

I was the nerd in a John Hughes movie but there was no way I could stay that way. There was no way I was going to spend the next three years with high school being my prison.

Dan O'Bannon gets the sole screen credit for writing *Alien*. Fellow writer and *Alien* alum Ronald Shusset joined him in a follow up horror called *Dead and Buried*. It hit The Sherman just near the end of my eight grade year—May, 1981. Before I got

time to see it, the film was gone. I don't think it lasted two weeks at our theater and it did not come to the mall.

I got around to seeing it late night on *HBO* and even bought the movie novelization ahead of time. That's how sure I was to getting a shot at seeing it on the big screen.

This was one of those after midnight movies that I thought I would sit down with some snack and see some boobs, maybe some sex. It would be a fast food kind of movie. That's not what happened and the opening scene of a guy photographing a beautiful girl on the beach turned to absolute horror when he is burned alive by some small town mob. It didn't stop there as he was finished off with a hypodermic needle to his exposed eye under a full-bodied bandage wrap. There was something about the scene where his immolated body was found on the beach and someone touched him and the burned guy screamed. It was horrifying.

They did an odd casting choice. , kind of like Grandpa Walton in that snake movie, *Sssss! Dead and Buried* featured Jack Albertson, "The Man" half of sitcom "Chico and The Man" but better known as Grandpa Joe from 1973's *Willy Wonka and the Chocolate Factory*. It was his last role, he appears ill and frail, and I think he just died by the time the film hit cable.

It gave me the same feeling as *Homebodies*. There was something visceral about watching *Dead and Buried*. It was dark and the effects impressive. Later the name Stan Winston would become synonymous with great effects and huge films. At this time he was working on lower budget horror like this, *Gargoyles* and the soon to be *Pumpkinhead*.

Dead and Buried is worth mentioning because it was an odd standout in horror at the time slashers were building momentum. It was a throwback to 70s paranoia horror, perhaps released just a few years too late. I think that's why it made such an impression on me. It would also serve as another film added to the list of "surprise ending" movies that armed me with the knowledge to guess the ending to *The Sixth Sense* within ten minutes.

I went to bed taking *Dead and Buried* with me. While not the greatest horror in my viewing experience, there was enough disturbing imagery to keep it in my mind all of these years. I made the mistake of watching it alone. My brother was asleep and not there to heckle the film to relieve some pressure.

HBO allowed me to fill in the horror gaps with all of the stuff I couldn't make it to The Sherman to see but also stuff that just didn't get much of a release. The magic of this time, which will never return, is that a small film like the cheese fest monster movie *The Boogens* could get some actual movie screenings. Stuff wasn't relegated to a "direct to video" release because home video just wasn't there yet. You planned sleepovers to the *HBO* guide and the good shit that went off after the parents went to bed.

Canadian director David Cronenberg benefitted from late night cable exposure. His *Rabid* and *The Brood* were nighttime staples and a lot of fun. The same went for *Basket Case* which got me so excited I found other Frank Hennenlotter films. The fact that this guy from New York City made some cool low budget horror AND his name was in the NYC directory. I learned all of this from *Fangoria* and read everything I could on Hennenlotter.

I called NYC directory assistance and asked for Frank Hennenlotter and there he was. The operator put me through. HE PICKED UP!

I told him I was from The Poconos. He asked how I got his number and I shot back that he was in the book. I think he gave me about a half an hour. It was not 30 minutes of fan gushing, but rather editing and sound

editing questions. Camera questions. Lighting questions. Almost 30 years later I would meet him face to face in New York City at dinner to honor him.

Late 70s eco-horror popped up with the bats run amok movie, *Nightwing*. What closed the deal for me was the same man who played the old, wide Native American in *Prophecy* fell out of that movie and into this one as another prophet of doom and bat manipulator. Must've been a casting run for these kinds of roles and this guy just went from one call to another.

Blood Beach was this awful John Saxon monster movie where you never really saw the monster (budget magic) and had a poster scarier than the movie. This was one of those "Do I? Don't I?" movies in the debate of spending money at the movies or wait for cable.

This was terrific late night heckling done right.

I was often left in charge of the house from sixth grade on while my parents went out for the night—usually to travel back to Bangor to play cards and drink with their friends back there. Not the time to watch *When a Stranger Calls*. I made that mistake once, and never stayed in my house alone again without thinking of that movie.

It was such an experience; years later I saw Carol Kane on a *Seinfeld* episode and was taken right back to her film. "The calls are coming from inside the house!"

George Kennedy took time off from flying doomed jets in the *Airport* movies to boarding doomed Nazi derelicts in *Ghost Ship*, an *HBO* after midnight gem that was perfect heckling material. A friend in school didn't feel the same as I held court around a table at lunch telling everyone how bad *Death Ship* was. She got angry at my flippant, laughing review of the bad horror film and her admission that it scared her. How could *Death Ship* scare anyone for God's sake? We were friends and I think she felt so hurt at the way I just scoffed at her fear.

She got quiet and didn't talk to me for the rest of class. It was in reading class at the end of the day that she passed me a note revealing that the whole Nazi thing was what scared her.

This was one of the first lessons I got in how personal horror could be to someone. What scares one doesn't necessarily apply to the other. Again… personal.

I apologized for being a jackass. I kept that letter from eighth grade to this day as a reminder of how the genre impacts us:

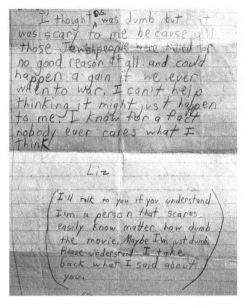

I thought[P.S.] was dumb but it was scary to me because all those Jewish people were killed for no good reason at all. and could happen again if we ever went to war. I can't help thinking it might just happen to me. I know for a fact nobody ever cares what I think.

Liz

I'll talk to you if you understand I'm a person that scares easily know matter how dumb the movie. Maybe I'm just dumb. Please understand I take back what I said about you.

Since we're on the subject, a quick diversion from *HBO*, even though I would torture myself further and watch this film again when it came to the platform. I saw *Motel Hell* at the same drive-in, the same summer that *Jaws* was re-released.

Motel Hell is a dumb movie but it scared the shit out of me. Better yet, it disturbed me. The images of those people buried to their necks in that "garden,"

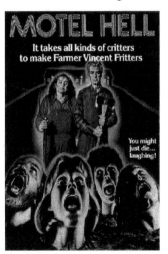

fed with the funnels, their vocal chords slit… what the fuck?

I sat atop a car with my cousins and pretended I was eating this up like the popcorn in my lap. In reality I wanted it to be over. I often shut my eyes but the goddamned sounds were just as terrifying. Chainsaws, screams and the whole concept of those poor people rendered helpless, force fed and then ground into food to be sold…

251

I came home unable to get those images out of the head that the dark comedy of the film went right over. I remember one TV ad said you just might die from laughter. I don't know where the hell that came from. Nothing in that movie provoked me to laugh. I know I had nightmares. I saw *Jaws* at eight years of age and didn't walk away as shaken as *Motel Hell's* effect.

If my cousins knew I was so scared they would have teased the Motel Hell out of me. I wouldn't hear the end of it for family reunions and holidays to come. I put on a good poker face but I hated that movie for the scaring it gave me.

Months later I would turn on my friend, Liz, with *Death Ship* and make her feel diminished, using her admission of fear as a bat to club her with. For her to turn around and so humbly write that letter of explanation put me in my place and taught me more of a lesson than if she had kept up her talking embargo against me.

I forgot how *Jaws 2* shook Michael, and how he asked me during that camping trip to just shut up about it. Liz's letter reminded me.

Say it with me: "Horror is always personal."

> I remember the first time I saw the original 1978 "Halloween."
> Back in those days, you had to wait a long time to be able to see
> movies on TV that were in theaters. It was 1981. I was sitting on my
> couch with a pillow near my face as soon as I heard the theme song. It
> made my heart beat so fast. It was so scary. Even today, when I hear it,
> it still brings me back to 1981.And seeing that pumpkin in the begin-
> ning get closer and closer and to hear Michael Myers breathing under
> that mask, added to the suspense.
>
> I knew right away that Horror was going to be my favorite movie
> genre and "Halloween" was going to be a favorite movie of mine.
>
> **Heidi Martinelli**

I worked on changing my image the summer between ninth and tenth grade.
I grew my hair longer. I allowed a mustache to fill out my upper lip. A weekend
at Michael's yielded an old safari bush jacket which I adopted from his dad who
was just planning to throw it away. I picked up *Ocean Pacific* (*OP*) T-shirts and
my official school uniform became T-shirts, jeans and that bush jacket.

My uncle got me a silent Super 8mm *Kodak* film camera for Christmas
1981. It was time to embrace the filmmaker in me. I went from carting a tire
chains box full of books to a movie maker and "The Horror Kid" by the end of
eight grade.

I was going to be popular by the time I graduated even if I had to bulldoze my way into it. Once again, Toni would be there to help me along.

I returned to Bangor that fall of 1982, just after my sophomore year started. I was in my safari uniform. I sat in the stand seeing how many old Bangor faces I would remember or how many remembered me.

It didn't matter, Lisa Heller did. She was in the band and puberty had been good to her. I last saw her in fifth grade and she was now this long-haired dirty blonde in a tight-fitting marching band uniform that held few secrets.

The night no one comes home.

She saw me in the stand, recognized me and came over to talk when she got a break. She was one of the few girls I talked with in fifth grade and we bonded over feeling like outcasts. I think we both fancied ourselves as ex-outcasts at that football game reunion.

I tested my new found confidence and asked for her phone number and if she would be interested in going on a date.

She was interested in me and very interested to see the third *Halloween* film. It just happened to be coming to The Sherman. I called

> *I remember going to see "Halloween H20" in theaters at four years old with my dad and my great aunt. They told me everyone around us was worried I would be scared, but I said "I hope this one isn't like "Halloween III". I love "Halloween III" now, but four-year-old me was all about Michael Myers. It's such a weird comfort movie, but I love it.*
>
> **Ashley Bialik**

her later that week and we made plans to go opening night.

My dad drove me to her house. We picked Lisa up in a his 1978 tan Ford Granada and he dropped us off at The Sherman's box office on Main Street.

The poster for *Halloween III: Season of the Witch* was intriguing. The stretched camera look of the kids against that red sunset. "The Night No One Comes Home," blared at us. I bought our tickets, treated her to the concession stand and we took our seats in the same theater where I saw *The Shining, The Amityville Horror* and *Dawn of the Dead*.

The place was packed for the first weekend. I tried to find a back row seat but no luck. We ended up somewhere in the middle but that was okay. I really did want to see the movie, not just make out.

The previews came and went and we buckled down for a good time. I listened to people before the show recap the end of *Halloween II*, wondering how Michael would return after he burned up at the end. Was Laurie Strode back? The person this guy was talking to said they didn't see her in any of the trailers. While it was *Halloween III*, no one really knew what it was *about*. The trailer and TV spots didn't show much.

The movie started. I managed to get an arm around Lisa. She laid her head on my left shoulder. Her hair smelled like *Breck* or *Wella Balsam*.

We had silent guys in suits chasing some dude with a mask. Were they like Michael Myers? There was no Haddonfield, so this was somewhere else? Some dude in a suit ripped mask guy's eyes out and then Tom Atkins showed up as a doctor. I could hear people muttering around me, asking just what the *fuck* was going on. What WAS this? They even showed a COMMERCIAL for the first *Halloween* film as Dr. Challis sat in a bar early in the film.

Then the aisle exodus started. You could see silhouettes grabbing coats, standing and leaving. I imagine it was going on behind us as well.

We heard someone ask, "Now what the fuck was that?" At the end Tom Atkins was forced to watch a horror marathon on TV. It's showing…you guessed it…the 1978 *Halloween*.

The theater held about 250 people. There might've been 50-75 people left by the end.

You could hear people yelling at the staff or manager out in the lobby every time the back doors opened. People were PISSED. This wasn't *Halloween*. This was some stupid shit with robots and masks. No Jamie Lee Curtis. No Michael Myers. No Dr. Loomis.

A second poster in the lobby said "All New!" What the hell did that mean? They weren't kidding. This was something entirely different. They just didn't tell anyone how different.

What I do know is we both LIKED it. It was not what we expected and the story felt more like the Halloween season than the last film. It was fun, a little silly, even at our young age, we knew that, but it was worth the ticket price. I told Lisa I would even see it again. I suggested that if they just called it *The Season of the Witch* it might've been better received. Would anyone have come to see it, though?

She kissed me. I didn't make the first move. She kissed me in that empty theater as the end credits to *Halloween III* rolled up the screen. Just for us. Little did I know that one day I would become the student of that film's director and writer. I would meet

John Carpenter, Nick Castle, Stacey Nelligan and become friends with Adrienne Barbeau.

What I did know is that I was in ass-over-tin-cups in love with the girl kissing me in The Sherman Theater, in that fall of 1982.

Disney tried to get in on the horror thing. The studio's *The Watcher in the Woods* was downright awful. I saw it on *HBO* and had no idea what I was watching. I would find out years later studio interference, script rewrites and Hollywood fuckery made the movie a total mess. They tried again with a classy move of adapting Ray Bradbury's *Something Wicked This Way Comes*. I saw it at the mall with a small crowd but the reaction was "meh" to say the least.

It looked good, had some atmospheric scenes but overall it wasn't scary and for the most part boring. Time has been a bit kinder to it, mostly for some of the imaginative cinematography, but many forget it was a flop when it came out in theaters. It was the wrong time to make that movie. The slasher reigned supreme in horror and Spielberg ran the rest of the box office. I saw *Something Wicked* and forgot it. That's how memorable it was for me until I revisited it decades later on DVD.

Lawrence D. Cohen, known as Larry Cohen was from the same stable as Roger Corman, George Romero, Frank Hennenlotter, Alan Ormsby, Joe Dante and the up and coming Lloyd Kaufman of *Troma Entertainment*.

Cohen did *It's Alive*, wrote the script for 1976's *Carrie* and went on to adapt Peter Straub's *Ghost Story* as well as the *ABC* miniseries for *Stephen King's IT*. His was behind the "sequel" to *Salem's Lot* which gave us Tara Reid. I would eventually connect with Larry to enlist his help for a gift for Tara—an original giant French one-sheet of her debut vampire film.

Cohen gave us *Q: The Winged Serpent,* a monster movie that rose above what would be considered fodder for *The Asylum* today. The Sherman kept its reputation as a solid horror house and ran this little gem that came out at the kickoff of the slasher. Instead of a masked psycho, we had a prehistoric flying reptile picking off victims from New York City rooftops while making its home in the top of The *Chrysler* Building.

This was a laugh out loud fun film and a perfect matinee film. Overcast and rainy, me and a few friends plopped down to be entertained in the decaying Sherman theater. It had a good crowd and people were ready for a good time. We got it. Silliness, a hot chick snatched from her penthouse pool, and a final confrontation that gave some great monster action for a film of this small budget. Candy Clark showed up, and once again gave legitimacy to a silly premise because she takes her work seriously. Dammit, Candy buys it and so do we. Her eclectic resume throughout her acting career has made her a chameleon. She can adapt to any role and showed it so well in *Q*.

What stands out to me was reading a review of this film by Roger Ebert a few weeks later in the paper. Ebert interviewed Samuel Z. Arkoff (the legendary *American International Pictures* producer who also did *The Amityville Horror*) and during their talk, they got to *Q*. Ebert commended Arkoff on the brilliant casting of its star, Michael Moriarty, whom Ebert felt gave a stellar method performance among the dreck of this cheesy monster movie.

Arkoff replied, "The dreck was my idea."

That response was perfect and summed up everything I loved about indie, low budget filmmaking.

Lloyd Kaufman remains standing with Roger Corman as the last of the great indie filmmakers. Kaufman's *Troma Studios* was all over the place in the 70s, making popular sex comedies, but also sex comedies with odd elements. He was

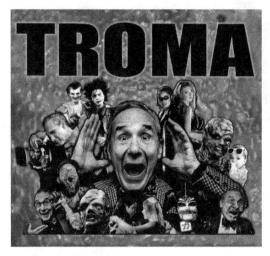

a filmmaking wild card who, like William Castle and Sam Arkoff, gave a number of filmmakers their first breaks. On one hand he could crank out Arkoff-style dreck then turn around and provide production to highbrow indie content like *My Dinner with Andre*.

I read about Lloyd in *Fangoria*, saw him on WPIX Channel 11 news. He was the New York spirit of indie filmmaking and a real character. His secret power was spying talented filmmakers and giving them a shot. He went on to write a series of "Make Your Own Damn Movie" books and lecture on the subject. Despite his comic persona, he is a hardened and brilliant filmmaker and showman who has stayed true to his roots and style. Lloyd Kaufman bent to no one.

He hit pay dirt with 1985's *The Toxic Avenger* which combined slapstick comedy with ultra-violent action with his anti-hero "Toxie" who would become the company mascot—a perverse parallel to Disney's Mickey Mouse.

I brought *The Toxic Avenger* on VHS to a party in my senior year. We watched after a number of people left or passed out. It got a lot of "What the fuck is this shit?" reactions and I loved it. Lloyd would be pleased.

Reading his books, listening to him speak brought me to New York City to meet him not long after my *6 Degrees of*

Hell was released. He was gracious, kind and most of all listened. His work was so important to me I demanded he make a cameo in my horror *Death House* which featured some of the biggest names of the genre. There was no way Lloyd could be left out.

I had him play "Dr. Challis" (a nod to Tom Atkins's character from *Halloween III*). We even did a special photo shoot where he played his cameo "Tromaville Janitor," donning orange coveralls and a mop. I had the honor of taking the picture with him, pretending to yell at him for doing a lousy job. It was one of the many high points in making that film. It's a life achievement to have had such an honor to share a movie photo with a hero of mine.

The word "fun" is often used to describe *Troma's* films. They are unpretentious and designed to do what good horror does: stimulate. Lloyd's brand echoes a time that has long been in recession. My concern is who will be there to carry on his legacy?

"The Toxic Avenger" was one of those late-night films I used to stay up late to watch on TV which introduced me to the magic of independent filmmaking.

I would often watch the classic Amicus and Hammer Horror films with my dad. The experience of watching "The Toxic Avenger" for the first time blew me away. I realized, horror wasn't just about the scares, it could also just be a lot of fun.

It would go on to change my life years later when I saw a social media post asking for someone to work with Lloyd Kauffman and play "The Toxic Avenger." I messaged and ended up playing Toxie for the night. I would go on to play Toxie again when Lloyd returned to London and after listening to Lloyd talk about how you should follow your dreams I decided to start writing.

A couple of days later I contacted a website and wrote a couple of articles, the following week I decided to do a review and then two weeks later I was working at MCM Comic Con and did my first ever interview with Jeremy Gillespie and Steven Kostanski for their film, "The Void." "The Toxic Avenger" has definitely had an impact on my life in more ways than one.

Philip Rogers

Rumors of a sequel to Hitchcock's *Psycho* circulated since 1981 (as far as I remembered). I saw *Psycho* in 1979 while in seventh grade and was knocked on my ass by the shower scene and the big reveal with Mother. Christmas brought books on film and horror history. I read everything (there wasn't much) I could on Hitchcock and the making of the film. I saw Anthony Perkins later that year in *Disney's Star Wars* wannabe misfire, *The Black Hole* and felt the casting was odd to

put Norman Bates in space. The public felt the same. It wasn't much later that I started reading blurbs in *Newsweek*, *Time* and *Fangoria* that Perkins was returning to the Bates Motel.

I saw the original black and white 1960 *Psycho* on TV and the shower scene kicked my ass. While I don't have any standout memory of viewing the first film, I loved it and was against a sequel the moment I heard about it.

I remember reading a *Time* interview in late 1982 or early 1983. Anthony Perkins gave us some scraps from Mother's tray on the new film. He described the upcoming *Psycho II* as Norman returning to motel to find it a flophouse and one night stand haven. "Mother doesn't like that," Perkins was quoted at the end.

Uh oh.

The "uh oh" feeling crept up The Suck Factor. I had this figured out: "Norman comes home, teens are screwing in the rooms and the film basically turns into *Friday the 13th* in a motel." *Fangoria* reported some cool behind the scenes stuff: Jamie Lee Curtis was approached. Christopher Walken was considered for Norman if Perkins didn't reprise the role. In the end, I would just have to see it.

By spring, 1983 my mind was made up: *Psycho II* was gonna be bad. I was fifteen and in tenth grade and jaded. The film was on my list along with *Jaws 3-D* and *Return of the Jedi*. My summer date roster was set.

I once again bicycled the seven miles to the mall with a group of friends and to meet a girl I was seeing. *Psycho II* was in *Music Makers* biggest house (This was before the *McDonald's* job and getting hired at the mall). I walked in ready to hate the film. I even killed the romantic mojo by saying that I expected this movie to be bad and she should too. "It'll be a *Friday the 13th* rip off." I knew everything. She asked why were seeing it if I knew it was going to be so bad? I didn't know. I had to see it. That's the only answer I had, and, I might get a good make out session out of it.

The lights went down, the coming attractions barreled over the screen and then it was time for our feature presentation. They did it, they opened with the shower scene and my prediction was confirmed. It was going to be bad. Why the shower scene? Was it necessary? Starting the film with it just reminded us of how much better the first film was. *Psycho II* was pure cynicism. We were in for a screw job over the next two hours.

Then something happened.

The screen went black, the opening titles came up with a striking blast of Jerry Goldsmith's score, surprising me and jolting me in my seat. Then the ominous tone took a maudlin, almost sympathetic turn, and from there on out I fell in love with *Psycho II*.

Psycho II is one of the best sequels ever made. It ranks up there with *The Bride of Frankenstein* in quality follow-ups to a classic horror motion picture. The film is almost a stand- alone story and in some ways not dependent on the first film. A good sequel builds on the characters and events of the previous film and takes us somewhere new. *Psycho II* does exactly that.

The best part was, it didn't have to. I expected it go down the *Friday the 13*th route. To be sure, it had to give you some blood and gore. Vera Miles's death delivered that in slasher spades. It had to because times had changed since the original film and audiences demanded more.

When the lights came up I was a changed boy. It was fantastic. It wasn't just a hack sequel. It was great. I walked out to the pay phones, called my mom and said I was going to stay for the next show. I bought another ticket, said goodbye to my girl and my friends and walked right back into the theater alone to sit through it all again.

The second audience viewing was equally a blast. People screamed and laughed in all the right spots. This time I was able to catch some of the more subtle dark humor. The movie was better the second time around and there even were a few satisfied claps of applause when the credits rolled up.

Years later I sat in a film course at Penn State. The professor asked if there were any film sequels that might be better than the originals. I offered up *Psycho II*, but with a caveat. I made it clear I didn't think *Psycho II* was SUPERIOR to Hitchcock's original. I just ENJOYED it more because I expected to hate it. He shook his head and started out calm enough but by the end had risen his voice in an angry, irritated way.

"The problem is you kids want blood and guts and sex. Story means nothing to you. To call *Psycho II* a great sequel shows how ignorant you and so many of your generation are to real cinema! It's worse than an insult to everything Hitchcock did!"

I defended my opinion and the film. Norman is a victim in this film, I told him. There is a conspiracy, and what could have been a straight up slasher, instead turns into an Agatha Christie mystery—a literal "Who Dunnit?" Sharp dialogue references the first film while also reminding us that what Norman did decades earlier was bad, worse things have since taken place. Mother and Norman are on the JV Murder Squad.

I said a lot more but he was having none of it. I was a dumb kid who wanted blood and boobs. I gave up trying and shut up. It was his class.

The 80s got better for me on the high school social scene. I got placed into an English class with some of the most popular people in my class. I liked them and they seemed to like me.

Toni urged me to run for class president as we saw our class was in some serious financial shit. Not only did I run at the end of my sophomore year, I won by a Reagan landslide.

I modeled my speeches after Reagan and I knew what Michael J. Fox's Alex P. Keaton was saying in his love for Reagan. I wasn't a Republican; I just bought into the whole style over substance motif that fueled the 80s.

The Sherman got another slasher flick a month after Toni's death. I was seeing another girl at the time who really didn't like horror movies, but she liked me. I was in a deep funk over Toni but thought I could re-create some of the magic with Lisa the year before when we saw *Halloween III*.

Sleepaway Camp was another low budget horror that would never see a movie screen if released today, not to mention its ending and how that would be received in today's social justice warrior cancel culture.

My date was a straight-laced girl. She liked me because I was "different," as she liked to say all the time. I wasn't the big, dumb jock that I guess she "used to date." She went for the opposite I guess. I could make her laugh and early on I knew that was a sure way to a girl's interest. Get 'em to laugh and you're halfway there.

I wasn't in love, but she was pretty, even with braces. She had these amazing green eyes, big hair and tan. She was tall, and that always worked for me. I think it's safe to say we passed each other's time even if it wasn't hot, teenaged passion.

We met at the theater. I had no idea what the film was about. This was a time before the Internet and saturated movie and entertainment news. It wasn't like I could go online and find out whatever I could about the film. Even if the director himself wanted to leak the ending of the film back then, few would have heard about it. *Sleepaway Camp* wasn't exactly the kind of film covered by *Entertainment Tonight,* which was about the only source of popular entertainment news aside from magazine. Maybe *Fangoria* might say something, but the horror magazine barely ran any coverage on it.

I was going in based on the poster and the one or two TV spots that I caught. I felt pretty secure it was a slasher and things were already fitting into a formula by 1983.

My date kept asking me what it was about as we got concessions I repeated that I honestly didn't know but to get ready for some *Friday the 13*th type deaths. She HATED *Friday the 13*th and when we got to our seats after she spent the entire walk to them listing why she hated that film, I asked her why she agreed to see this with me.

That was the first red flag that the night would not end well.

The movie started and it seemed to fall right in with the *Friday the 13*th pattern. Counselors were picked off in a variety of gruesome ways. This time we had the picked on the girl, was she doing it? Was it this guy? I did take note that the gore effects were becoming stronger and stronger as the years moved forward. Things changed from the original *Halloween*.

Then we saw that ending. There were around fifty people in the theater and they gasped. There were a few "what the fuck's?" I looked at my date. She was slack-jawed. She stared at the screen, mouth open and with a look of absolute repulsion. *Sleepaway Camp* was not what she expected.

The lights came up, the credits rolled and she stood, got her coat and motioned for me to move out of the row so she could get to the aisle. She seemed in a hurry. We walked out to the lobby and you could tell she couldn't wait to ask me: "What did you think of that?"

Did she mean the whole movie or the ending? I was still processing it myself and was kind of hoping she might want discuss and give her point of view. "I thought it was a fun little horror movie," was all I could offer.

She nodded and you could tell she had things she wanted to say. After a few moments as people exited past us she said, "You know, I don't think I could date someone who thought THAT was a "fun" movie."

She wasn't scared. She was disgusted. I went on to explain I would love to make horror movies one day and have people react to them the way that group did or even how she was reacting. She laughed—that kind of sarcastic "You gotta be fucking kidding me" laugh.

I dug my grave deeper when I shared my thoughts on Felissa Rose, saying she was the best actor in the film and it would be cool to get her into a movie one day.

She didn't need any more time to think. "Maybe we should take a break. This was a little too much." She was breaking up with me in the lobby of The Sherman over a movie.

"Okay." It just came out of me. Just like that. She nodded and said I didn't need to drive her home. She would call her parents. I drove her home though. It was a long, quiet ride.

We never got together again. Now here I am all these years later. Maybe she bought this book?

If so…please enjoy this photo of me and Felissa Rose in Hollywood as she not only became my business partner but also my close, personal friend. We met when I cast her as one of the leads of my *Camp Dread* and it was *Sleepaway Camp* that influenced that decision.

I started my first real job at 15 washing dishes at a diner. Toni waitressed there and got me the job. I moved up to *McDonalds* and worked the grill. That didn't go so well.

Let me give you some local historical context before I move into *Jaws 3-D*, *Poltergeist* and *The Thing*.

From about eighth grade on, my mother dropped this threat at least once a week at the dinner table: "You better plan on getting a job once you get up to that high school. Because if you think for one minute we are paying for your car insurance and gas you got another thing coming."

My first car being restored at my father's house.

I got a 1975 *Ford Maverick* for my 16th birthday. My biological father restored it himself, adding a spoiler and mag wheels with a hot candy apple red paint job and black racing stripe.

Just after tenth grade ended Toni put in a good word for me to wash dishes at the nearby diner. I didn't mind the work. It was better than sweating my ass of mowing lawns and pulling weeds but the hours really sucked as it was open 24 hours and they paid me under the table. That meant to them they could work me at whatever late hours they pleased.

The McDonald's uptown where I once worked. Briefly.

I figured I would risk offending Toni and move on up to the *McDonalds* across the street from the mall. For whatever reason, the two female managers didn't like me. I was still riding my ten speed as I couldn't drive until September. My first day at the Golden Arches started at 4 AM as I was asked to come in to blacktop the parking lot with buckets of this tar black sealer.

I biked the seven miles in the dark and was greeted by Deb, one of the managers at the back door. She had buckets of that sealer and these big push brooms. She pointed to a leaf blower and told me what to do. Blow out the driveway and start sealing the one section of the parking lot before the breakfast drive through crowd started.

Linda was the other manager, a short plug of a woman with thick *Brillo* black hair and beaver incisors. She had favorites on the staff. I was not one of them and to this day I do not know why.

Brian and Scott were two seniors that I knew from school. They led the kitchen team. Brian was a stoner, one of our overnight Jeff Spiccoli's who appeared in the wake of *Fast Times at Ridgemont High* the year before. His long brown hair was pulled back into a ponytail and he wore his triangular paper hat with a certain amount of pride and yet indifference. He smoked while he flipped burgers and seemed pleased to have another burger buddy to talk to.

Scott was higher on the echelon. He seemed a favorite of managers Deb and Linda and was given the coveted job of running the fry and Chicken McNuggets machines. Scott deep fried them all and in my experience, laid claim to deep frying anything from *Hershey* Bars to Brian's cigarette, long before stores in NYC found it trendy to deep fry *Twinkies* and candy bars.

"After 30 minutes you throw 'em out," Scott said in a bored voice. He was a tall blonde guy with short-cropped hair and Rutger Hauer glazed blue eyes. He held a screen full of brown breaded chicken nuggets before me. He had slid them out of some giant warmer that was dotted with red LED counters.

"You throw them out? They're still good!" I was in shock.

"It's the rules. Don't let them catch you selling these after half an hour."

"Why don't you freeze 'em and give 'em to the Salvation Army in their kitchens. Is this the way it is across the country? I can take food down there."

Deb walked up behind me. "Any food that leaves this building goes into the dumpster. It will be considered company theft if you take any of this off these premises. You'll be fired and prosecuted." She made eye contact with me on that one. She looked to Scott to back her up.

"It's true." He shrugged and walked back to his fryer.

"Brian! Burger Grill!" Linda yelled this from up front where the cashiers manned the picture menu registers.

"Fuck me," he grumbled. He hated "burger grill" orders.

A Burger Grill was a special order by a patron. They usually came from the drive-through. Brian saw them as a personal attack and a way to slow him down as he cranked out his burgers. Each "Burger Grill" meant wasted time.

"Fuckin' people think they're at Tavern on the Green," he would curse. "Motherfuckin' grill orders. I'll give you something special." He would cough hard and break loose an impressive chunk of tar-flecked mucus. After giving a quick look over the counter, he dripped a watery gob onto the special burger order and capped it off with a bun. "There's some extra special sauce."

I watched him stick a cooked burger down the back of his pants and beneath his underwear, wiping the crack of his ass with it. He dropped ash and phlegm onto Big Mac's, Quarter Pounders, hamburgers and cheeseburgers and mixed it with ketchup and mayonnaise. He later told me his goal was to ejaculate on a Burger Grill special order, but was stymied with the logistics on that one.

I made the mistake of telling Linda, underestimating her affection for him.

Right after I was hired, Deb gave me my first assignment for my first day of work. "You're the new guy," she gruffed.

"Yeah?"

"You need to be in here tomorrow by 4 AM." She was checking something off of the clipboard that never left her hands. She managed to always look busy.

"Am I working breakfast?" I was told in my interviews that no one is entitled to work the breakfast shift. Only special crew got the honors. Deb's favorites were the breakfast crew because she opened the building and liked certain people around her. I was not one of them.

"You're going to seal the parking lot," she told me. "You need to be here early before the sun gets hot. Otherwise it really sucks." She gave me a small smile as she looked up from her clipboard.

I woke up at three that morning, showered, rolled my uniform into a backpack and hopped on my blue Fuji ten speed and biked uptown. It was dark when I arrived, but Deb's pride and joy, brand new blue Subaru car was in the lot. She met me at the door when she unlocked it and never let me in.

"Take the leaf blower. You know how to use one?"

"Yeah."

"Blow out the entire lot first. No stones or garbage on the ground. Once you do that, come see me." She closed the door and locked it, leaving me framed by the giant yellow golden arches painted on the glass.

By 5 AM the lot was blown free of debris and she supervised my opening of the five gallon sealer buckets.

"Sun's just coming up. You're in good shape." She went to go back inside.

"Hey Deb."

Surprised, she turned around. "What?"

"Am I the only guy doing this? No one else is coming in to help with this giant parking lot?"

"You're it." That's all she had to say. What the fuck did I do to piss these people off?

She came outside later to inspect my work and seemed impressed that I was finishing the last section. Black sealer spattered my legs and burned from absorbing the warming sunlight.

That whole job sucked. The people sucked. The customers sucked and my bosses sucked.

I had an hour for lunch. I walked across Route 611 to the mall.

I saw "Poltergeist" at a slumber party at my house. I was around 10 years old. I have no idea how we ended up renting it on VHS. I have no memory of actually watching it and being scared. I don't remember having any problems with nightmares that night, surrounded by my friends. For the next week, I would wake up, curled under the frame of my parents' bed. She found out that we had watched "Poltergeist" and made me re-watch it, in the light of day. I was horrified this time. As I watched it, I realized why it terrified me so much. Once she made me confront this, I was able to sleep in my own bed. I never forgot the psychological awakening in re-watching that movie in the day.

Kelly Heeg

The movie theater was the hub for teenage social life inside Stroud Mall. There were no other multiplexes within fifty miles and the two remaining local movie theaters were in sad shape. The Grand Theater had become a porno house by 1982 and was closing down because the video industry was wiping out theatrical porn films.

The Sherman Theater downtown was destroyed by the *Music Makers* multiplex that came with the mall in 1977. As the town grew, so did the need for parking, and the Sherman just didn't have the space. The mall lured away patrons from a downtown burdened with parking meters and exposed shops that could not compete with the discount chains that made their home in the new, air-conditioned, heated and covered mall.

The last several horror films I saw at The Sherman before my defection to the mall were *Creepshow, Sleepaway Camp, The Dead Zone* and *Poltergeist.*

We went as a group to see *Poltergeist* in 1982 and found the theater packed with a

crowd that was over-the-top psyched to see it. *Poltergeist* was like a rollercoaster. It lured you in. It made us laugh and then when the scares started, it was relentless. Five of us sat in a screaming theater, slowly cranking up the coaster to the first drop. Then the car flew through the story and led to massive laughter and applause at the end when Craig T. Nelson throws the TV cart out of the motel room.

The film played us with highs and lows, feeding into our real fears of the dark and the things that reside there. The stuffed toy clown looks scary but the real fear was what every child had that goes from what's in the room to what's under the bed.

Out to dinner in Hollywood with Adrienne Barbeau.

No one dies in *Poltergeist*. No bloody kills as the slasher movement ramped up. Good, fun scares all worked on the personal level. Nothing is more terrifying to a parent than the loss of a child or worse yet…one that goes missing. *Poltergeist* got personal and that's why it worked and its subsequent sequels will not.

I remember the audience screaming as the one ghost hunter ripped his face apart in the bathroom only to find it was the ghosts fucking with him. That was

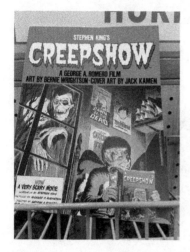

a Tobe Hooper moment if there ever was one. As horrible as it was, the result said: it was okay, it was just a dream.

Creepshow struck me on another level. I went with Michael (our friendship surviving my move to Stroudsburg) over Thanksgiving break. One of our tenth grade English assignments was to keep a daily journal.

I did it and kept both volumes to this day. My entry on my theater experience seeing *Creepshow* was dated 11/28/1982:

"Creepshow was a movie laid out in comic book format. It was like the old Tales From the Crypt comic books. They have a version of Creepshow in comic format up at Waldenbooks in the mall. Five different stories were put into film format and it was really interesting. Stephen King is incredible and he teamed up  *with George Romero who did Dawn of the Dead. I really liked it. Hardly anyone was in the theater but I think the movie has been out since the start of the month. I want to make a horror movie one day just like that. It was fun."*

I still feel that way and saddened to read hardly anyone watched it with us on the big screen.

The following year, with the new ability to drive, I would skip off school grounds and drive uptown to *Video Jones*, THE video rental store to rent a copy of *Creepshow* to bring back and entertain my study hall. Mr. Adams would sit in the back grading papers while Adrienne Barbeau told Hal Holbrook he sucked in bed, Carrie Nye got her head twisted 360 degrees by Nathan Grantham looking for his cake, and E.G. Marshall told his employee he could take his whole family to Disney on his fucking welfare check.

Good old Mr. Adams couldn't have cared less. Imagine that happening today.

The Dead Zone was another Stephen King adaptation as Hollywood jumped on the King Train. We would start to see King translations and original films with his name on them. It wouldn't take long to understand they weren't always the greatest. His name above the title didn't guarantee quality.

I was becoming familiar with David Cronenberg after seeing *The Brood* and *Rabid* on *HBO* a few years earlier. This gave me a bit of expectation for *The Dead Zone* and knew to expect the disturbing and offbeat.

He didn't disappoint. This was one I saw alone and again, in an almost-empty matinee theater and it was better that way. The theatrical experience of *The Dead Zone* was way different than seeing it a year later on home video. Cronenberg brought you into Christopher Walken's world. It enveloped you. It was immersive. It really was. The theater was quiet, no laughing or even talking. The others were as engrossed as I was.

When the horror moments came, they did so quietly with understatement, and then presented themselves matter-of-factly, leaving you to *think* about them. The horrific rape and murder scene was followed up by a "you are there" police raid on a corrupt deputy's home. When Tom Skerritt kicks in the bathroom door what we see is quietly disturbing. Cronenberg then threw in a few small death

277

twitches just to top it off, searing the image in your brain. I can see it now, on the big screen, as I write this.

I left the theater contemplating and for the first time, consciously pondering my political standing and about what I wanted out of life because it could all change in a moment. *The Dead Zone* made me THINK. For me, it remains one of the absolute best King adaptations ever made.

An American Werewolf in London hit cable around March of 1983. It moved me enough to write an entry about it as well:

"Well, I sat and watched a movie that was totally different from any other I've seen before. An American Werewolf In London premiered on HBO tonight. It was the yarn and string of the typical werewolf movie woven into a modern story. Two American tourists are attacked on the British moors by a werewolf. One is killed but the other survives to carry on the tradition. The movie was put together nicely. The photography was way above what I expected and the acting was fresh and alive...

...A wise-cracking corpse of the murdered friend of the afflicted young man (David Naughton, the Dr. Pepper guy) comes back to warn his buddy of the "treats" that await him. Jokes and humor are added to these scenes. The effects are incredible. I couldn't believe how they turned Naughton into a wolf! The movie just kind of ended. It doesn't really build to a giant climax. The special effects were amazing and blood-chilling and it's a fresh change from other werewolf movies or all these psycho killer movies."

1981-82 were odd years for horror as two different trends were at odds. *Dead and Buried, Creepshow, Ghost Story, The Howling, American Werewolf* and *The Thing* bucked the slasher trend. Adrienne Barbeau once told me years later that she and then-husband John Carpenter landed in Hawaii and saw a giant poster for *E.T.* on the building wall. He turned to her and said, "We're done."

He was referring to the release of his *The Thing* which came out after *E.T.* This was the Reagan 80s and Americans wanted their aliens friendly with upbeat endings. He was right. I saw *The Thing*, by myself, in an almost empty theater summer 1982.

Some call *The Thing* Carpenter's greatest film. Others, like me, call it one of the greatest films ever made for any genre. Carpenter's film was buried in 1982 by that candy pilfering alien and Spielberg. Between a lackluster marketing campaign by Universal Studios and Reagan America's pop sugar desire for heart glowing aliens, *The Thing*, 1982, never really had a chance.

Universal dropped the marketing ball in 1982 with the original *The Thing*. They were more focused on *E.T.* and the cash rolling in. Carpenter's film got kicked to the curb and left to fend on its own. Universal leaned toward connecting Carpenter's movie with the 1951 film, *The Thing from Another World.* The original was a creature feature fan favorite and remakes were not taken as kindly as they are today. So for many it was blasphemy that the James Arness classic would be remade. Instead of hyping up the difference of this new film and the positive spin of truly being based on the original short story, the film could have been marketed better as a whole **new** film instead of a remake. It was more of an original telling of John Campbell's novella, *Who Goes There* than the 1951 film which bares only a cursory resemblance to the written work. You can argue Carpenter's *The Thing* is less a remake than it is a direct translation of the original written material.

Doing that would take actual work and imagination. The Imagination Capital of the World is lacking in this natural resource to this day. They threw the film out there at the end of summer after *E.T. The Extraterrestrial* became the biggest movie of all time. The little alien clobbered Carpenter's shape shifting monstrosity and Kurt Russell.

They would go on to do the same thing with the film's 2011 prequel, which was stupidly also named *The Thing* leading people to assume it was remake. Who

> *I was at a friend's house, watching "The Thing" on VHS. There were three of us watching it, but I was the only one who never saw it.*
>
> *As the film started, I asked the ultimate question of a novice who hadn't seen this epic: "Why are they shooting at the dog?" To which my friend simply replied: "Ohhhhhh, just wait."*
>
> *Little did I know that I was seeing a film that not only would become my favorite horror film, but one of my favorite films of all time. It's a movie that I love more each time I watch it.*
>
> **Daniel J. Dudyich**

the hell was and still is running things at *Universal's* marketing department?

There was no real theatrical experience with a crowd, but the feeling of paranoia and claustrophobia in Carpenter's film spilled out into the almost empty theater. Rob Bottin's special effects blew me away. My mouth dropped open with the dog kennel scene and it only dropped further to the floor as the film progressed with each new horrific discovery.

I knew I was watching something unique and brilliant. The film's effects still hold up against the very best CGI today and are even more amazing because they were done by hand, not designed and executed by computer. When *The Thing* emerged at the end as what fans call "Blair Thing," the few people around me yelled in awe. There were several "What the fucks" thrown around that matinee showing.

I left the theater with a heavy exhale. Wow! That was fucking something! Looking back, remembering the almost vacant theater, it only makes it more special because I was one of the first champions of the movie before the Johnny Come Lately's years later that saw it on video.

> **It's difficult to talk about horror and not think of John Carpenter's The Thing.**
>
> *As a kid, on first watching it, I'll admit I simply watched it as another creature feature with amazing special effects, and it scared the shit out of me.*
>
> *As I got older and re-watched it more and more, I started to see more than the alien monster and saw a survival story of isolated characters and an environment that aided the alien creature.*
>
> *It terrorized them and turned this group of men from friendly to forcing them to their limits, turning on each other and reminding you the whole while, it (the horror) could be anyone.*
>
> **WoodsWalker X**

Time and home video have been kind to *The Thing*. I think it's safe to say that it now has the respect and audience it so deserved all those years ago.

I saw it at the mall *Music Makers* Theater in its smallest house. It was 1982 and *AIDS* was just starting to cross into the mainstream dialogue. Looking at the way *The Thing* replicates itself to take over host cells, we were seeing a real-life monster portrayed in this film. It sat quiet for hundreds of years and then once it came into contact with just one person…it started into the bloodstream and threatened the entire planet.

Now back to my *McDonald's* exit and jumping ship to that movie theater. I approached the box office in the mall and was greeted by a short girl with thick wire blond hair.

"Could I have an application, please?" I smiled at her and looked to the floor. She smiled and offered her hand.

"I'm Karen." She gave a warm smile and I wanted to quit *McDonald's* that moment. I penned out the application, filled in the annoying little blocks with all of that pertinent information. I handed it back and a door slammed from inside the lobby. A tall man, slightly stooped with a matted, almost nappy perm and scraggly beard came walking toward the box office.

"You have a job right now?" His voice was dry, slow and again…tired.

"Yes, sir."

An eyebrow went up when I said "Sir." He chuckled to himself. That amused him.

"Are you planning on leaving your *McDonald's* job?" He was looking at me with a tired stare that made me feel he could see right through me.

"Yes, sir."

"When can you start?"

"I'd like to give some notice if I could, please."

"Come see me after you are done with *McDonald's*. We'll talk then." He left.

Karen in the box office flashed a toothy smile and a gave me the "thumbs up."

"You're gonna love it here!" she whispered. She was excited.

The 80s saw a brief revival with the 3-D movie (*Friday the 13th Part 3, Parasite (With Demi Moore!), Comin' at Ya* (Good title for a 3-D porn, don't'cha think?) I asked for my first night off since starting at *McDonald's* to catch the opening night of *Jaws 3-D*, the second sequel to my favorite film of all time. I had never seen a 3-D film, and the articles I read in *Fangoria* magazine promised screams in the first five minutes of the opening credits. Plus, it was *Jaws* and I wanted to see how their *Jaws 3* stood up to my sixth grade masterpiece.

I saw *Friday the 13th Part III* in 3-D with Michael the year before in Easton. It didn't have the red and blue glasses, but instead these new "polarized" specs. I swear the 3-D was fantastic. The movie wasn't so great but it's now beloved because it's the installment where Jason got his hockey mask.

The audience screamed and laughed with the 3-D effects, especially the harpoon gun gag and the eyeball popping out of the skull and out to us. It was summer, throwaway fun. I thought for sure that this was the last one. Jason got clobbered in the head with an axe, and despite the retread ending of Mrs. Voorhees leaping from the water, it seemed like the whole thing had run its course. I was wrong. Really wrong.

Back to *Jaws 3-D*.

"You can see the movie any time! Why do you have to see it opening night?" Linda asked. She was seated at her desk in the nook she called an office. She wasn't even looking at me. "That's just stupid."

She had no idea I was about to give my two week's notice.

"If you find someone to cover for you, I don't care. But I am not taking you off the schedule on a Friday night." She went on writing. The silence told me the conversation was over.

Scott covered for me but he wasn't happy about it. I had to promise to cover for him the following Friday night, which turned out to be until closing which was after 11 PM. That meant my mom would have to come into town late to get me. I would never hear the end of it. However it was *Jaws* and Troy and Eddie and Scott were set to see it with me or without me.

I made the deal.

The star of the *Jaws 3-D*, Dennis Quaid, told a story in 1988 about a moment that changed his career forever. That summer of 1983 he had been

283

shopping in New York City when a woman approached him and asked, "Are you Dennis Quaid? You're in *Jaws 3-D* aren't you?"

"Yes I am," Quaid replied, expecting an autograph request.

"Why do they make shitty movies like that?" the woman asked in earnest.

It was that moment, Quaid later said in an interview, that made him go back to his Montana home and re-evaluate his entire film career.

Karen saw me in line for *Jaws 3-D* with Troy, Scott and Eddie. She gave an excited wave and her big white smile. We were at the separate two "little theaters" on the other end of the mall by the *J.C. Penney* store. There were a total of five theaters at the time, but the three on the other side of the mall were known as "the big theaters" because they held the most people.

The two small theaters on the *J.C. Penney* side held *Jaws 3-D* because they were the only projectors capable of showing a 3-D presentation and they were outfitted to run one movie in two theaters with a complex system of rollers, belts and highways as one projector fed its film to another across the room.

She let me in for free. The others had to pay. She felt that I was pretty much hired, and one of the perks for working the movie theater was free movies. I didn't work a single day and yet I got my first free movie.

We were excited. The theaters were sold out. Over 500 people had their 3-D glasses stuck to their faces. You could hear excited chatter…people really wanted this to be great.

The lights went down, the previews were flat 2-D not 3-D and then the blurry Universal logo came up telling us it was time to put on our glasses.

Maybe my memory fails me, but the 3-D in *Friday the 13*[th] seemed way better than the murky, headache-inducing 3-D in *Jaws 3-D*.

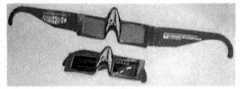

The opening kill was the first sign of trouble. Director Joe Alves told *Fangoria* that there would be screams in the first minute. Not quite.

The shark point of view shot closed in on a big Grouper fish. There was a "crunch!" sound and blood in the water and they cut to the first 3-D effect, the still moving fish head floating out of the screen toward us.

I would find soon enough that the entire 3-D process was wasted on this movie. It didn't add anything because the movie itself was a floating pile of shark shit. Nothing was going to make it better.

The picture color was washed out. Shadows flitted top and bottom of the screen. I closed one eye and watched with the other and reversed.

Sometimes the picture was so dark you couldn't make out what was going on.

This was a rip-off. No wonder they opened it so late in the summer. Later I would learn about a "hit and run." That's when a studio knows they have a stinker and they release it as late as possible, get a solid opening weekend and maybe one more and get their money back before bad word of mouth got around.

The fish head opening was an "uh oh" moment and we got the next one right on its heels. Bright orange and yellow 3-D titles rose up and then made a bite sound as the words *Jaws 3-D* snapped together.

It went downhill. People around me chuckled. Many scoffed or groaned with the quality of the effects. When we got a 3-D inside view of the shark swallowing Simon MacCorkindale whole; it was almost too much for all of us.

I was angry. How could they fuck up *Jaws* like that? It wasn't just bad, it was AWFUL. A few people walked out. By the time we got to the end and the infamous 3-D shot of a fake shark that looked like someone scored it from the *Sea World* souvenir shop, floating stationary toward the camera, I was ready to stand up and scream "THIS SUCKS!" I was so pissed. This was like a 60s *Godzilla* movie when the series was in decline.

The lights came up and no one applauded. No one cheered. People got up with that "let's get the fuck outta here" way that showed they knew they had been screwed. I heard so many around me grumbling, "That was bad, that sucked, holy shit that was awful."

As we inched down the aisle toward the exit doors some kid around my age said to his dad, "That was pretty good!" I wanted to give him a 3-D punch to the face.

"That movie sucked so bad, I saw it for **free** and I want my money back!" That was my review for *Jaws 3-D* as I left the theater.

I was scheduled for the afternoon shift at *McDonald's* the next day. It rained through the late afternoon and when I walked into the restaurant I thought I was at a concert. It was standing room only. Two charter buses parked on my new, sealed macadam and their passengers were lined up twelve deep at the ordering counters.

Linda was in the back helping Brian shoot the ketchup with a giant condiment "caulk gun" onto trays of burger buns.

"Get in here," she snapped.

I went to work, zapping the burgers with ketchup and throwing down hockey puck frozen patties onto the grill. Brian and me scraped the hot surface between burger sets and instantly turned to zap the burgers with ketchup while the new patties fried.

"Faster!" Linda barked as she passed by on her way to the freezer. I looked at her as if she couldn't be serious. "Yeah!" she leered. "You heard me! We have two buses out there and two more are pulling in. So move it!"

"What are you doing, Bruce?" She tossed the frozen burgers to a metal table and looked at me in disbelief.

Before I could answer she snatched the burger zapper out of my hands and manically started splotching ketchup in big red dollops all over the lined up buns.

"Faster! Faster! It's gotta be faster! It...has...to....be...like...THIS!" she hissed as she showed me the ways of squirting ketchup.

"This is nuts," I answered her gaze. "It's burgers! Does it look like anyone out there is starving, Linda?"

She yelled. I can't remember her exact words but it was so over-the-top and over dramatic that I decided to fuck my two weeks 'notice. I pulled off my ridiculous paper hat and walked for the back door. My bike was out there chained and waiting.

"I'm yours," I said to Mr. Hankins at the box office. I had biked across the street to the mall. "When can I start?"

That's how I got my job as an usher at *Music Makers Theaters*.

A few small shout outs to some overlooked 80s horror films before I wind up this chapter.

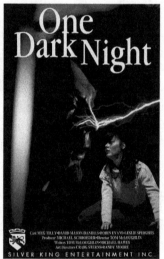

One Dark Night squeaked out there into a handful of theaters. It played at the mall for maybe a week. I saw it only because Meg Tilly of *Psycho II* was in it. I don't think there were twenty people in the theater with me. It got almost no advertising and there was already limited press as it was promoted without an Internet.

One Dark Night is a great example of the opportunity small films had in the 80s. Even with no real marketing, the film managed to get on a handful of screens. No kidding, if you didn't see it in the first week of release, you probably missed it.

This was a perfect make out movie. Horny, wise assed, good-looking teens stumbled upon a supernatural force. It wasn't a slasher but it was goofy and allowed me and a date to sit in the back row, make out and stop long enough to take in the good parts and follow along.

My best memory of this was not just the film being fun but a small reminder of the rush of being young. A low budget, cheesy horror movie with such a great title, a beautiful girl in one dark theater who was totally into me, popcorn, driving on my own…it's something that is hard to convey to many these days.

I was fortunate enough to realize it at that time and know these times were not going to last forever.

The Keep wasn't as much fun. This was kind of like the monster movie version of *The Shining*. It felt way longer than what it was and when I thought about it in hindsight, it seemed like the whole movie was in slow motion. Later I found that there was studio fuckery with this one too and not only was the adaptation of the book screwed, the film's edit was a mess resulting in a slow, stylistic horror film that made little impression.

It made little impression on the audience as well. There weren't a lot of people in the theater. I remember when walking out no one was talking about the film. They just left.

I was now an usher at *Music Makers Theaters* and now I could see movies for free. I could see them multiple times, and when it was slow, catch parts of them as I checked the houses and stood at the back to open the doors. I was sixteen years old and living the horror dream.

We had a local mom-and-pop video store located in the back of an auto parts shop. They would set up a television that played a series of custom trailers for the VHS tapes they had in stock. The trailers were provided by the video distributor, and featured a voiceover describing the movie: what it was about, who was in it, how amazingly great it was, why we should rent it right away.

When "The Keep" came out, the trailer started with the voiceover solemnly intoning: "The Keep...!" Then followed several random scenes from the movie, during which the narrator was silent... and at the end, as though he had no idea what else to say about it, the voice-over just repeated: "The Keep...!" That was it.

That was the best they could do. Even the video company had no idea how to sell this film. That's when I first fell in love with that amazing mess of a movie, which, despite its budget and its stunning production design -- is in many ways more akin to the other flicks I fell in love with from that same grimy location: SPOOKIES, IT CAME, THINGS, BRAIN DAMAGE, THE HOUSE BY THE CEMETERY.

Will T. Laughlin

A BRIEF WORD FROM DEE WALLACE

It's funny. I didn't go looking for horror. Horror found me. And when it did, I realized I loved all the opportunities it gave me: the emotional rides, the arcs to play, the intricate relationships. I was hooked--not that I don't love the *Hallmark* and *Lifetime* movies, and amazing opportunities like *E.T.* I do. Horror asks more of you. Horror serves a real purpose in people's lives. Watching a horror film decreases your anxiety, strengthens your DNA, floods you with good hormones, and empowers you to handle your fear in a safe place. Why do you think all the Disney movies have scary characters?

I enjoy the role of Scream Queen. If people knew how much talent it takes to make all those scenarios real, without overacting, they might bring horror films to the Academy Awards more often. If they understood the mental, emotional, and physical expense it takes to do a film like *Cujo*, they would appreciate scream queens a hell of a lot more!

-- Dee Wallace

HORROR AT MUCUS MAKERS

My first "free" movie as an employee of *Music Makers Theaters* was *Cujo*. I started in August of 1983, only several days before the film opened. I took my mother to see it, on me. Since seventh grade she'd been my Stephen King conduit so it was time to pay it forward.

I will start this chapter saying Dee Wallace was robbed of an Academy Award nomination at the very least for *Cujo*. I still argue she should've been nominated and WON The Best Actress award for 1983. Years later when I worked with her on *Zombie Killers: Elephant's Graveyard* she shared that Stephen King told her the same thing himself. *Cujo* did the rare hat trick—it was an improvement over the book.

Dee's work on *Cujo* is nothing short of combat pay.

This was a "dog days of summer" (as my boss liked to call them) release, thrown out at the end to get past the big blockbusters. Studios either do this because the film is bad and they have low expectations and try for a "hit and run" or they want to give the film a chance. *Cujo* was the latter and surprised many by its quality and great direction. *Cujo* took full advantage of a light late summer line up.

The woman who transformed into a werewolf at the end of *The Howling* became "America's Mom" after *E.T. The Extraterrestrial*. She followed up her wholesome, family friendly role in the biggest film of all time with a cheating, flawed woman who puts her son and herself in mortal danger as a culmination of bad choices. Dee Wallace took risks with her career and her turn in this film gave the entire adaptation legitimacy.

The theater was packed—surprising my manager boss who didn't miss a moment to call the film "a dog." His cynicism was profound for a man that loved movies and ran a theater. The business side jaded him. He was a miserable bastard but sardonic and funny. He called the theater chain *Mucus Makers*. He seemed to delight in that every time he said it.

He was wrong. He didn't want to admit it. The film was fantastic and it was making money, going from a smaller theater to the largest.

People chattered approval on the way out as another long line waited for the next matinee show. I saw a school friend who saw it the show before me. She gave it a thumbs down and when I asked why, saying how much I enjoyed it, she said "they changed the ending."

That's a reason why I liked it so much. King's book ending was downbeat, nihilistic and a middle finger to the reader. There was no redemption. Years later I would read that he felt the film's ending was a complete improvement upon his as he barely remembered writing *Cujo* from the alcohol and drug-fueled hazed that consumed him at that time.

Directing Dee Wallace onset of *Death House*.

Years later I would direct Dee Wallace in my *Zombie Killers* as well as *Death House* as I wrote both parts for her. That's how much I wanted to work with this legend. I am proud to say that she's become my adopted second mom. *Cujo* is a shining moment for her.

I would watch her stoned out of my mind around 1986 in Los Angeles with *Critters*, blasting those little fuckers off the front porch with her shotgun and loving every minute of it. Seeing *Critters* in the theater with a packed house (I'll bet a lot were in the same as me and my friend) was a hoot. When two Critters discuss humans having weapons and the one says "So what" all in subtitles, Dee's gun barrel pops out the front door and unloads. BANG!

The one Critter is blown away, leaving only his feet and smoke next to his pal. The creature screams and the subtitles say: Fuck!"

 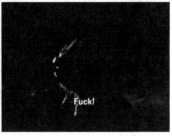

We lost it. The audience lost it and applauded and cheered. Holy shit that film was fun to watch in the theater. One of the best "I was so stoned" theatrical experiences for me.

Let's catch up on a little history as we move toward the mid-80s. Here are some highlights between 1982-1983.

The "Reagan Revolution" was yet to knock back inflation. Unemployment was coming down but prices remained high. The poverty level was its highest since 1967. While he championed to cut taxes, a 98 billion tax hike was passed through Congress August 1982.

Reagan told a group at a speaking engagement he always wanted to make a funny gesture to the media and famously claps back at the media, endearing him to the American public. In school we loved this moment and talked about it. Reagan was giving it back to the system.

The *Tylenol* killer was on the loose, killing seven people through product tampering. *Tylenol* reacted fast, and pulled its product, giving rise to "tamper proof" packaging that we have today.

Disney's EPCOT opened even as the recession continued through 1982.

John Landis ordered the descent of a helicopter while shooting a scene for his episode of *Twilight Zone: The Movie*. The chopper's blades were disabled by the blast of pyrotechnics and special effects, causing the machine to fall on top of actor Vic Morrow (Jennifer Jason Leigh's father) and two illegally employed Vietnamese children, slicing them to shreds and decapitating Morrow.

AIDS continued to move through the nation and its blood supply, readying for its big reveal. Little attention was paid as it appeared to affect only the homosexual and drug addict communities. Televangelist Rev. Jerry Falwell calls the disease a "gay plague" and God's way of "spanking us."

Cable TV continued its growth. The top shows on TV are "Diff'rent Strokes" with Gary Coleman as its breakout star. *Dallas* and *Dynasty* celebrate wealth, power and greed, with "Dallas" at the top of the ratings with its "Who Shot JR?" episode, leaving America on edge for the next season to find out whodunit.

John DeLorean, the now famous car maker, was arrested in Los Angeles as part of an FBI sting operation for buying cocaine from undercover agents.

Michael Jackson captivated the country and world "Moonwalking" backwards as he performed *Billie Jean* at the *Motown 25th Anniversary*. It becomes a phenomenon.

Reagan continued his very public rebuilding of the US military. The armed forces revamp their recruiting commercials to slick, *MTV*-style spots to entice new recruits. The United States steps up its incursions into Central America. By 1983 Reagan declared the Soviet Union an "Evil Empire" and the nation rejoiced. Reagan was giving it to the Russians. The flipside was the Soviets shot down a Korean passenger jet for straying off course into Russian airspace, killing all 269 on board.

Our education system was revealed to be far behind the rest of the world when the *A Nation at Risk* report was released.

The United States invaded the island of Grenada to overturn a seizure of power. It is hailed as a military victory, furthering our excitement that "America is back" even as a truck bombing at a Marine compound in Beirut, Lebanon killed more than 200 sleeping Marines.

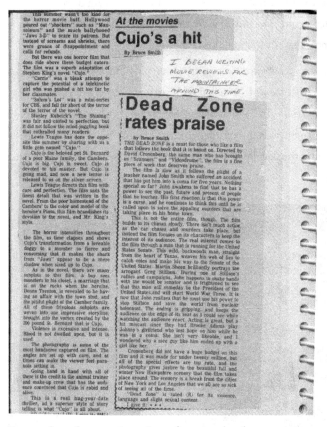

Some of my first movie reviews for our school newspaper as
"Pop Culture Editor."

I was writing movie reviews for our high school paper, *The Mountaineer*, and moved up to its "Pop Culture Editor."

I was president of my class and tasked with raising almost $9000 for our coming senior prom. This is a whole other book, but I knew we had to do more than just sell candy and do car washes. By the middle of my junior year I had joined forces with the school's popular crowd to throw giant keg parties, charge at the door and found a way to launder the money through school activity groups and back into our class account.

I now worked at *Music Makers* August, 1983. Toni died October 8th. I sunk into a depression, jeopardizing my class presidency with rumors of impeachment and removal of office. I had given up.

Horror was always on my mind. Stephen King's new *Pet Sematary* novel resonated with me as I struggled with such intense grief. That was the same fall we got *Amityville 3-D* and as cheesy and awful that movie was, there were a few things on the personal level that connected with me. I have to step back a year to 1982 and the equally bad *Amityville II: The Possession*, a "prequel" to the 1979 film.

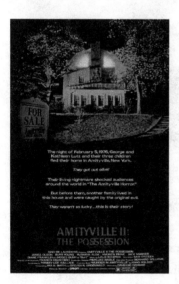

The only *fact* about any of the *Amityville Horror* films is that the DeFeo family was murdered in their sleep inside the house on 112 Ocean Avenue. The real horror is what the surviving relatives of the murdered DeFeo's must endure every time one of these lousy films is made.

I caught this one on cable, with no intention to get screwed out of another ticket price. The film focuses on the events before The Lutz family endured their alleged 28 days of terror. The filmmakers changed the last name from DeFeo to Montelli. The success of the book and the 1979 film publicized the DeFeo name. Why they bothered to change the name for this film is beyond me. The damage was done.

The film goes on to rip off *The Exorcist*. You have a haunted house movie. You have ghosts. Is there any justifiable reason to have incest between the brother and sister? Aside from the fact that you have a poorly made film (*Rocky's* Burt Young headlines) what purpose does incest serve?

I don't think it was to titillate, but rather to compensate for the lack of genuine horror and scares in the film. While real horror comes from dark places, real horror is identifiable. When we can relate to it, we connect. When we connect, we react. The incest subplot becomes a major plot point by the end of the film. It is the equivalent to the "hypodermic scene" where a needle injection is inserted in gratuitous close up to elicit a response from the viewer because the script is lacking the ability to do it.

With Ladies of the Eighties, Amanda Wyss (A Nightmare on Elm Street) and Diane Franklin (Amityville II) at the premiere of my action-comedy *Garlic and Gunpowder.*

It's shameful that cynicism fueled the exploitation of the family that had to not only deal with the murders, but also have people thinking incest was committed in that house. Just changing the names doesn't help and the filmmakers knew it. The filmmakers allegedly had "professionals and experts" (The Warren's of future *The Conjuring* fame were said to be "advisors") on the real murders and Lutz story consult with the writer. All knew incest was never a factor and never substantiated. Didn't anyone speak up and object to this being not just in bad taste but defamation? I guess not. The filmmakers should've known better, and they did.

The true star of *Amityville II* was Diane Franklin, who went on to break a lot of hearts in *The Last American Virgin*. Diane's role was so powerful, the ending to *Virgin* made me distrust her as much as Nurse Ratched would do for Louise Fletcher. Even when she appeared in *Better Off Dead* as the spritely optimistic and sweet as all-get-out French foreign exchange student, Monique—I still expected her to break John Cusack's heart.

One of the last films of the short-lived 3-D revival was in Theater Four, the same house where I saw *Jaws 3-D*. Toni was dead that fall. I walked around like a zombie. One slow, weekday evening, I walked into a house with a dozen people sitting in their glasses and stood in the back at the doors and watched *Amityville 3-D*. The patrons who came had little to no reaction during or after.

There was never time to watch a movie straight through. There were floors to sweep, trash to take, butter pumps to clean and another theater to patrol. I had a manager named Cathy who hunted you down if you disappeared for too long.

Here's the thing…I LIKED *Amityville 3-D*. It was awful, but in some weird way, it had the feel and tone of a good haunted house movie. There were moments. I still stand by the fun factor.

I am going to say this might be the "best" one in the series because it's so bad it's brilliant in a William Castle kind of way. It might be the only film that captures the atmosphere the original book tried to present. While the house blows up at the end, no one goes running around with an axe. There are some moments when it works. They are brief and they are quiet.

Meg Ryan debuted in this film. Woody Allen favorite Tony Roberts and pre-"Lonesome Dove" Tess Roberts headlined. The always cute and "I wish she got undressed" Lori Loughlin was the doomed victim inside this full house. Horror stalwart Candy Clark makes the whole thing worthwhile, because she takes it all so serious. Clark, as I have gushed, is a wonderful actress who classed up Stephen King's *Cat's Eye* just before this and had too short of a presence in 1988's *The Blob* remake. She remains on my "Ten Most Wanted" actors to work with.

The cheesy Dino DeLaurentiis poster featured a disclaimer for this 3-D mess. It made it clear this had nothing to do with the previous two films. Not quite…Meg Ryan's character leads us on a tour of the DeFeo murders and names the family by name. Again, here was a third installment to a money making franchise and, again, no one could be bothered to put in the effort. The special effects are laughable. I invoked William Castle because of its *13 Ghosts* feel. The 3-D aspect was a low rent 80s gimmick and the film itself is a mess from script to screen. From murky picture quality to editing…zero fucks given on the making of this third installment and to the DeFeo family.

The cast seemed game, though. They were really trying and the script throws a few bones to them. It opens by taking a swipe at famed ghost hunters Ed and Lorraine Warren and Robert Joy's character gives a nod toward Stephen Kaplan, a paranormal scientist who claimed to be the first to debunk the *Amityville Horror* and called out The Lutz's as hoaxsters.

The opening of the film could have set the tone for the rest of the movie. Tony Roberts and Candy Clark are investigative journalists looking to expose a husband and wife team who con people in their grief. Clark is game for the movie and we like her from the first scene. We identify with Candy, we enjoy her

character and I want to know more about her.

The opening effects were bad, then the lights go on in the house and we see they were SUPPOSED to be bad. They were used to fool Clark and Roberts pretending to be grieving parents. Unfortunately when we do see the actual film effects at the end they look just like the amateurish ones used by the fraud psychics that opened the film.

Roberts has a great talk with the realtor looking to unload the famous house. The actor does a sincere job expressing fear and frustration as he tells the history of the home succinctly with good dialogue. By the end of the conversation he convinces Roberts to take the house off his hands. It's just a good quiet scene with the house looking over it. Lori Loughlin's death is well done even though it oddly takes place off camera. We really feel it when Roberts discovers his daughter lying dead in the back yard. Tess Harper's experience inside the house at the same time is a quiet and creepy moment. It totally works and the lighting works with it to create an atmosphere that conveys true dread.

This is where the film made it personal. For some reason I equated Loughlin's character with Toni. They were both brunettes with a natural beauty look to them. They were the same age. They both died. The grief expressed by both Tess Harper and Tony Roberts had more of a 3-D effect on me than the visuals. That's what came off the screen to that 16-year-old boy watching *Amityville 3-D* in the back of the theater. It was grief. I got what Tess Harper's character was saying— part of me refused to believe Toni was gone as well. Maybe she could return, too. Just like *Pet Sematary* showed in King's book. The drowning scene of Loughlin's character and her appearances in the house, walking all wet and cold back up to her room in the overcast daylight made me react in a way that the other films did not. Grief made me connect with this silly 3-D movie.

Candy Clark needed more to do and, consequently, the film should've been about her. She had two good moments. One was her introduction to the house as she investigates a blown fuse. It was a quiet moment, and because we liked her character, we were engaged in her exploration.

Clark's other moment came when she examines her photos of the house. Her magnifying glass reveals a startling little image and a brief...moment. Then it's gone. Her subsequent death is nothing short of horrifying and marred by the substandard 3-D. We liked her and the way she perished in that car fire was upsetting and unnerving. Her performance was that strong because you could tell Candy took it seriously and because she did, we took her seriously and we liked her. She played a great "every person"— so much that her burned alive death scene disturbed in the theater and does on home video viewings.

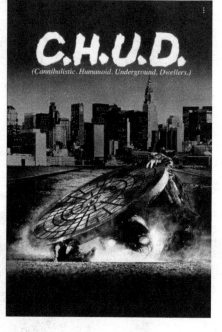

I went way too long on this movie. The score is haunting and fun, at times subtle and then right over the top. All they needed to do was throw a Theremin into the mix. With all of its cheese and bad effects—this is the only film out of the entire *Amityville* franchise that connected with me on a personal level. It's my "favorite" of them all.

Walking the theaters allowed me to catch other horrors on the "installment plan." You caught some of the beginning, some of the middle and some of the end during the time of the film's theatrical run. One of these was *C.H.U.D.* It was a brief run but I caught it all. This was one I didn't get to watch from beginning to end until it hit home video. Few people came and for some reason it was in our largest house. I guess Mr. H thought it was going to do some business opening weekend. It didn't but it was a hell of a lot of fun.

The Evil Dead returned for some kind of re-release for a limited engagement and since The Sherman was all but dead, *Mucus Makers* got it. It played only a week or two but I remember people walking out repulsed by it. One woman stormed out of the theater demanding her money back for the "pencil through the ankle" scene. She was disgusted and she made sure to let everyone in the lobby know it. The only other time I heard someone announce their disgust for a movie was a woman complaining about the concert film, *Richard Pryor: Here and Now.*

I wrote earlier about the protest crowds for *Silent Night, Deadly Night.* They gathered outside the smaller theaters down by the *JC Penney* side of the mall. They carried signs and wore sandwich board-type placards over their shoulders and walked in front of the gate. When we opened for business they were forced to stand at least ten feet back from the box office to allow allow paying customers through.

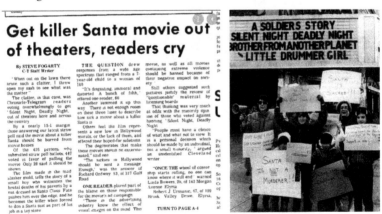

Security patrolled or stood by. People who got their tickets were heckled or harassed. The local paper and TV came to the mall to cover this "event." I thought the whole thing was stupid. All these protestors were doing was drumming up more interest for the film. If they'd just left things alone the movie

305

would have come and gone in a week or two. Instead, business ticked up enough for it to stay a good four weeks.

When the movie left, they did as well, no doubt to get back to their book burning club.

Some weekend nights the crew would have movie parties. They selected a film, and Mr. H allowed one of the projectors to get threaded up with the film of choice.

We did "food runs" for these, often a trip to *Mister Donut* across the street. The night we chose John Carpenter's adaptation of *Christine* was also my turn for the "food run." I saved one of the lists. Everybody threw their money at you and then you got the honor of driving over, waiting and then coming back with bags of shit and hope no one fucked it up because it would be YOUR fault. Mr. H always got his *Sanka*.

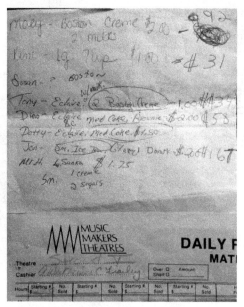

Christine opened at our smaller theater side by *JC Penney* and never moved up. I remember there was little turnout, likely from the stigma of a killer car. Even when I read the book, cheesy vehicle movies like *The Car* and *The Hearse* came to mind. The only good killer vehicle movie I saw was Steven Spielberg's

TV movie *Duel*, which got him the *Jaws* job. That didn't really count because the truck in that film was controlled by the unseen driver.

King's book was good because he knew that the human characters are the real framework, not just a monster automobile that can regenerate. The book also made it clear that most of the time the spirit of Christine's previous owner was driving her. Arnie Cunningham was possessed by the previous owner but King made it clear Christine was also autonomous and sentient.

About 12 of us sat in the theater. We popped a giant 50-gallon bag of popcorn and left it in the middle of the aisle. We would get up, fill containers and sit back down. We had unlimited popcorn and soda and the entire theater to ourselves. The show usually got started about an hour after the

Me with Keith Gordon in Los Angeles

last movie let out, Mr. H left and the gates dropped.

Being invited to these after-hours employee screenings was a sign my social stock had risen. I tried to hide my emotional slump at work—knowing if I showed any kind of slacking Mr. H would be quick to shit can my ass.

Christine was slick and beautifully shot. Some called it a work for hire by Carpenter. I thought Keith Gordon (best known to me as "Doug" from *Jaws 2*) was an odd choice as I pictured more of a pimply, fat kid rather than Gordon's intense, serial killer meets Robert Carradine's nerd look. Gordon made it work and the cast across the board was stellar.

Harry Dean Stanton was underused. I asked a female co-worker if she felt like there was a lot cut from the film. She didn't read the book. She shrugged, drank a beer and watched.

I was entranced with Alexandra Paul's Leigh Cabot. I totally got what Dean Stockwell's pal meant by wishing he was the eraser of the pencil she chewed. Leigh Cabot was my type, my image and a new onscreen horror crush.

The smell of pot smoke wafted up from in front. In about five minutes a joint made it to me. It wasn't my first pot experience but it was the first time I got stoned in a movie theater in public.

I ate a lot of popcorn. A lot.

It wasn't public. It was just us—the *Mucus Makers* crew. The boss was gone. The place was ours. I took several good drags and soon the need for salty, buttered (it was real butter not that flavored oil that was to come) hit me. I gorged myself.

We had fun, especially for a first time employee experience. I missed out on the *Night of the Comet* screenings. I heard they were a blast. We had the whole theater just to ourselves. I needed it. It helped with the depression and funk that hung over me.

I did want more and after the pot, I really got to thinking about the differences between the book and film. A lot of back story was left out, and I understood why, but wondered if there would ever be another version of the film one day. I am still asking if deleted footage exists and if a restored cut will ever surface.

> For my 15th birthday my dad, who was a Matr'd at Shawnee Inn and never around; decided we needed a father-daughter movie night. He let me pick the movie. Being he was the one that got me hooked on Jason I thought he'd like "MY BLOODY VALENTINE." We got to the theater and did the snack attack ritual: popcorn, soda and snow caps. The movie began; dad was talking to me trying to catch up on my life and such ....within 10 minutes his happy go lucky demeanor has changed. He actually looked pale and started breathing a little heavy. I was getting worried and asked him if he was okay. He said yes, covered his mouth and told me "Stay here be right back." I sat through the rest of the movie alone. Where was my sweet ,hard working father? In the bathroom puking. My father had a blood phobia and NEVER told anyone. He damn near passed out in the theater. We laughed about this for years.
>
> **Patti Granahan Kirk**

I found out that Temple University was showing a screening of the original 1973 *The Exorcist* on campus. While I did see the film on home video (and its awful sequel *Exorcist II: The Heretic*), uncut, there were no real memorable moments. Whatever way I got the information the film was playing on a big screen (this was not an official studio re-release) I knew I wanted to see it with a flesh and blood movie audience.

My best friend packed three others and me into his car and we set out for Philadelphia. No GPS. No *Waze*—just us with a gas station map figuring it out as we went along. I never drove to Philly before.

I would see *Fright Night* a few years later with a college crowd just like *The Exorcist*. The film was open to the public and students. It was not a 35mm print but none of us cared. We got our tickets and went into some arts building to see the show.

Keep in mind, I read the stories of the original 1973 release. It almost got an "X" rating. People fainted. One woman claimed she miscarried and tried to sue Warner Brothers. Others puked. People screamed and some fled the theaters. How much of it was true, who knew?

I relayed all of this horror history to my friends on the road trip down.

This is probably bad memory, but I believe we might have been five of maybe twenty white people in the whole place. What I do know is it was the first time any of us were really outside our suburban element and introduced to an urban vibe.

I sat in the middle of a row, next to a large African-American man who looked like an out of shape boxer. He gave me a nod as I plopped down next to him. He was with a woman I assumed was his wife.

The lights went down. There were no previews. The movie started.

No matter how I write this. No matter how careful I am to not sound racist or offensive, the best way to describe this is to just say it. I learned that night that watching a horror movie with a largely non-white audience is an experience all in its own.

Unlike white people, I discovered that black people talk back to the screen. They can talk loud or sometimes they just outright yell. They try to warn the characters, offering advice to not go into dark rooms or to watch out behind them.

I wouldn't see and DO *The Rocky Horror Picture Show* until the late 80s, but this might've been the closest I got to *Rocky Horror*. When Ellen Burstyn is moving through the old attic looking for "mice" after hearing noise up there, people all around me were yelling to get the hell out. The man next to me kept shaking his head, muttering "uh, uh, uh…" A denial that he would ever do something like that. I could hear him and he was as scared as I was.

I knew what was coming. I bet a lot of people in that theater with me did too because of cable and home video watches. It didn't matter. This was like *Jaws* all over again. All of these strangers, white, black, brown…who fucking cared? We were all PEOPLE in that auditorium—scared people all united by the images coming from that screen.

When Dick Smith's special effects gave us Linda Blair projectile vomiting in Jason Miller's face the guy to my left screamed: 'GODDAMN!" His huge frame shot up out of that seat and he fucking ran down that aisle. No, he BULLDOZED his way down that aisle. "I'm fucking done!" he yelled to the woman seated behind him. He never came back.

That guy did the same thing I tried in *Alien* back in 1979, only he had no one to grab him by the back of his pants and force his ass down into the seat like my mother did. No one was going to stop that guy's stampede out of that movie.

We made it through. I was glad we did it. The way home was discussion on evil, if the supernatural really existed and *The Rain Boy*. That's right, Stroudsburg had its own demonic national headlines. It wasn't on the level of *The Exorcist*, but just *Google* "Stroudsburg Rain Boy Don Decker" and see what comes up. We even got an episode of *Unsolved Mysteries* out of it.

That's what a theatrical screening can do. Seeing *The Exorcist* in that auditorium gave me something far more entertaining and culturally educational than when I watched it on VHS with Michael on his living room TV.

I opened a cardboard poster tube and pulled out the latest sheet. The caption read: "Friday, April 13th Is Jason's Unlucky Day."

The fourth installment to *Friday the 13th* was on its way. It carried the subtitle: "The Final Chapter." I thought for sure the 3-D excursion was the last one, but wadda ya know? They were squeezing out one more.

The Final Chapter promised payback to Jason Voorhees. It didn't get me revved up, but my friends in school were getting pumped.

I shook off my depression and managed my grief better, averting impeachment charges and turned things around. Our class was making money, I was popular with some great friends and…I was the kid who worked at the movies. That meant the power of free access. I told a number of my friends clamoring to see this final *Friday* to just find me. I would hook them up.

We had two roped-off exits that served as under the radar entries. My friends would pop over to the side; I would unhook the thick red rope and let them pass. Opening night of *Friday the 13th The Final Chapter* had about thirty freebies in that first show audience.

This was the first *Friday the 13th* where I had a true theatrical experience. There was a vibe that Friday the 13th night. Jason was going to die and people wanted it. This was the film that brought Corey Feldman to my attention as Tommy Jarvis, the only character to truly kill Jason. One day I would make *6 Degrees of Hell* with him.

I could see my friends…the dumbasses waved to me as I patrolled the theater. I caught bits and pieces of the film and knew I would get to see the whole thing eventually. This one would have an afterhours screening for sure.

There was no way I could miss the ending. I didn't care. It wasn't like I was missing some heavy plot or mysterious ending. I stood in the back, and let me tell you, that audience fucking screamed. From the moment Jason smashes through that front door and the big finale started, the audience was going nuts in its seats. Some stood and cheered, you could see girls thrusting their heads into the arms of their boyfriends unable to watch the bloody carnage. Corey Feldman came down the steps with his shaved head, clutching that machete. There were gasps of shock, laughter and then, WHACK! Feldman split Jason's hand with that machete! The entire theater was SCREAMING! Tom Savini was back and it showed. His effects were bringing down the house.

It didn't stop there. Feldman took another swing, planting the machete into Jason's head, and the mask came off revealing the adult mama's boy for everyone to behold. More screams as the camera held on the dazed, enlarged cranium of the Voorhees kid. Jason took another hit, and then fell on the embedded machete that pushed up through his eye and out the back of his skull.

That did it—the audience was out of control. The screams were so loud the audience waiting outside in the lobby heard them. I stood in the back BEHOLDING this. Holy shit, I wanted to do this to an audience one day. This wasn't a movie, it was an amusement park ride.

Several girls pushed past me, fleeing for the doors behind me. They threw them open and screamed, running into the lobby. The people waiting for the next show had to be thrilled. They were gonna get their money's worth. The film delivered on its promise to be the big ending. Tom Savini brought it all home.

A few of my friends found me afterwards. Several hugged me, thanking me for a great movie and time. Like I had anything to do with it. I just let their asses in for free. People on the way out declared they would be back to see it again. That movie cranked right to summer.

That's why the franchise went on. To Paramount's surprise the "final chapter" made huge money, showing the blood had not run out of the body just yet. There was still more life in it.

Decades later I got to tell Tom Savini this whole opening night to his face as I sat in his home and studio. It's not often you get a chance to meet the makers of your memories.

My folks couldn't afford to take me to see "Jason Lives" at the theater, so they bought me the novelization. I read that book until I had to tape the cover back on. I was in 6th grade and would hide the book and read it at my desk. My grades dropped, three D's on one grade card. She still says I'm the only person that she knows who could read so much and still get failing grades. My father would take me to see every horror movie on opening night. He said that he hated those blood & gut movies. However taking me made it an experience and an event. I remember him taking me to the Drive-In to see "Fright Night" and he would excuse himself to the concession stand--only to sneak up on the other side of the car and scare the hell out of me!

Horror Orman

With Tom Savini at his home.

I have a confession. I didn't see much of *Firestarter* when it was in our theater. That doesn't mean it wasn't a great theatrical experience or memory. Let me explain.

Dating took on a whole new life once I got the job at the theater. I had a base of operations you could say. A free movie was always the fallback and there's just something so cool about being 16 and getting into the movies for free.

I liked a college girl that worked with me. As my star rose in high school, I got bolder; asking out this beautiful blonde-haired, blue-eyed student teacher in our health class. She attended East Stroundsburg University, a major education school. I was attending college frat parties by the end of eleventh grade. I stayed after class one morning and asked if she might be interested in dinner and a movie, a FREE movie. I was so out of my depth, what a lame thing to say. She politely declined.

Since she let me down gently, I thought I had some mojo, and turned my attention to a college girl that worked with us. Stacey was tall, with a Sigourney Weaver kind of thing going on. She really wasn't my type, but she had a great sense of humor, a calming voice and was laid back, really laid back. I asked her out. A number of people, including Cathy, my assistant manager, knew I had a

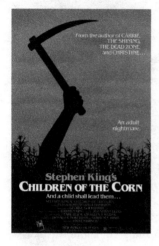

thing for Stacey, so she wasn't too surprised when I finally worked up the moxie to ask. To my surprise, she said yes. I just got my first college girl date. Spring and love were in the air.

What to do? I offered dinner in the mall's only Italian and somewhat classy restaurant, *The Italian Delite*. It was this corner store, all dark, lit with candles in its attempt to recreate the atmosphere of some New York bistro. Stephen King had yet another movie coming, *Children of the Corn*. I read the short story in his *Night Shift* collection and wanted to see it just to find out how they took a nine page story and turned it into a full-length movie.

Stacey was game. That sounded just fine. I know…you're thinking how unimaginative—a date to the place we worked. She didn't seem to mind and our assistant manager and Stacey's good friend, Cathy, encouraged it. I found that a bit odd because I didn't think Cathy liked me all that much or really anyone for that matter. Cathy had a few pets, all girls and anyone else outside the circle seemed tolerated. I didn't think much of it either way. I did my job and tried not to piss off Cathy. Simple.

When Mr. H heard I was taking Stacey out, he gave a sarcastic smile and patted me on the back. "Good luck, Brucie," he said with an amused chuckle. I didn't know what that meant and I didn't ask. We had dinner. I remember it being a good time. She liked my vocal impressions of celebrities, especially my Ronald Reagan. She laughed, asking me to say things in the President's voice. Any time I did Reagan, I always started the sentence with "Well…"

We headed down to the smaller theaters by *JC Penney*. There seemed to be a welcoming committee led by Cathy at the box office. Cathy shared the box office with one of her groupies. The girl behind the candy counter was from Cathy's inner circle. She waited on us and I swear I saw her trading looks with Stacey and the two of them traded small smiles. I was being paranoid, but in a horror movie, this is the first sign of trouble for the protagonist. Three sets of eyes were on us. We went into Theater Four for *Children of the Corn*. It had a decent crowd for opening week.

This was pre-*Terminator* Linda Hamilton. About ten minutes in I knew it was going to be a long 80 more. The film had that low grade 70s feel and while I read somewhere that the filmmakers wanted it to be a commentary on the Islamic Revolution in Iran four years earlier, it fell way short of that mark. Creepy kids, blood and some bad practical effects with something behind the corn rows that when revealed was a flat moment.

I held Stacey's hand and she held it back. Our fingers kind of traced each other and toward the end I moved to kiss her and she accepted but there just weren't any fireworks. It seemed like she expected the kiss and returned out of... well...courtesy. I knew before the movie was over there would be no second date. The goal was to make sure none of this got weird or as they say nowadays, "awkward."

We left the theater but the second show was so busy we didn't see any of the women that greeted us on the way in. We walked out into the mall and said goodnight. I offered to walk her to her car but she said she had some things to buy and would see me at work later that week.

I walked through the mall up to what we called "The Big End" where the theater's biggest houses could be found. Mr. H was at his usual perch, right behind the box office watching what he called "the wave of human debris" float by out in the mall.

He saw me and waved me over. He was smiling, cigarette in the corner of his mouth.

"Well?"

I told him it went just fine. She was a lot of fun. The movie wasn't so hot, but I had a really nice time and hoped Stacey did too.

"The movie sucks. That's why I put it down there. It will be gone in another week." He knew his shit when it came to booking films to houses. One year later he would make a major booking mistake with *Fright* Night, but more on that in a bit.

"You know now that she's a lesbian, right?" He waited for my reaction with a kind of hunger. He fed off this kind of drama.

No. I didn't. If she was a lesbian, why would she go out with me? Plus, I kissed her and she kissed me back. It didn't add up, but Mr. H was happy to do the math.

"Cathy has the college crew down there." He was referring to the small theaters or "The Little End" down by *Penney's*. "They're all dykes, Brucie. You've been working here long enough to finally know the truth."

He went on to say he didn't have a problem with it, but he didn't want to see me being so naïve. They were all using me to keep up the appearance of being straight.

In his mind, he was doing me a favor? Being a father figure, maybe?

If Cathy wanted these things kept secret, he didn't help her cause. I took it all in and left. I felt stupid and used, just like he wanted me to feel. What the hell do you say to that? To this day it's the worst aftermath to a date aside from the time I ended up packing a girl's front teeth into ice after she fell and face planted into a cement floor when living in Los Angeles. That wouldn't happen for almost three years at that time.

Bet you weren't expecting that ending to a *Children of the Corn* memory. I was a beard.

My junior year was coming to a close and by May things were humming along nicely. Our school had a whole day event known as "Maroon and White Day," which was field day—high school Olympics if you will. The junior class was assigned one of the concession stands. We got the honors of making hot dogs and we shared the large stand with the sophomores.

One sophomore stood out. She had long, blonde hair which was feathered and layered so well, it was a work of art. Think Kelli Maroney meets...Alexandra Paul from *Christine*.

Night of the Comet counted as a horror film. A comet turns people into killer zombies but instead of a band of rag tag fighters, you had two hot girls, Kelli Maroney and Catherine Mary Stewart as quasi-Valley Girls charged with saving what's left of the world. I caught the film with a sold out house one evening, just myself, and found myself thinking it would not be a bad thing to be one of the last people on earth stranded with Kelli Maroney or Stewart.

The audience was in a good mood, as this was horror light. Some fun moments with a stylistic look that transformed Los Angeles into an *MTV* video set. This film took me back to the fun days of Doc Shock. It would have been a perfect Saturday afternoon creature feature.

Night of the Comet became a cult late-night, after hours hit with our theater staff. It's how I first learned of employee screenings after the place closed. Mr. H allowed them every now and then. *Night of the Comet* was that midnight movie. The staff drank, smoked pot and enjoyed a movie all to themselves. This one was a repeat late night showing. *Comet* was a multiple after hours hit.

Back to the Kelli Maroney blonde working the concession stand. She had this lilting, sweet voice and when she laughed, it was a sexy whisper. She wore a grey, school hoodie and tight designer jeans. I was struck and knew I had to get this girl's number.

I made all the requisite hot dog/wiener jokes that I could muster (see what I did there?) and worked my charm. The key was getting them to laugh. I was a charmer. She said her name was Regan (pronounced like the President) and I knew it had to be fate. I did my Reagan impression and asked if she was named after the girl in *The Exorcist.*

"No," she replied with a smile. She looked at my safari jacket. "Are you supposed to be Indiana Jones?" She gave me her number. Memorial Day weekend was coming up. After the weekend (I had to work it as the summer blockbuster movies were starting their onslaught. *Indiana Jones and the Temple of Doom* was opening in our two houses by *JC Penney* because you could thread the film on one side of the theater and it would run all the way to the other across the booth. It was called "Interlocking" It was the summer of '84. Look it up) would she like to see *Firestarter* with me? She said she would. Date secured. Her phone number was on a slip of paper in my pocket. We went to the movie that following weekend. I picked her up at her house, met the parents and we headed off to the mall. No dinner, we went straight for the movie.

Mr. H was at his spot behind the box office. "Your name is Regan? Well… that's a name." He was dry, dragged on his cigarette and made sure to bust my balls although he was taken with how cute Regan was. "She's a lot better than your last one," he smirked. He was poking the Stacey wound. "I think you'll have better luck."

I got the popcorn and soda and in we went. Regan did not ask me what Mr. H meant about "the last date."

We got to about the first half hour. We managed the back row to ourselves, sitting among fifty people or so. It was hard to buy George C. Scott as Native American and odd to see Art Carney and Louise Fletcher together. I explained to Regan that I never trusted Louise Fletcher after *One Flew Over the Cuckoo's Nest.* Her Nurse Ratched was one of the most evil villains ever put on screen. She was too good in that role. I went further. I believed *Cuckoo's Nest* was a social horror film. She was fascinated. I thought for sure Fletcher showing up at that farmhouse spelled doom for Drew Barrymore and David Keith.

That was about it. Regan made the first move, kissing me. It was like she was eating my face. I went right with it and while Drew fucked shit up and burned shit down, I got to second base. When the lights came up we both had wild sex hair. I exhaled as she buttoned her shirt, "That was interesting!"

I would have to fill in the movie plot blanks after that first half hour with walks through the theater and standing at the back doors when I was working. I saw *Firestarter* on the installment plan.

Google "Summer Movies of 1984." See what you get.

I was tempted to classify *Indiana Jones and the Temple of Doom* as a horror film. The prequel took a lot of people by surprise with its nasty, dark edge. These days social media gets all lit up with people trying to re-classify films like *Die Hard* from action to Christmas, *The Nightmare Before Christmas* as Christmas instead of Halloween and so forth.

I said earlier that *One Flew Over the Cuckoo's Nest* is a social horror film akin to *Invasion of the Body Snatchers* 1979. Louise Fletcher's Nurse Ratched is just short of some cold alien bent on the assimilation of her victims. The patients in her hospital, on her floor are victims of horrible experiments that culminate in the terrifying electroshock

321

treatment of Nicholson at the end. I am told the ending was uplifting, but in reality, Ratched won. Nurse Ratched is a sociopathic monster. The death of Billy Bibbit is horrifying and Ratched draws cool satisfaction from her complicity in his death by his own hand. The film shows the real monsters are us, and they often hide behind a guise of complete normalcy. While a drama and dark comedy, for me, *One Flew Over the Cuckoo's Nest* will remain by my estimation… a horror movie.

I tried explaining this to Regan that night in *Firestarter* before she proceeded to eat my face.

Corey Feldman and me onset of my *6 Degrees of Hell.*

We will keep *Temple of Doom* in its action/adventure category. *Gremlins,* however, was another story. The poster arrived with little fanfare and went into the display stand at the front of "The Big End" facing out to the mall walkers (The Living Dead as Mr. H called them. He saw *Dawn of the Dead*). I studied it and something cute and fuzzy seemed to be coming out of that box. The jeans button had *ET* on it for Spielberg's *Amblin* production company. Spielberg's name was all over it. It looked like a fun, crazy family film.

Joe Dante directed. I knew his name from *Piranha*. Dante made Spielberg's favorite *Jaws* rip-off and rewarded him with *Gremlins*. Die hard *Jaws* fans know Spielberg led a legal crusade in the 80s to shut down as many *Jaws* rip-offs that he could. The most known casualty was the Italian shark clone, *Great White* which was later re-titled *The Last Shark*. The poster caught my attention. It might've played U.S. screens for a week before Spielberg banished it. I saw it years later on home video somewhere and Spielberg was right to slap it down. It was a blatant copyright infringement and the filmmakers thought they could just get away with it if it wasn't for that meddling kid.

The *Gremlins* preview was on our screens by April; right around the time Jason was getting his in *The Final Chapter*. The trailer went out of its way to present an *It's a Wonderful Life* setup. Christmas. Wholesome kids, Phoebe Cates in  lots of heavy winter wear and not her infamous red bikini from *Fast Times at Ridgemont High*. There was something cute and fuzzy and then later the trailer shows what happens if they eat after midnight. You never saw the final stage Gremlins, but you heard lots of devilish laughter and that Jerry Goldsmith "Gremlin Rag" that was comical and a throwback to the slapstick comedies of the 1930s. The trailer made it very clear that while there could be some dark comedy moments—this was a family summer film.

The film opened on June 8th, 1984, the same day as the original *Ghostbusters* (another film The Internet has tried to rebrand. It's not a horror film. It's a comedy). I planned to see it with Regan after opening weekend. The gates went up at six and the lines for the movie were down the hall and all the way back to one of the anchor stores up at "The Big End." It was *E.T.* business.

The first sign of trouble dropped about 45 minutes in. Several mothers pushed through the double doors with crying children, their eyes were on fire. They wanted a manager. They wanted blood. I told them I would get the manager and two more moms along with dads came out.

This went on for the remainder of the first show and all throughout that opening week. "Have you seen it, yes?" one mother demanded of me. I told her I had not. "It's not a kid's movie! It's a horror movie!"

What the hell could be so bad? The few clips in the beginning looked harmless. Gizmo was this furry little thing that would sell a shitload of toys that Christmas. Hell, even I wanted a Gizmo. I knew I had to see it right away, and this time I would wait to watch it all from beginning to end.

I set expectations with Regan. We were WATCHING this movie. We could make out later. This wasn't going to be a repeat of *Firestarter*. We did pretty well in *Indiana Jones and the Temple of Doom* earlier that week even with it being an evening show. That's because the place was so crowded we were in the middle of the theater and not a dark back row.

Gremlins was packed for the matinee show. We got our seats and it started. As I saw on opening night, there was nothing to complain about 30 minutes

in. Then…those green fuckers hatched out of their cocoons and people started to die. The kitchen scene was the turning point. Billy's mother goes on a rampage to rid her home of its invaders. She stabs one to death, minces one in a juicer and blows another up in a microwave.

The audience screamed, moaned, groaned. Some laughed, but as I sat in that theater I watched the parent-child exodus as kids left the theater in tears.

There were lots of laughs and screams and the ending got some good applause. Even though Stripe, the bad guy was vanquished, his final death scene terrified kids. I heard crying around and even little kids screaming as the sunlight killed him Dracula-style.

I want to take a pause here to offer a theatrical impression. *Gremlins* was not a low budget film. It came from the king of the 80s box office: Spielberg. Its cousin blockbuster, *Temple of Doom*, was playing right next door to sold out shows as well.

I'll just say it, I was surprised at how CHEAP the movie looked. Was this by design as a tip of the hat to Dante's low budget roots? The town was clearly a movie set, the snow extremely plastic and fake right down to the matte painting that opens the movie with the main title.

While Gizmo was a charmer, his animatronic limitations were accentuated on the big screen. The nasty gremlins themselves looked like rejects from Jim Henson's Muppets. I felt I wasn't part of some inside joke. By the age of 16 I thought I understood "so bad it's good" and left my first screening with Regan a bit confused.

There were clear editing and continuity mistakes. The metal panel affixed to stunt cars back then to make them go nose-first into the air before flipping was clearly seen on the bottom of the cop car. The gremlins marching en mass into the town was low grade stop motion animation. It HAD to be deliberate, right? How does this kind of stuff that you would expect from Roger Corman come from Spielberg's company?

It was almost like we HAD to love it. Would the film have done as well if "Steven Spielberg Presents" wasn't over the title? The whole movie looked and felt cheap.

The power of hype was an ongoing lesson. This was a time when you waited a full year for something and got small tidbits, not saturating Internet coverage. You took what you got and they really turned it up as the film got closer to release date.

Over the next several weeks I walked the *Gremlins* theater just to watch the audience and their reactions. To this day I can see one little girl, on her mother's lap, crying, putting her hands to her eyes when Gizmo was pinned to a dart board as the newly-hatched bad guys lobbed darts at him. She was terrified little Gizmo would die.

Stripe used a gun, a chainsaw and a crossbow on Billy Peltzer. Kids hid their eyes, ran out of their seats and didn't know what the hell to do in a dark theater with these things playing out before them on those giant screens and booming sound systems. They were immersed in horror under false pretenses. They thought they were seeing a funny movie. The joke was on them, kind of like Cochran's plan in *Halloween III: Season of the Witch.*

Stripe's death was a double punch. His meltdown had kids barely able to look at the screen. Then, just when you thought it was done, his skeleton leapt from the fountain and right into the camera then dissolved on the store floor. Even after turning into steaming goo, one last breath bubble inflated and exhaled for good measure.

The content of *Gremlins* wasn't so much the issues as its disingenuous marketing. From the time the first poster arrived to the dropping of its trailer this movie was packaged as a family film. There were no hints of the genuine horror moments it would contain.

The creation of *PG-13* was to remedy this kind of thing with *Red Dawn and Temple of Doom*. *Gremlins* should've had a *PG-13* rating and I spent the summer of '84 seeing that firsthand.

It might surprise some that I saw *A Nightmare on Elm Street* in an almost empty theater. Many today think it was this massive hit when released. It was not. The film was an after summer offering, dropping that November of 1984. It arrived with little fanfare. The poster didn't generate much excitement and I don't remember a lot of advertising on TV.

I was working a lot, partying and driving all over, and TV was kind of a wasteland to me at that time. I do not remember watching much TV from late 1983-1985. "The Cosby Show" exploded onto the scene. I saw maybe half an episode and pretty much can say that to this day.

The only memory of *Elm Street* in the theater was sitting once again, in our smallest house, where horror usually ended up. It was not what I expected—nowhere near as bloody as *Friday the 13th* was and it had fleshed out characters. I took immediately to Nancy Thompson and loved the cat and mouse game that grew between her and the undead Freddy Krueger.

The film was imaginative, clever and understood teenagers (likely because Craven was a former high school teacher). It was a far cry from director/writer Wes Craven's offbeat and for me, middle of the road *Deadly Blessing* that I caught on *HBO* a few years earlier.

I knew about Craven having seen *The Hills Have Eyes* and deeply disturbed by *The Last House on the Left*, which I still hold to be his most horrific film because it was the most personal for me. What made *A Nightmare on Elm Street* stand out to me as I sat in the same theater where I saw *The Thing* two years earlier was the even-handed, low key performance of its star heroine, Heather Lagenkamp as Nancy Thompson. We had something new here. She was horror's Ripley before *Aliens* made Ripley an icon for strong female horror characters in 1986's *Aliens*.

Lagenkamp brought grit to what could have been another "dead teenager movie." Instead she's the girl next door—the typical suburban teen who gets the good grades, is a good daughter and sometimes a tad bad with the boy across the street. I felt I was on a journey with Nancy. It was more than just kids facing a killer. Nancy was on a quest and *A Nightmare on Elm Street* transformed into this low budget hero's journey.

Other slasher films had their "final girl" (that term was not a thing at this time) but they were mousey, introverted girls whose survival to the end owed more to luck than skill. Nancy bucked that trend. She was smart, strong and emerged as the leader of her troupe. She might be the last one standing, but she refused to let the monster take her friends without putting up a fight.

Me with my safari jacket and trusty blonde, Regan.

Nancy's final confrontation with Krueger is understated rage as she realizes all that he has taken from her. In turn, she will now take all she has given him. Heather Lagenkamp's performance elevated *A Nightmare on Elm Street* above the usual slasher fodder which would pay off with a second life on home video. Lagenkamp's Nancy set the stage for Ashley Laurence's Kirsty Cotton in 1987's *Hellraiser* and its sequels. Laurence was not only attractive, she was attractive in that Girl Next Door Kind of way. She was believable—an average girl thrust into incredible circumstances and against a formidable evil male.

What made Doug Bradley's sardonic Pinhead work was having a good nemesis and Laurence was it. The cat and mouse relationship forged by Nancy and Freddy was at work in Clive Barker's film.

The audience around me liked Laurence's character.

I saw *Hellraiser* with a date and listened to the audience around me as it played out. The images disturbed them, especially the living skinned body. We never really saw anything like The Cenobites before, but what connected all of this imagery to that audience was Laurence. They got behind her, cheered her on, yelled back at the screen hoping she would listen and often she did. *Hellraiser* was a good time and a nice interactive horror experience at a time when horror was in a weird place as the 80s drew to a close.

> *There were certain visual scenes in "A Nightmare on Elm Street" ingrained in my memory: Amanda Wyss's Tina dragged through the hallways in a body bag or butchered up the walls and across the ceiling. These weren't just people getting stabbed, strangled, or bitten like most of the Hammer horror films, these kills were really imaginative and for me as a kid, created a real visual nightmare.*
>
> **Philip Rogers**

I left *Mucus Makers* at the end of 1984 to work at a new video store downtown called *Main Street Video*. The money and hours were better but I kept the door open and stayed on good terms with Mr. H. That would prove to be a smart move.

I wasn't as smart with Regan. I broke up with her just around New Years, 1985 because I wanted to be free my senior year.

The John Hughes teen trope was invoked. I broke her heart and she deserved better than the "It's not you, it's me" bit. I broke up with her in an empty classroom, pulling her in between the switch. My English teacher walked in right in the middle of the breakup with her crying, me hugging her and being the shit I was. He turned around, coffee mug in hand and let out a Steve Martin "Excuuuusssse me!" and left the room.

She was my Leigh Cabot, right? But we didn't have a killer *Plymouth Fury* to unite us. We made out in a number of those mall theaters. We had some steamy summer nights, but I felt, somehow, my senior year was going to offer the better deal.

I left her in the room as classes switched and hoped I would not see her in the hallways for the rest of the day or...for the near future.

She would move on. I wasn't that hard to get over, was I?

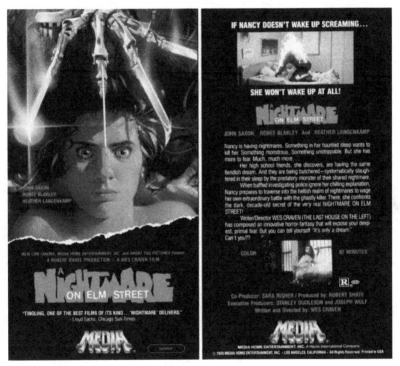

By summer of 1985 *A Nightmare on Elm Street* hit home video from "Media Home Entertainment." It was a cranked-out copy with a basic transfer and pretty grainy even by pan and scan standards. I snagged a VHS copy at my store and called a few friends to have a watch party. It was brand new on video and I got the goods.

I was still "The Horror Guy" in between making movies; I would often bring a VHS VCR to a house with a horror film from the video store. Once the party wound down, I would sit up late with a few kids to watch. It was the best way to flirt and get some action with girls.

My best friend had a giant *Mitsubishi* projection TV at the time. I got a bunch of kids hooked into *The Abominable Dr. Phibes* after a night of drinking; leaving them wondering just what the hell they watched. They did, however, get into it, trying to figure out the final curse. I loved it.

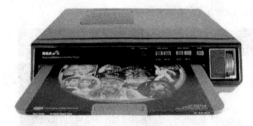

I had a blowout at my house in my junior year that left me and a handful of friends stoned as hell to watch *Psycho II* on *RCA Video Disc*. While a lot of fun, it was hardly the theatrical experience that inspired me to walk right back in for the next show.

It was a hot summer night, 1985. We'd all just graduated only a few weeks before. A group of girls and a few guys came to my house after I got off work. One of them was my best female friend, who kind of stepped in for Toni over the last few years. Another was Annie, one of the sweetest girls in my class. She was idealized by my best male friend, Chris, who perceived himself as the class Bad Boy.

If John Stamos and Rick Springfield had a kid, it was Chris. His scent was *Drakkar*, his black hair complimented blue-grey eyes. He wore turtlenecks and a black Members Only Jacket and drove a brand new, white and gold 1985 *Trans Am* with the flaming eagle on the hood. Chris was head over heels for Annie but I think he enjoyed the chase. She was sweet to him but not sure a love connection was there.

Annie hated horror movies as did my other friend who brought her, Heather. Both girls were good friends, smart, funny and middle of the road. They didn't party and they didn't watch horror. Tonight they did the latter.

My parents were gone for the weekend and the house was mine. I offered pot, beer and chips. Annie and Heather politely refused. Heather was one of the most objective people I knew. While she didn't go for the wild lifestyle, she did not judge her friends who did. She was ahead of her time. I had so much respect for her.

The movie went on and for the next 90 minutes we were entranced around the 25-inch screen. When it was done, the lights came on and I did my customary, "Well? How did you like it?" Heather's hands went up. She was very clear that she would not be sleeping tonight. In fact, it was way too late and she needed to get home.

Chris tried to make moves on Annie throughout the film and left just after it ended. He was sulking and I knew why he was making such a quick departure.

Annie, however, was shaken. At first I thought it was an act just to garner a little attention, but as she started to talk about the film, it was less a critique than it was a therapy session or even confession.

Her voice cracked when she got to talking about Amanda Wyss's death. Wyss was known for *Fast Times at Ridgemont High* and that summer of '85 had *Silverado* and *Better Off Dead* in theaters. She would be known as "Beth" the girl everyone wanted to date in that John Cusack comedy film.

"The way he killed that girl (Wyss) in the bedroom, he BUTCHERED her, Bruce and she was aware of it." The scene was haunting her all over again as she described it to us. Heather got even more shaken. She was driving her parents' *VW Vanagon* and while only less than a mile down the road, she said she was terrified for the entire short trip driving that bus by herself.

Amanda Wyss's death in *A Nightmare on Elm Street* is, in my opinion, the most horrific out of the entire series. It was played straight as this was before Freddy became a wisecracking, standup comedian. Krueger was a monster in the first film, the creeper who abducted kids, vested with horrid supernatural powers.

> *Tina's death scene really shocked me. I had never seen anything like it up to that point. I begged my dad to record it off the TV for me to watch with my friend's during a sleepover. He agreed, on one condition. He would watch it first and decide if it was suitable. I knew straight away that after watching it, he would not allow me to see it. Luckily, my dad forgot about viewing it first. The day my friend's came over to stay, I asked if he had watched it yet (knowing he hadn't).*
>
> *Anyway, he caved in to the pressure of potentially disappointing us and ruining our plans and gave us the tape to watch.*
>
> **Andrew Wardlow**

Craven shot that scene with the revolving room and inventive camera work was akin to combat footage. Annie was right—Tina wasn't just killed—she was slaughtered like some barn animal. Annie asked me to drive her home since Heather had to leave. Chris missed out on his chance for one on one drive time. I had no designs on Annie as she was a good friend, but my teen male ego was flattered. Sure, I would drive her home.

She was quiet the whole way and when I parked outside and asked if I could walk her to the door, she asked if I would come in. She also had the house to herself for the weekend. Where was this going? Not the way I thought it was.

She turned on every available light and we sat at her kitchen table. "I can't get that movie out of my head, Bruce." She seemed angry at herself for letting it get to her. "That girl."

I explained how they did the effect, trying to downplay the horror for movie magic. She wasn't having it. That's when she told me of a memory from when she was a little kid. A boy disappeared near the town where she lived. The person who abducted him likely managed it by using the boy's name that was printed on his T-shirt. They were popular back in the 70s.

They never found the kid and that made one hell of an impression on her. Death scared her. We were young, but it could come at any time. She invoked Toni. One day she was there and the next she wasn't. I don't think she saw a single slasher film before *A Nightmare on Elm Street*. The entire formula escaped her. The genre was alien to her, but this film made it personal.

Annie feared dying in her sleep. She wiped tears as she let all of this out to me. What if one night she went to bed and just never got up? What happens? Where do we go? What if we go nowhere? After the *Death Ship* incident five years earlier in eighth grade with my friend, Liz, I knew better than to just dismiss this. I listened.

Amanda Wyss was not just an 80s "Horror Girl"—she transcended into "Beth" in *Better Off Dead* which made her America's dating ideal. She was the tanned, smiling blonde that caught your eye in school or a Friday night at the mall. This entire wholesome image would be shredded before us…again, slaughtered before America and there was nothing we could but watch.

I would think of my conversation with Annie decades later as I sat in Mike Flanagan's *The Shining* sequel, *Doctor Sleep* and listen to a hospice patient express the same fears. My mind went right to Annie.

I stayed with her until the sun came up. We talked. Listened to music—anything to clear her head of Freddy Krueger and Tina Gray's death.

The summer of 1985 was coming to a close. I would be heading to Penn State for film in less than two months at the end of August. There was one more horror film coming to close out the summer of 1985.

It would change my life.

> I was old enough to see "A Nightmare on Elm Street" by myself in the theater, and that experience was so powerful, it has stayed with me my entire life. It is the reason I'm a lifelong horror fan. I will never forget what it felt like to sit in the darkened theater alone and watch Tina's death scene. There was so much blood. I was afraid to sleep for weeks afterward and that was what made the film so brilliant to me. Today it not only amazes me how many filmmakers have tried to recreate Wes Craven's magic, but it also makes me smile and remember how it felt to experience "A Nightmare on Elm Street" in a theater in 1984. It was wonderful.
>
> **Michelle Swope**

WELCOME TO FRIGHT NIGHT

We were halfway through the 80s. I was not the same person I was at the start of the decade. Before I moved to Stroudsburg my life played out like an *After School Special*. After that it turned into a John Hughes movie.

Summer 1985 didn't offer a lot for horror. Reagan handily won re-election and it was all about action movies and comedies. *Rambo: First Blood Part II* refought the Vietnam War and won it. *Weird Science* followed on the success of the previous year's *The Breakfast Club*. Then there was this little film about that kid from that family sitcom who goes back to the 1950s to change the past to ensure his future. You might have heard of it.

The name escapes me right now. The slasher was receding from screens. *Friday the 13th* stumbled with its lackluster part five after the promised final chapter. *A New Beginning* came and went fast—apparently the filmmakers didn't take notes from *Halloween III*. Don't make installments to your popular slasher franchise without its killer. The series would survive but none would ever have the box office impact like *The Final Chapter*.

"Friday The 13th Part V: A New Beginning" was the first in that series I saw. I think I was about eight at the time. My uncle from Alberta was visiting and rented it. Debbie-Sue Voorhees' boobs left an impression on me and I got in shit at school for talking about Jason. Good times. Love that flick.

Scott Stringle

Mr. H asked me to come back to *Mucus Makers* after leaving a movie with a date. He offered me an assistant manager position. I told him I would be leaving for college soon. I was heading to the Hazleton campus of Penn State. While I could commute, it was still a good hour away.

He didn't care. I could work when I came home on breaks. I gave it some thought, and with the increase in pay and the coveted assistant manager title, I returned to the mall movieplex for my last summer in town.

I took a week off after graduation to go to the Jersey shore with some buddies. We had a beach house rented and, of course, according to 80s comedy movies, I would lose my virginity to some hot pink bikini babe I meet by accident in an arcade or along the boardwalk.

The next day the house phone rang around ten in the morning: it was my mother telling me my grandfather died. I had to come home that day for the coming funeral. I wasn't at the shore 24 hours and I was catching a *Greyhound* back to The Poconos.

I had to route through Philly and bought a paper for the ride to The Poconos. I read about Reagan's polyp surgery and the Philly police just bombed a neighborhood where a radical group called MOVE made their headquarters.

I got home—but instead of staying at my own house, I stayed at Annie's. She had one of our just graduated high school friends staying there. I crushed on that girl since sixth grade. We pretended we were adults. This was the second time I had an extended stay with two girls in a house all to myself. Just a few weeks earlier another female friend and her future college roommate stayed at my house while my parents camped over Memorial Day Weekend. No romance bloomed from that, but the two nights I was at Annie's would have brought Jason Voorhees to crash the fun.

I attended the funeral. Instead of going back to the shore, I lied and went back to Annie's and my summer fling. I also went back to work because, what else was I gonna do? It was a taste of some freedom before college. I worked and then went home to a place not home with two attractive girls, and one of them was waiting for me to spend the night.

Then I met Jen. Mr. H hired her around graduation as I took a week off for all that came with it. When I got back from the shore, Mr. H introduced us and it was an 80s movie moment. Time froze, light fell upon her. Some wind came from somewhere and billowed her hair as she turned to smile at me and say, "Hi" in slow motion.

She was Leigh Cabot from *Christine*. Same color hair, the right style and those doe eyes. She was beautiful, even in our ridiculous theater uniform. Mr. H told her I was the assistant manager.

She knew who I was. She went to a rival high school but her friends had come to a few of my parties. Mr. H was impressed. I told her I looked forward to working with her, and as we walked away Mr. H muttered, "And playing with her."

This was my last summer to be a kid. I would be 18 in September and away at Penn State, living the adult, college life. It was all about to change and I knew it. I lost my second grandparent, leaving Nanny and Pappy.

The *Fright Night* previews started running around June. The trailer left me unimpressed and now that I was an assistant manager, part of my job was learning which houses to place movies. You had to take your best educated guess on what you thought the opening weekend would be like.

Fright Night was set for an August release, "The Dog Days" as Mr. H liked to say. Based on the trailer, I felt this would arrive and leave out of our smallest house. Mr. H nodded his approval. He felt the same. Two new theaters were built on to "The Big End" making it five full theaters up there and turning the two at "The Little End" into theaters six and seven.

The trailer looked cheesy and underwhelming. A kid finds out a vampire moves next door and it all looked tongue-in-cheek. By the time *Fright Night* arrived at our theater, I was in a full-blown love affair with Jen.

About a week after I returned from the shore, a co-worker and high school friend since sixth grade spilled the beans that someone we worked with liked me.

"I know someone who likes you," she teased. I was closing her out of working the box office. She was doing the closing sheets and I was counting the money.

"So who is it?"

She shrugged. "Someone who works here."

Damn her. "You can't do that to me! Come on!"

"It's so obvious! You can't be that dense!" She was starting the closeout, writing down her ending ticket series numbers. "Let me close out."

The conversation went on hold until the cash closeout in the office. Once the money was counted and verified with the ticket sales, I sat back and pressed her again.

"So who is it?" I wanted an answer. No more games.

She shook her head. "I can't believe you don't know."

"You can't do this to me."

She looked outside the office. The place was locked down, the gate had been dropped and the two candy girls had gone home. It was just us in the tiny office. "If I tell you, you can't tell her that I told you. Promise?"

"Yeah, yeah, I promise."

She waited as if for me to brace myself. "It's Jen."

340

"Jen who?" I drew a blank.

"Duh! Jen who? Think you fool!" She threw her hands up in amazement.

"Jen…" Then it hit. She meant OUR Jen.

"Yes!" she exclaimed.

I didn't believe her, thinking she was messing with me. She assured me she was being serious.

A few nights later I asked Jen out. It took off from there. The last two months of summer was a summer of love for me.

I discovered her sense of humor when we saw *Pee Wee's Big Adventure* as our date that let everyone at the theater know we were an official *Mucus Makers* couple.

Since I was "The Horror Guy," she asked if I had interest to see *Fright Night* when it arrived? The poster went up sometime after July Fourth. She thought it looked interesting.

> I vividly remember being nine or ten years old and the opening scene of "The Lost Boys" with Lucy, Michael, and Sam, then having the TV remote snatched from me by my older brother as he changed the channel.
>
> For many years I would remember that scene and not the actual name of the movie. I found it when I was 13 on a VHS tape and plopped down on the sofa, watched and fell deeply, madly in love with it. I have since re-watched it around 125 or so times; for me it never gets old and it definitely parties all night.
>
> **Lana S**

Fright Night was my first solo film I "stayed after" to see. I approached Mr. H and asked permission for Jen and I to stay after the theater closed. *Fright Night* just opened that day. He shrugged, smoked his tenth cigarette of the evening as recorded organ music pumped through his *Radio* Shack speakers in his office. "Don't do anything I wouldn't do. Actually, DO what I wouldn't do. Have fun."

The tag line to *Fright Night* was: "If you love being scared, it will be the night of your life." Audiences responded. The film moved from our smallest house to the biggest by the end of opening weekend.

I had the keys to the entire theater. Jen met me at "The Little End." It would show in Theater Seven, our smallest (Formerly Theater Four), and she too thought the trailer looked downright silly. Didn't matter…we were in love and we enjoyed horror films. I took her upstairs to the projection booth and showed her my mad film projector threading skills. The 35mm film pulled from one of three vertical platters over the projector, through it and back down to spool on another platter.

We lugged a giant bag of popcorn into theater six a little after midnight and fired up the show. We had the entire theater to ourselves. The mall was empty. The whole place was ours.

Fright Night became our movie.

I realized about thirty minutes in that *Fright Night* would graduate to our largest house at the other end of the mall and do some serious business. It was fucking good.

Aside from the cool casting of Chris Sarandon as vampire Jerry Dandridge and Roddy McDowell as broken down B-movie actor Peter Vincent, I locked in on the eulogy Tom Holland had created.

Fright Night was a goodbye letter to the great old days of horror—a more innocent time when there were three channels with affiliate channels that signed off around midnight with the National Anthem. There was no cable, no VCRs to glut the movie menu.

Fright Night is about mourning. It is a sad reminder that our better days are behind us. When I watch it now, I feel maudlin when it's done. Not only do I miss the summer of '85— I miss my childhood that was perfectly tapped by Holland's film. This whole book is about those memories.

Roddy McDowell's Peter Vincent (a play on Peter Cushing and Vincent Price) admonishes William Ragsdale's Charley Brewster that his generation doesn't appreciate the creatures that preceded the 80s run of slasher films.

"Apparently your generation doesn't want to see vampire killers or vampires either! All they want are demented madmen running around in ski-masks hacking up young virgins!"

Why sit up late to watch the old chillers when you could rent them (then for 99 cents) at any grocery store or gas station? Cable and home video had eroded the fun late nights and horror movie afternoon matinees on TV and affiliate stations. Everything I wrote about in the previous chapters of this book was vanishing from the nightmare landscape by that summer of '85.

Doctor Shock was dead by the time I saw *Fright Night* and *Creature Feature* matinees were replaced by political pundit shows. My middle school days were behind me. High school was officially dead.

I was within weeks of leaving my hometown where I was the favorite son and king of all I could see. The Internet was still 15 years away but I saw *Fright Night* as Tom Holland's sad, sentimental swan song to a pop culture era dying in the sunrise of a new technological age.

I was a little bit Charley Brewster, trying to get laid with my girl but I was also Peter Vincent, an old soul, lamenting better days—waxing nostalgic before it was time. Roddy McDowell's performance as Peter Vincent is nothing less than fantastic. From the deliberately bad grey stage hair coloring to his over-the-top "I am Peter Vincent, Vampire Killer!" (A nod to Roman Polanski's *The Fearless Vampire Killers*) McDowell's unique voice and British accent, his meek yet dignified manner gave credence to his broken horror movie star.

Vincent now had to slum on late-night local cable, hosting his own low budget films, having his face rubbed nightly into the fact that his best days are now behind him. He nails the cheesy acting in his own *Hammer*-like films and as a horror host but transforms into a genuine hero when forced to confront Jerry Dandridge, the real vampire.

The hit list soundtrack was poppy and very 80s, but Brad Fiedel's instrumental score was so operatic and sad...*Fright Night* didn't scare me— it made me mournful. I was grieving for a time that was dying before me. I grieved for my childhood. All of the old *Hammer* and horror tropes were there. The repressed, virginal girl, the cuckolded boyfriend/human suitor forced to watch the vampire take his girl, the vampire hunter, the special effects, the boundary-defying sets… all the proper ingredients were in place. *Fright Night* was a labor of love.

Those days were already in the rear-view mirror by the summer of '85 as the VCR and cable had pretty much wiped out the old-time shows as people now chose their programming. The film's success resurrected the vampire film. Without *Fright Night* there would have been no *Buffy the Vampire Slayer* or (and this would not have been a bad thing) no *Twilight* as well.

Fright Night was the number one horror film shown on college campuses around the United States. I know because I saw it at Penn State and Bloomsburg and talked with others who were catching it as a college night fright flick. Why?

Fright Night was fun. The audiences that came to my theater summer '85 thought the same. Here are some actual questions I got from people over the years. Most were convention goers, some were students. Almost all of them were 30 or younger.

Q: So like, why is this kid watching all these old movies and why does he like them so much?

A: In the days before texting, *IM*, *Xbox*, and *Warcraft* there were things called three channels, basic cable, and imagination. People also watched old movies because Hollywood had not really caught on to the cynical idea of recycling the same stories with slicked-up newer versions to fool you.

Q: The vampire seemed gay to me. Why was he dressed like some 80's model?

A: And sparkling, feminine, shirtless underwear model vampires who are prettier than their female counterparts are any better? Throughout vampire lore, the vampire's sexuality has always been a blur. *Dracula* hints at homosexuality as well, whether male or lesbian attraction. Vampires are dead from the waist down. Intercourse for them is feeding. The exchange of fluids for a vampire is a transfusion and this goes back to the earliest vampire tales.

Oh yeah, it also takes place in 1985, hence his 80's fashion. Not to mention vampires are almost always fashion plates (except for those animalistic brutes like in *30 Days of Night* or similar films).

Q: Why does the girl's hair suddenly get long after she is bit and then back to normal when they kill the vampire?

A: In the old *Hammer* Film vampire movies like *Brides of Dracula, Dracula Prince of Darkness, Terror of Dracula*, the female victims are usually sexually repressed, conservative British types who literally never let their hair down. They have boring fiancées and lead stuffy, boring lives. Then along comes that sexy undead Count who shakes things up a little and does a little tooth sex romp on her neck, and before you can say *Twilight* she's liberated. This transformation was usually shown by an increase in the woman's bust line and her hair was not only down, it seemed to gain inches in length overnight. It's a stylistic thing, not a continuity error, and it became a hallmark of those old-time films. When the vampire was killed, things went back to normal. It's intentional.

Q: What do you mean *Hammer* films? What's that?

A: *Hammer* was and still is a British film studio that put out unique spins on old horror material and basically created a whole new subgenre in horror that was built around grand old actors like Christopher Lee, Vincent Price, and Peter Cushing. Many consider Lee's portrayal of Count Dracula superior to Bela Lugosi's iconic count.

Roddy McDowell's character, "Peter Vincent" is a play on words from the old *Hammer* days. It's a combination of "Peter Cushing" and "Vincent Price." Of course, if you never saw any of these films then you wouldn't know that. PETER Cushing on the left. VINCENT Price on the right. Put 'em together and you get PETER VINCENT.

There are plenty more but hopefully, you knew a lot of this after reading this far. *Fright Night* was meant to be a fun tribute for people who remembered a better time in their entertainment.

I got Peter Vincent. He was in my soul. When he held the award for one of his old films, gazing at it with longing and sadness, he was talking to me. I could feel his nostalgia. I could smell the sentiment. I was holding the old cardboard Academy Award my friends made for me in eighth grade, only five years earlier.

Jen and I watched the full movie. No sucking face, necks or other anatomy. From opening to closing credits, the film had our attention. She loved Peter Vincent, enjoying his line, "And I have always WON!" Jen got the old-school horror inside jokes and references.

I swear I was more in love with her when we left that movie at three in the morning than when I threaded the machine and started it. I had to get her home before six in the morning as her mother usually got in from her late nursing shift by six-thirty.

The sun would be up in a few hours. I told her how the movie made me feel. I was leaving for Penn State in weeks. My life was different, but I had such a great time in high school. I openly wept at the biggest award ceremony, "Moving Up Day." It was considered a bigger event than graduation. When the chorus sang some song about time flowing like a river, I broke down. It was pure grief.

I led my class out of the gymnasium at the end in tears with a number of my classmates doing the same.

I loved my class. I loved those people. I wasn't 18 yet and already felt old.

I told her I feared the same with our relationship. I was never in love with someone like her. I was being so honest with her it hurt. She was moved. When we parked at her house she kissed me and held me for so long. She wasn't going anywhere she promised. Even when I left for school we would stay as in love then as were now.

No Jerry Dandridge was going to seduce her. There were a lot of them out there and she was a perfect vampire target. She told me no guy ever talked to her the way I did. She said I had so much passion, so much feeling and it was contagious.

We said "I love you" a dozen times before she got out and walked inside. I went home and slept most of the following morning away because of our midnight *Fright Night* screening.

The following weekend was spent at my house. My mother was working the night nursing shift and my dad was out of town. We had the house to ourselves. I still had the old RCA Video Disc player. I kept it because I had a number of movies on disc. One of them was *Jaws* and…it just happened to be Jen's favorite movie as well. Jen was on the couch, I was on the floor. It was a hot August summer night. I was well aware the loud crickets outside were summer's final concert.

Fall was coming. Summer was dying.

Right around the time the shark scared Brody while he tossed chum, she leaned off the couch and whispered into my ear, "Guess what we can do?"

I looked at the clock, saw it was almost two in the morning, and everything in our little town, save for a handful of diners and the old Perkins restaurant were closed. She smacked me on the head and said it again, fluttering eyebrows, and then gave me her "come hither" look.

Sex. Holy shit. She meant SEX. She was on The Pill long enough.

It happened that night, in my basement rec room and a factor was *Fright Night* and how my sensitive side spoke to her after we watched the film one week earlier.

A comic I drew for Penn State's newspaper that shows how change was not a good thing for me.

It transformed me. I was no longer a virgin. Charley Brewster hounded his girlfriend Amy for sex, but look what happened when vampire Amy came for him. "What's the matter, Charley? Don't you want me anymore?"

I drove her home as the sun came up. I was different, like the theme song to *Fright Night* said: "You can wait your whole life for the sun to rise. When it finally comes up, it's gonna hurt your eyes."

On the way back to my house, just as the town was waking up and the first light was growing brighter, I blew through a red light at a four-way on Main Street.

Some big, fat guy with white or grey hair who looked a lot like Porky from those films in a boat of a car, veered and avoided my car T-boning him on his driver's side. I slammed on my brakes; he did as well and we skidded into the center of the intersection.

The guy rolled down his window, mouth already screaming. He yelled something like, "Don't you fucking stop at red lights?" Something like that.

My hands shot off the wheel and up, warding him off to not get out and come to my car and pummel me.

"I am so sorry," I yelled. "I wasn't thinking! I just lost virginity last night and—"

I never got to finish. The guy's face went from a mask of anger to "What the fuck?" He shook his head, cut me off in mid-sentence and drove away, dismissing me with a hand flip.

Not the answer he was expecting. I imagined him telling that one to his wife.

It was after six in the morning when I got home. My mom was at the kitchen table as I came through the door. She had her cigarette in hand, the newspaper before her, and a half-empty glass of orange juice before her. She just got in as well from her night nursing shift.

"Someone's slinking in." She was amused.

There was no sense in hiding it. I was rattled about my near-death experience on the heels of being de-virginized. I needed to talk. I sat down and waited.

"So…what'd you do last night?" She pretended to read the paper.

It was a huge benefit to have a mother I could tell anything. "I had sex with Jen for the first time." I said it just like that. No frills. No long, roundabout tale.

She paused and took this in. She exhaled her smoke. "Sex for the first time? Or sex with Jen for the first time?"

"Both," I replied.

"Oh yeah, how was it?" Her eyes never left the paper.

I wanted to go into detail about this whole feeling of loss. Instead I said, "It's not like they portray it in the movies."

She smiled, took a drag, exhaled and said, "It never is. Pass the orange juice."

I did. I got up. Kissed her on the head and went to my bedroom. I was a boy going back to a bedroom once decorated with *Star Wars curtains and bed sheets.* Now it seemed too small for a man. I mean, the movies said I was a man now, only I didn't feel it.

I was Peter Vincent, adrift in a brave new world that held all kinds of surprises that I was not ready to tackle.

I left for college two weeks later. I did organize a roommate road trip to a neighboring university that was showing *Fright Night* in their auditorium on 16mm. My new friends loved it. That 1300 seat auditorium screamed and cheered. The final confrontation in Dandridge's house brought so many screams and when it ended there was applause.

That's what good movies do. Those are the memories they give us.

Nothing was the same. It all changed in just over two weeks and now that bygone era is the core of my horror filmmaking soul.

It's why I wrote this book for you.

AFTERMATH

I never married Jen. We broke up by Halloween, 1985. I understood the term "heartbreak" because I literally felt that pain in my chest when it happened.

The 80s moved forward. Tobe Hopper had a swing and a miss with *Lifeforce*. It stayed two weeks at our theater and was gone. His follow up to *Poltergeist* was an expensive flop. He would make it a bomb triple play with his remake of *Invaders from Mars*.

Tom Atkins returned for *Night of the Creeps*, but it came and went so fast in theaters, I missed it and caught a terrific and fun 80s horror on home video. I wish I'd had the theater experience for that one.

I flunked out of Penn State by January, 1986. I did get to see *Day of the Dead* and *A Nightmare on Elm Street II: Freddy's Revenge* at Hazleton's equivalent of The Sherman—a rundown old theater called The Hersker.

I saw both films stoned and it was just my roommate and me. No big crowd events and I left both feeling they lacked something, yet also had something cool as well.

Audience reaction to both were subdued. Part of the problem is both films had big shoes to follow. As said, the original *A Nightmare on Elm Street* came and went in theaters but built up its reputation through home video. *Dawn of the Dead* transformed zombie movies, and maybe an audience at another theater would have been different, but The Hersker was quiet. Both *Day of the Dead* and *Nightmare 2* have been rehabilitated in a number of ways and properly appreciated and assessed on their own merits, instead of in the light of their predecessors.

I caught *The Hitcher* with another roommate and left it feeling disturbed by the sheer nastiness of the film. The Hersker was close to empty that night, too. That paranoia factor returned and one year later I would spend a night of drinking with C. Thomas Howell telling him all about it.

> *I watched "Freddy's Revenge" at my cousin's house. I was only nine. My parents didn't know, and I wasn't sure I wanted to watch it. It terrified me, but had me realizing I liked the feeling of being scared. The rush and prickled skin were sensations I enjoyed because I was in a safe environment. I was intrigued my how they made everything look so good.*
>
> **Gfox**

I moved to Los Angeles where I lied my way onto the Universal Studios lot and got a job as paid production assistant thanks to Norman Bates himself, Anthony Perkins. I saw *Psycho III* and while I enjoyed it, the theatrical experience was flat, and the film flopped. Its dark tone took years to grow on me. I have since rediscovered it and love it.

I saw the giant tank where *Jaws: The Revenge* would film its big ending, not knowing it would be the worst motion picture ever made.

I dated an actress who worked some soap operas and was one of the bikini girls at the end of *Freddy's Revenge*. She would appear in 1988's Lovecraft horror, *The Unnamable* as well.

We saw *Aliens* in San Francisco in a giant movie theater. It had to have at least 500 seats and it was sold out. The crowd went crazy throughout but the ending when Sigourney Weaver's Ellen Ripley comes to Carrie Henn's defense in the giant mechanical exoskeleton to kick some alien queen ass—the crowd stood on its feet. "Get away from her you BITCH!" That brought the house down.

Top Gun was number one at the box office. Eddie Murphy and Tom Cruise were kings. Arnold was edging out Stallone as the new action overlord.

The *Challenger* space shuttle exploded 30 seconds after liftoff and President Reagan gave one of the best speeches of his presidency in its aftermath.

AIDS held the country in its death grip as the United States had its reckoning for ignoring it for so long. The slasher film continued to recede, never fully vanishing, but just staying out there.

By 1988 Reagan was looking tired, his second term rocked by some damn big scandals. The Gipper signed off in a memorable farewell speech that ended with: "All in all not bad. Not bad at all."

That's how I felt about my life as I wandered Los Angeles—wondering just how I was going to make a real go of it. Would I ever become a real filmmaker?

I returned home in 1987, just barely two years after I left and returned to the same mall multi-plex I worked in high school. *Mucus Makers* was now *Loews Theaters* and Mr. H was gone. A new manager ran the building and I was hired as part of the assistant management team.

I started August 1988 almost five years to the very day I started after leaving McDonalds.

Memories were everywhere. Jen and me in *Fright Night*, *Gremlins* with Regan…so many memories and adventures happened in these seven movie theaters.

We were up to a fourth *Elm Street* by 1988 and a fourth *Halloween*. I was managing the cinema when both ran. We had our after hour employee nights where I caught those films, *Pet Sematary, Jacob's Ladder, Deep Star Six, Leviathan*…the list goes on. We did get a *Fright Night Part II* but distribution problems and believe it or not, a connection to The Menendez brothers murders cut the film off at its knees and the film was barely a blip on theater screens. Fortunately it has received a second life thanks to home video.

Peter Vincent had it right.

The 80s ended and a new decade would bring new types of horror.

I discovered "Mystery Science Theater" on *Comedy Central* and it helped me make the transition. Those guys got it. They got everything I grew up with. I also learned a lot about what NOT to do in filmmaking.

The "MS3TK" guys were the new Doctor Shock.

It was all over—but what a ride.

WHAT'S THE SCARIEST MOVIE
YOU'VE EVER SEEN?

The better question is…what really scares you? I hate the water but I don't fear sharks or piranhas or giant alligators getting me. It's drowning that gets me. I fear an early death but ghosts, demons and the supernatural don't scare me. Nanny made it clear: "Be more afraid of the living than the dead."

My fear lies more with 70s paranoia horror. When you have that one person who sees things have changed—people have changed, their friends and family have changed…that's what scares the shit out of me.

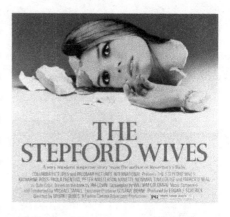

The Stepford Wives scared the hell out of me. It is not all that scary a film. It was unnerving—the concept of replacing women with compliant androids—the film was a rebuke of the growing feminist movement. Katherine Ross senses something is really wrong with the idyllic little town her husband found. She's not

much different than Jessica in *Let's Scare Jessica to Death*—fearing her own sanity as she questions the reality around her.

Invasion of the Body Snatchers 1979 is the scariest movie I have seen. While star Donald Sutherland's *Don't Look Now* is one of his most disturbing, *Body Snatchers* hit me the hardest and I carry it with me to this day. The horror for me is that in some ways, the movie came true.

Look at our world now. Cancel culture, everyone offended, social justice warriors—step out of line with any of their group think and the offended screech and sound the alarm.

As I write this Dave Chapelle is one of those who hasn't fallen asleep and is under attack for his comedy and branded with all sorts of labels.

The woman who stood up after my screening of *The Fields*—remember her? The *Disney*-loving mother outraged by the content of my film and my life— there are now millions of her. Call them Karens, Social Justice Warriors, Cancel Culture Fanatics, Trumpers, Leftists, Traitors, Racists, Nazis…we can go on.

My point is, no matter where you reside on the political spectrum, individual thought is paid lip service. It's either absorbed in a collective group think or on the other end it is branded as the selfish right to have what you want and fuck everyone else. COVID showed us better than ever before just who and what we are. It will be interesting to see how our reaction to this global pandemic will be reviewed fifty years from now.

Express individual thought, critical thinking or anything that diverts from the various narratives and you get this:

Sometimes I feel as if I am Veronica Cartwright screaming her head off, realizing that the fight was for nothing and all is lost. That, my friends, is what horror is to me: hopelessness.

These memories…these are my own experiences but they were shared with thousands over the years. We became something more than just individuals with tickets in those dark theaters. We were Americans. We were stitched together with a common cultural fabric.

I hope for a return to that.

Technology has changed the way we make and view movies. The theatrical experience has been marred by the fear of mass shootings and of course, COVID.

Share your memories and experiences. Share that joy. It means you're alive.

Demand better of your entertainment and try to understand film and its rich history. I think you saw in the way I laid out this book that it was a gradual learning process with horror but it made me a better person.

Horror shielded me from real issues at home. It helped me deal with bullies and gave me the tools to become a well-adjusted young adult who rose to the top of his class.

Despite what the headlines want to spout, the horror genre is not the reason for the awful things that happen in our world.

It is a reflection of them.

We are the monsters. Rod Serling knew it with *The Monsters Are Due on Maple Street*.

It's the awful realization at the end of a good horror story.

Be more afraid of the living than the dead.

EPILOGUE

I moved to California in the fall of 1986 after failing out of Penn State. After getting a job at *Universal Studios* and dating my *Freddy's Revenge* actress, I became close with a family who lived north of Los Angeles and became my adopted kin.

They had a younger daughter (I called her Little Lee) just hitting her teens, and I thought I would recreate the summer of 1985 dynamic and magic, and rented the original *A Nightmare on Elm Street* for them. This girl became my tagalong, kid sister sidekick and she wanted a scary film for a weekend sleepover party with her school girlfriends. I was happy to oblige. Her folks would be going out to dinner that night. I had a plan.

A houseful of teen girls gathered around the TV and VCR to watch the film for their first time. What they didn't know was I was outside the house, readying to scare the hell out of them once the film got cranking. I was able to station myself in the backyard with a clear shot of the TV. I knew the film well, and when the right time came, I transformed into "The Man."

Instead of moving through cornfields, I skulked around the side of the house to a small tool shed flush against the garage. I climbed on top, then grabbed the rain spouting and shimmied my way up to the roof. I can't believe I got up on that roof without falling and breaking my back.

Once I got on the roof, I moved overtop to the point where I was directly overhead of the viewing room. I started scratching the shingles, then rubbing my feet to make as much noise as possible. It was like "The Monster" all over again.

There was nothing at first. Then I heard the TV go quiet. They either stopped the tape or muted it. That told me I had them. They heard something. Enough to stop the movie.

I went nuts, and ran over the roof from one side of the house to the other. The screams came not long after.

So did the police.

I saw flashing red and blue lights coming down the street. There was no siren, but the car was coming for our house—the house I was standing on.

I dashed to the chimney and hunkered down. The police parked out front and got out brandishing flashlights right away. They went to the front door. I could hear the girls' panicked description with the words that made the acid reek in my gut: "…up on the roof!"

I lowered my breathing as much as my panicked self would allow. My breath was making vapor in the cool California night air. Dammit! The lights splashed all around me. I didn't move. They would hear me.

"I got him!" A cop yelled from down there in the back yard. His torch was on me and he held it steady. It was joined by two others.

They got me, all right.

I thought guns would get drawn so I called down loud and clear. I saw myself getting shot atop that house, my blood spattered all against the chimney. I told the officers I was a close friend of the family. I was just playing a prank. I would come down, just don't shoot me. I raised my hands but was afraid I would slide down the roof.

"Bruce?!" Little Lee squealed. I dropped down to the back patio in front of several cops and a squad of girls. I offered a wave and embarrassed smile. She slapped playfully at me, giving me a playful kick for good measure. "You jerk! You scared the hell out of us!"

The police relaxed. The flashlights went out and they confirmed one more time that she knew me and I was no threat. They gave me the sound advice to never try to scare someone again by climbing on a roof.

The next step was to exit gracefully as I am sure the police didn't want an 18-year-old guy hanging behind with a bunch for middle-school teenagers. I followed them out as the girls laughed and went back inside. I could see them at the front window as I got to my car. They wanted to make sure I actually left.

I got my balls busted by her parents the next day but everyone thought it was pretty funny. When I asked Little Lee what scared her about the whole thing; her answer was pretty simple: Freddy Krueger. He was out there—up on the roof and he came for HER.

I messed her hair with a smile.

"Be more afraid of the living than the dead," I told her.

THE RELEVANCY OF MONSTERS

Our walk is about done. One of the biggest gripes I hear online, in interviews and at conventions is "Aren't there any good ideas anymore?" Why all the remakes? From horror to *Ghostbusters*, why is Hollywood obsessed with remaking and rebooting their original classics.

Money. It's a cynical move overall, however remakes are not inherently bad. There are a number of terrific remakes that come to mind. In horror, Zack Snyder's *Dawn of the Dead* comes to mind as a remake done right. The same goes for Tom Savini's *Night of the Living Dead* remake discussed earlier.

This topic could be a book all its own, but I want to wind down with a look at three specific horror franchises and go beyond the simple question of "why remake something?"

If you go back to my chapter "The Universal Big Bang" you'll see I offer a reason for why the old classic monsters eventually fell into cheap, satire fodder. The times changed but the monsters didn't. Movie-going experiences shifted from the darkness of the economic depression in the 1930s to the fear of war and the horrors it brought as World War II kicked off in 1941.

Universal tried to "reboot" their classic monsters into a *Marvel*-style extended universe called "The Dark Universe." Their hope was to update and refashion their old properties as *Dracula, Frankenstein, The Mummy* into action-style films with wild revisions to canon to make their monsters more like comic book superheroes.

It didn't work.

It didn't work because these types of monsters had nothing to say in this modern day. They were removed from their respective times and the historical context around them. *Marvel* is *Marvel* and the obsession with Hollywood to fit whatever they can into this Disney-*Marvel* model has been met with mixed results at best. *Star Wars* is an example of a franchise remolded into this format.

Watching Michael Myers, Jason Voorhees or Freddy Krueger on the big screen allowed us to watch as the times changed around them. All three original films were made before, at the start and the middle of the 1980s. *Halloween* dropped in 1978 with *Friday the 13*th on its heels in 1980 with *A Nightmare on Elm Street* dropped into the middle of the decade.

Each film had its own unique place in history with events around each respective film a major reason why they succeeded the way they did.

Michael Myers is a tornado. He touched down in a small town; hit a few houses while leaving others untouched. He was a random force of nature that arbitrarily chose his victims, which for the most part were attractive women.

Michael was the last vestige of the Manson hippie movement. He was a product of the suburbs gone dark, returning to his home town to kill it. America had just come out of the *Helter Skelter* era, Vietnam and Watergate. Michael was a Gen X'er gone bad, a product of all that came before him.

His Haddonfield rampage was a representation of what was coming for America—the 80s and a return to 1950s conservatism that would be the backdrop to the coming AIDS epidemic. Michael Myers was an Angel of Death for promiscuous teens. The only one to make it is the virgin which, as we discussed, will become "The Final Girl" mythos and trope almost every horror film will embrace in the 80s.

America was out of the "Free Love" movement and a new wave of feminism emerged in the early 1970s. Michael was horror's answer to that. He was a product of his time and it clicked with viewers as The Carter Years drew to a close. Victims were powerless against Michael, much like how Americans felt against staggering inflation, America's new decline in world stature and its distrust of the government.

Halloween II would reflect the changes of just a few short years and up its body count and violence and gore. It did this to stay relevant, no different than how *Psycho II* played the same card to keep in line with the slashers hitting their peak by 1983.

Over ten installments later (including Rob Zombie's remakes) is Michael still relevant? The series was ret-conned again in 2018, ignoring all other films in the series save for the 1978 original. This included 1981's *Halloween II* and its silly sibling plotline.

I sat in a theater of fanboys. This wasn't just a normal audience; these were people my age, with very few younger kids in attendance. These were fans that saw every other film, knew some of them word for word in their dialogue. They were ready for their monster to return to the screen 40 goddamned years later. Michael should be stalking nursing homes, not the streets of Haddonfield.

Just what is Michael's purpose this time around? Since Haddonfield last saw him, the country went through the AIDS epidemic, the crack drug wave, Columbine and the terrorist attacks of September 11th, 2001. We saw a shift away from monsters being symbols of fear to them becoming ourselves. Our own children are now the new monsters.

Want to make a new *Halloween* film? Put Michael up against the school shooters we have seen over the past twenty years. Something tells me Michael might get a run for his money. In fact the person I saw *Halloween 2018* sitting next to me insisted we pick seats bas close to an exit as possible in the event of an "active shooter" inside the theater.

What if "The Boogeyman" doesn't wear a William Shatner mask? What if he dyes his hair bright pink? What if he wears a black trench coat? What if he is willing to die for his god and take thousands with him or behead his victims online for the world to see?

Friday the 13th's original message was "have sex and die." This was a world pre-video games and pre-cell phones and applications. I have heard kids ask, "What was summer camp?" The original film was made a ta time when if you wanted to know where all the kids in the neighborhood were, you just looked for the pile of bikes in someone's yard.

Now you can go through almost any neighborhood and be led to believe they have no kids at all. Where are they? Inside. Texting. Online gaming. Social chat hubs.

In a post-AIDs world we see the physical act of sex supplanted by virtual "sexting" or online gratification. Dating is hard. Real-life relationships are hard. It's easier to just send nudes and masturbate and be a couple online.

Just who does Jason have to stalk these days? If kids still do come to summer camp, what if they're not screwing? What if all they do is the counselor mandated activities and then sit in their cabins on their phones? Is the hulking killer in a hockey mask all that scary anymore? Again, in a world of active on campus shooters, COVID, domestic terrorism, is the Voorhees kid scary or silly?

Jason is a zombie in athletic wear. We now have zombies on several different cable and streaming shows. We are inundated by walking dead. What makes Jason so special and why hide behind the mask. We've seen scarier stuff since Savini created shrieks of terror April, 1984 in that movie theater I ushered.

Just what does *Friday the 13*th have to say? Apparently not a lot. The 2009 remake offered up slick production value, some more fornicating teenagers. It tried, like Rob Zombie did with Michael Myers, to give Jason a more detailed background.

Living in a world where major, big scale horrible things happen, as humans we want answers. Nothing can just be random can it?

Rob Zombie's remakes had Michael Myers coming from a bad family. He was abused. He was sick. He tortured animals. If you remember the 1978 film, Dr. Loomis gave us a single sentence reason: Michael was evil. That's it. Nothing else. Nothing about his mom, dad, sister. Nothing.

There was no *Phantom Menace* Midichlorian explanation for The Force here. A vast, indefinable energy source is quantified as a genetic condition. I think we are close to a *Halloween* film where Michael's seemingly dead body is on a lab table. A doctor studies his genetic structure to find his cells regenerate rapidly for some unknown reason just before Michael awakens and grabs the guy by the throat.

Does Jason need a back story? Yeah, he's a momma's boy, but do we need to see remnants of his past? Doe we need to explain him? Because if we do, then how did he come back from the dead? How did he go from some weak, deformed kid to a hulking monster?

It seems that people now crave answers to anything because sometimes we can't just accept the fact that bad shit happens and there are often no reasons let alone a singular reason for them.

We saw this in 1981's *Halloween II*. Laurie was asked to define fate by her English teacher in the original 1978 film. It was a small, light hint that sometimes we are fated to things because that's just the way the universe works. Michael and Laurie collided by a chance of fate. Not because they were brother and sister. Audiences just could accept the fact that Laurie was a random target. We had to have some kind of reasoning behind it all. She had to be his sister… yeah! That's it! That's why Michael was after her. You know, she lived in that same small town that had that big killing of Judith Myers and nobody seemed to know at all that Laurie Strode was really a Myers kid. Right.

The Internet comes along and we have answers to everything. Even batshit crazy ones like the kind we saw in the rise of COVID. A virus shuts down the world needs an answer. It couldn't be just a random event. It had to be a bio weapon. It was population control by the wealthy elite or even Reptilian Lizard People. It didn't exist at all and was part of some elaborate mind control scheme. I could go on and you could list a few of your own.

We need answers because as human beings we can't accept that there are things bigger than us out there and they don't always have answers.

The times changed and the monsters didn't. Michael stumbles around Haddonfield, but we really don't know what he wants. *Halloween Kills* showed this without doubt. What did he come home for? The sheriff speculates Michael came for him. Laurie insists he came for her. Neither is confirmed. He wanted to be back at his house. Why? He's smart. He knows this is where police will come for him because that's where they got him the last time.

I suspect, at the time of this writing, we are going to find out why Michael comes back in the coming third film, *Halloween* Ends, and it's going to explain a lot to us. The sad part is; I don't think it should.

Even the previous *Halloween* sequels threw in some kind of Druid cult of Thorn. Michael was some weird experiment, driven by some supernatural, ancient force and Haddonfield townsfolk were in on it and it goes on and on.

The original idea was better. Michael was evil. His ability to resurrect was never discussed. We didn't need it explained.

Freddy Krueger had a tougher time of things. *A Nightmare On Elm Street* struck a chord with my friend because of her personal fear of missing children. Freddy emerged in the light of America's realization we had a kid gone missing problem. Freddy arrived in the age of the milk carton pictures of missing children. The country was also seeing a rise in anti-social and aberrant behavior in teens. Schools were changing, with teachers admitting that something was happening but they just couldn't say what. We had a rising mental health issue on our hands and with the rise of mass media, stories of teen suicides spread with it. What was once happening in the shadows was now out there for millions to know.

Freddy wasn't a "sex and die" punisher. He hated children or maybe he desired them in the way good people shouldn't. Freddy represented "Stranger Danger" to the extreme. Once a school janitor, then a child murderer kept as a dirty secret by the people who killed him.

As the sequels to *A Nightmare On Elm Street* rolled out, they reflected more of the dark side of the party 80s. Freddy adopted pop culture phrases, looks and icons. By the time *Freddy's Dead* came around, he was a gaming monster using a power glove and Nintendo-type game system to kill his victims.

The reboot tried to take Freddy back to his roots, even reversing then, un-reversing the whole child killer thing. It was slickly made. Good green screen effects could now give us better nightmare visions for an audience, but it lacked Robert England's "panache" shall we say? The new film also did nothing to connect its present day audience with the material.

In other words, the horror of the new *A Nightmare On Elm Street* wasn't personal. It was a rehash of the things from the 80s that made the original an eventual hit. There was a disconnect with the material and the audience.

Kids had other worries by 2010. They saw New York and Washington attacked. They watched two new w2ars erupt and take family members into their maelstrom. They feared the monsters that sat next to them in their classrooms and something else that Freddy would have trouble with: these kids tuned out of reality and willingly entered the fake, digital world which in itself was a kind of dream like place that Freddy couldn't penetrate.

What happens when kids no longer fear monster like Freddy? If it's like the ending to the original 1984 film, they take away the monster's power. It is rendered irrelevant.

That's what happened to the remake

of *A Nightmare On Elm Street.*

The new *Halloween* films are not remakes or reboots. They are continuations of the original 1978 storyline. *Halloween 2018* and *Halloween Kills* were financial successes. They served their original fans well. They were not made for new audiences. These were films made by fanboys for fanboys. They are chock full of Easter eggs and tiny details only the most ardent *Halloween* fans will get. If they happen to pick up some new viewers on the way (which they will) then that's a bonus.

I have heard a number of kids say about the new films and even the originals: "I don't get it. They're boring." They watch them because they're told they're classics but overall the reboots and remakes are created to wring out the dollars of the original fans with the hope they bring their kids.

The times changed. The monsters didn't.

What happened to Universal's monsters happened to the 80s horror gang as well. They've had a better run, I think, than their Universal counterparts

but the whole thing now feels tired and running out of gas.

The key is not spending more money on these films. It's finding what connects these monsters to the kids of today and what taps into their fears.

What makes it personal?

THIS TIME IT'S PERSONAL

This book was written out of a love for film and the joy and experiences it gave me growing up. Film shaped my future. It's given me a career. Horror has made me somewhat of an expert on something and that's a good feeling.

Film is art. I think I sufficiently expressed my love for some of the cheesiest bad movies as well as the terrific. Many of you might not realize, but it takes a lot of effort to make a truly bad film. On the flipside, it takes little effort to make a mediocre one and even less effort to make a cynical one.

I have a podcast called *Cynema* that was inspired by a single film: *Jaws The Revenge*. I use the word "film" loosely in describing *Jaws The Revenge* aka *Jaws 4*. The word "Cynema" is a mash up of "cynical" and "cinema" invented by me. My definition is as follows: "The cynical contempt for an audience by making product devoid of creativity, respect for production value or having the intent to entertain; while having the financial and intellectual means to do so."

This final chapter brings everything full circle. We started this journey with my love of film, my reliance upon it. We end with my contempt for the very industry that creates it.

I have to back to the summer of 1983 and *Jaws 3-D*. My love for *Jaws* brought me to my film career. *Jaws 2* supplanted *Jaws* for awhile in its appeal to my burgeoning teenage hormones. After I hit high school, I re-evaluated the two films and *Jaws* was restored to its proper position on my film list. However, *Jaws 2* was not a bad film. As I wrote, the film's biggest crime is simply that it wasn't *Jaws*.

Jaws 2 was a solid sequel. It had excellent production value. While it lacked the excellent script and cast of its predecessor, its production team wanted a high quality film made with the intent to entertain and thrill.

You might not have liked *Jaws 2*, but it doesn't mean it was a poorly made film or even a cynical one. Yes, it was made to capitalize off of *Jaws* and its massive success. I guess you could argue there's some cynicism there, but its producers Richard Zanuck and David Brown were committed to make sure they brought forth a sequel of quality.

They also knew if they didn't make it, someone else would, and *Jaws* was a legacy picture for both men. They took the job and gave us a worthy sequel.

After the success of *Jaws 2* and its overall crowd-pleasing reception (the audience I was with screamed, jumped and applauded) the producing team was offered a third *Jaws* film. Universal Studios president Sid Sheinberg came to "The Sunshine Boys" (Zanuck and Brown's nickname) and asked for lighting to strike a third time. Both men felt everything that could be done had been done. Roy Scheider made it clear he had non interest to return to Amity's police force. In fact, he deliberately accepted the film *Blue Thunder* to ensure he could not be available for any *Jaws 3*.

Sheinberg was determined. "I've got plans for *Jaws 3* right now," he told the author of *The Jaws 2 Log* production diary, Ray Loynd. Many don't know the story of how we got that *Jaws 3* and I won't go into too much detail, but this was the slippery slope that led us to the non-movie that *Jaws the Revenge* would be in 1987.

Whether it was Sheinberg or some other Universal suit, the idea was floated to make *Jaws 3* a spoof. The title was *Jaws 3, People 0*. It was written by Matty Simmons (who would go on to write the original *Vacation*) and Joe Dante of *Piranha* fame was rumored to be the director of choice.

Zanuck and Brown were offered this sequel of sorts. I imagine they read the script, but in the end they declined to produce *Jaws 3* whether a straight up film or spoof. David Brown likened the making of a spoof to their two *Jaws* films to "fouling your own nest." They departed the project and moved on.

The spoof/satire idea was abandoned and through a series of unfortunate events, *Jaws 3* was shopped out to schlocky producer Alan Landsburg. The 3-D craze briefly returned in the early 80s and it was decided the third *Jaws* film would shoot in the third dimension.

Here is where you may be surprised. As bad as *Jaws 3-D* was (and it WAS really awful) I don't classify it as "Cynema." I hated the film that opening night back in July 1983. I was appalled at how such a shitty installment could follow not just a good previous film, but stain the name of the first, classic motion picture.

Like *Halloween III*, *Jaws 3-D* has been rehabilitated somewhat over the decades. I grew to love it as much as that dopey rubber mutant bear movie, *Prophecy*. John Frankenheimer set out to make an important horror film with environmental messages. His alcoholism had other plans.

I think Joe Alves set out with every intention to make a great third installment to the *Jaws* franchise. He knew the film was in trouble early in development. Former *Jaws* editor Verna Fields (the real unsung hero of *Jaws*) told Alves he needed to get involved because Landsburg and his people were making a mess of things.

Alves was a top notch production designer for the first two films. His ingenuity was a major contributor to the success of both motion pictures plagued with production problems. The third time would not be a charm.

The film was shopped out from Universal to Landsburg's company which cut the budget, moved up effects deadlines and made a mess of the original script and its subsequent revises. *Jaws 3-D* was released with some major effects scenes not even finished. If you watch the film you will see people in the underwater tunnels walking against blue screens with nothing matted in. It's a scene where a little kid walking with their father yells something like "Daddy! Look at the fish!" The guy turns around and yells "Holy shit!" Only there is nothing there. We see nothing. That's because the special effects were never finished. Landsburg rushed the film into release.

I think Alves had every intention of making a good film. I really do. I think he got a great cast: Dennis Quaid, Bess Armstrong and an Oscar winner with the always solid Louis Gossett, Jr. Gossett just came off of an Oscar win for 1982's *An Officer and a Gentleman*.

Michael Caine would echo this with an Oscar win for *Hannah and Her Sisters* and follow that with *Jaws the Revenge*

Jaws 3-D is a lot of fun. It's my "go to" background movie when I am cleaning the house or just need something to put on because I laugh at it. I enjoy the cheesy effects and that bad, growling mama shark.

If you had told me I would do this back when I was 15, I would've taken a swing at you.

Here's what most people don't know: *Jaws 3-D* made money. A lot of it. Maybe it didn't make original *Jaws* money or even *Jaws 2* money, but it turned a profit and was still making money when it was pulled from theatrical release.

This was not lost on Universal President Sid Sheinberg. That fish still had some life in it and it was only a matter of time before a fourth installment was on the books.

Now…how did we get there? With a film as awful as *Jaws 3-D*, you would think that should've halted the plans for any more sequels. You would be right had the film flopped. While it rightfully took a critical beating, *Jaws 3-D*, to remind you again, made money.

There was something else too…this time it was personal and it goes all the way back to the troubled set of *Jaws 2*.

The original director on *Jaws 2* was John Hancock. He came to the film with dark ideas and a darker vision. The suits at Universal felt otherwise, but there was another point of contention. Sid Sheinberg was president of Universal Studios back then as well. He presided over the original *Jaws* and he just happened to be married to one of its stars, Lorraine Gary who played Ellen Brody.

Sheinberg wanted to see his wife's character expanded and a point of contention between the studio president and the director of the film and its two producers Zanuck and Brown was Ellen going out to sea at the end of the film to face down the shark with her husband, Chief Martin Brody.

See where I am going with this?

Richard Zanuck said something like "Over my dead body." Director John Hancock sided with his producers and what do you know? Not long afterward Hancock was fired. Could be coincidence, but Sheinberg wasn't happy with being rebuffed. He kind of got his way, as Ellen did accompany Martin on the first leg of his journey, but was left to tend to Tina Wilcox and in Deputy Hendricks's care.

This time around, Sheinberg was going to get his way. This time it was personal.

An ad appeared in a Hollywood trade magazine announcing *Jaws 4*.

Here's where I get speculative. I have no proof it happened this way but I suspect it went something like this. Just on that trade announcement where Sheinberg let us know his wife will not only confront the shark, she will kill it; it tells us there's a grudge still nursed. Lorraine had technically retired from

NOT EVERY MAN can give his wife just what she wants. But at Christmas, movie tycoon **Sid Scheinberg** did just that. He wrapped up the screenplay currently titled "Jaws '87" for his actress-mate **Lorraine Gary**, promising she'll get to reprise her original 1975 role as the wife in a small New England resort. What's more, in this sequel to the sequels Lorraine will not only co-star with the great white shark; she'll get to **kill it** in a violent episode of woman versus nature.

acting after Spielberg's *1941* comedy fiasco (one of my favorite comedies for the record).

She was allegedly "lured" back into acting because of the "people person" script that ensured this would be a film about the human characters, not about the shark like the ill-fated previous film.

The article says Sheinberg himself wrapped up the screenplay. However nowhere in the film's credits does he get screenplay credit. Michael DeGuzman gets the "credit" for this shit film's script, if that's what you want to call it.

Sheinberg was retiring as studio president. While I have no proof of this, I suspect he allegedly saw a chance to wring a few more bucks out that shark and made *Jaws 4* one last big payday for him and the wife. It would also be a paid three month vacation to The Bahamas and get them out of Los Angeles for the winter.

I remember the fiberglass shark heads all lined up for shipping when I worked at Universal. Someone there told me they were for *Jaws 4* and then walked me to where the giant tank was being prepared for the films ending. A crew was spraying this huge white wall that looked like a drive-in movie screen to look like a sky.

That might've been my first "uh oh" moment.

Don't tell me this film was pitched to anyone. Imagine that pitch session: "Okay, the shark is psychic..." Right there any self-respecting head of development would stop that person and fire them or clear them from the room. However, that is the central plot to *Jaws the Revenge*. The shark is psychic and is hunting down members of the Brody family, presumably for killing the other sharks or maybe the original one.

The film was rushed into production, with Sheinberg demanding the whole thing be ready for summer, 1987. In fact he had titled his original opus, *Jaws '87*. Sheinberg trotted out Joe Sargent who worked with Lorraine Gary on a previous project years earlier to direct. He even offered him a producer title and creative control. Whatever, buddy, just get this made so we can justify these paychecks.

It is fair to mention that Universal had a pretty lousy 1986 at the boxoffice. Expensive bombs like *Legal Eagles* and the now synonymous with boxoffice bomb, *Howard the Duck* gave Universal Studios a couple of black eyes. There's the possibility Sheinberg wanted to go back to the fish tank one more time... anything to get a hit movie up on the screens.

I heard a theory that this film wanted to ape the "woman action hero" success of Sigourney Weaver in *Aliens*. I call bullshit, If you really wanted to do that, you don't trot out grandma Brody for the task. Why not make a fresh new story with a younger female lead to take on the shark?

No, it is my opinion, and only my opinion, that Sheinberg saw one last chance to make a few easy bucks for him and his wife before he departed the studio. There was a lot of nonsense about this being so character driven and that's why everyone rallied around the script. How anyone didn't get past the first ten pages and not throw this "script" into the trash is beyond me. Again, I think Sheinberg wrote the original, stupid story and it was shucked off onto DeGuzman to make something out of it. That's not the official record; it's just my filmmaker's hunch.

The summer of 1987 was part of my "lost years." I was still reeling from failing at Penn State. I moved back home from California, chalking up another life failure. I was working jobs and wandering aimlessly about my home town while my friends were at college, in the military, having families. I was this loser at almost 20 years of age living back home to save up money to move back out… again.

There was still a little bit of that teenager still alive in me. He still had that excitement for a summer of movies. While I had great theatrical experiences in California with *Aliens, Little Shop of Horrors, Star Trek IV* and even *King Kong Lives* (for its sheer big screen awfulness that only Dino DeLaurentiis could deliver) my return home left me adrift and with low expectations for just about everything.

There was some article just after New Years 1987 in *Rolling Stone* announcing *Jaws 4* was on the schedule for a summer release. I had some hope. I allowed myself to get excited for something.

There were no spoilers. No plot leaks. There was nowhere to go to get any kind of inside information. You read what you could find in magazines, tabloids, whatever. The only real entertainment news source was *Entertainment Tonight* and its puffball pieces…they liked everything. Even if *Jaws 4* was a dog, they wouldn't say it. Spring came along and the trailer for *Jaws the Revenge* surfaced. Did I catch it in a theater screening or on TV? Not sure.

I do know I had almost no feeling for it. It didn't tell you much, which was fine, but I couldn't help but think they were hiding something. A lot of fast cuts, Percy Rodriguez returned as the narrating "voice." This offered little assurance because he did the same for *Jaws 3-D* and I still couldn't get past the pop culture trauma caused by that movie.

The 80s were coming to an end. Reagan was winding down, and there was more talk about his mental competence. Scandals were cropping up. AIDS was in full force throughout the nation and across the globe. Governor Michael Dukakis thought he would take on Reagan's heir apparent George Bush, but America knew in its heart of hearts, even if Reagan was fading and not entirely in control of his office, George Bush was going to be Reagan 3-D. Dukakis had no chance, even with his cousin, actress Olympia Dukakis using her *Moonstruck* Oscar win to cheer him on. I felt I was lost in a lost nation. *Jaws* provided some kind of comfort, is that the right word? Maybe it allowed me to feel more comfortable in my retreat. I kept the hope the film might be good.

Hank Searls, who did the novelization for *Jaws 2* returned for *Jaws The Revenge*.

Searls did a terrific job with *Jaws 2*. He took the original screenplay and fashioned it into a book that outshined Benchley's original novel. He was given a solid screenplay to adapt from Howard Sackler and Dorothy Tirstan. This time…it was terrible. The "screenplay:" for *Jaws The Revenge* originally called for Brody himself to die at the jaws of the shark. From there a widowed Mrs. Brody would travel to The Bahamas to be with her eldest son, Michael, now some marine biologist. The family would encounter a bitter voodoo witch doctor named Papa Jacques who had some kind of supernatural connection  with the Great White shark (which also was the offspring last seen at the end of Searls's *Jaws 2* novel. For the record the original shark in *Jaws* hooked up with the female shark in *Jaws 2* before he was killed).

Searls worked with the whole voodoo thing as best as possible, and the idea that this shark had some kind of psychic bond with Ellen Brody and was looking for…well, revenge.

I read the book before I saw the film, just like I did with *Jaws 2* back in 1978. While Searls again deftly handled the material, you couldn't help but feel he was handed a stinking turd to polish. I just couldn't get past the supernatural elements no matter how well-grounded Searls made them.

I found out that Matt Hooper was written to return. This would mean Richard Dreyfuss would don the knit cap one more time. Fortunately both Roy Scheider and Richard Dreyfuss smelled a stinker and declined to return. This turns my attention now to the stupid title of this movie.

Incepted under Sheinberg as *Jaws '87*, working title or not it sounded like an *Airport* disaster movie title, it moved to the title of *Jaws The Return*. Note that I use to no colon punctuation, no hyphens, ellipses or dashes.

It's one verbal vomit: *Jaws The Return*. Somewhere along the line "return" was swapped out for "revenge" and that's the fascinating story of how we got this grammatically bad film title.

As was done with *Jaws 3-D* a quick "making of" TV special was churned out to rev people up. *Jaws 3-D* had some dumb title like "Sharks Never Die." This one did something similar, working in the whole "this time it's personal" tag line. It wasn't an improvement.

I left a family picnic to get home in time to watch this special for *Jaws The Revenge*. It was opening in less than two weeks. They showed enough of the shark to tell me we were in for a rough ride. The fish's gums were unnaturally extended and looked like stitched fake car leather fastened around the fake unnaturally perfect, white teeth. The big takeaway was Mrs. Brody's return and the movie was going to be about the characters.

I was just catching on how to decipher Hollywood bullshit code. All of the actors interviewed, led by Lorraine Gary seemed really hellbent to convince you this movie was going to be good. Their spots seemed desperate as they talked of the characters and most of all, the heralded return of Lorraine Gary to the Ellen Brody role. It was like Sean Connery returning to James Bond one more time in *Never Say Never Again*, but actually not. It wasn't like anyone out there was waiting for the next Lorraine Gary film. Aside from *Jaws* fans, her name was unknown except when you saw her face it was, "Oh yeah, that lady."

The cynicism was palpable. Gary's return was a cynical ploy to separate this film from the stain of *Jaws 3-D* which had none of the original *Jaws* cast. By simply bringing back Ellen Brody the studio was sending a false message of a return to quality to the *Jaws* fanbase. How could this movie suck if Mrs. Brody returned? She came out of RETIREMENT for this!

Easy. Hubby came home from the office and in my mind said, "Lorraine, what say we get out of town for Christmas? How would you like a fully paid, free vacation to The Bahamas for three months and make a big fat check to boot?"

The plan to bring back Scheider and Dreyfuss was a triple cynical threat. The filmmakers admitted Scheider would be back just to be killed off. He would be in the film for ten minutes tops. You could see him in the proposed trailer. They would cut it all around him, Gary and Dreyfuss. Dreyfuss's cameo was planned as a phone call to Michael on Christmas day. The two would talk about the recently deceased Chief Brody and that would be it.

Yet, you know if they got these cameos they would have built that trailer all around them to show a return to the old *Jaws* territory and the fans would come in droves.

This was a pre-packaged cynical piece of product disguised as a motion picture. Director Joe Sargent, in my opinion, was picked because he was friends with Lorraine and Sid. He would be easy to use and would take the marching orders to make this corporate cash grab a legitimate venture. Sargent tried his best to sell his belief in this hot mess. He echoed the "it's about the people" bullshit. This was going to have a spectacular shark, doing spectacular things. If you saw the film, you know we got neither of these things.

In my opinion *Jaws The Revenge* was a deliberate con job. Or a joke. There was no intent to entertain. It was made to justify paychecks and who knows, maybe even some kind of tax write off to the tune of almost 30 million dollars. The desire to bring back Scheider and Dreyfuss was nothing more than a cynical ploy to fool audiences into the belief the film would be on the same creative and quality level as the first two films. Instead, they got Gary and that's because the president of the studio who made this dung pile was married to her.

You will never convince me that *Jaws the Revenge* was made with any intent to be a fitting component in the original film's legacy. Rushed into production from a stupid psychic shark idea to a slapdash, might as well have been impossible production schedule; if the intention was quality, it would have been done right from the moment the idea was pitched.

If the goal was to ape *Aliens* and Ripley's woman of action, the result would not have been pasty white grandma with a terrible 80s lid wandering around islands believing a shark was hunting her family. No one paid to see Gary and Michael Caine engage in romance either.

There was every opportunity to make something great with a fourth *Jaws*. The issue was, no one really wanted to. Everyone came out and did their bit, said the right things to the press to create and maintain the illusion.

Then the film opened.

I was there opening night, just like I was for *Jaws 3-D* four years earlier. I went with a friend and chatted up the film and my belief that we might be in for something decent. This friend also *Jaws 3-D* and had his doubts.

While not exactly sold out, the largest theater in the mall cineplex was packed. People were excited. They were also hopeful, and this might be *Jaws the Revenge's* biggest sin—it destroyed hope and faith in the film industry to do the right thing.

I've said in interviews that the only good thing about this movie was its score by the late Michael Small. I also said he deserved something better than this movie. The opening theme, set to a kind of military, action kind of march was catchy. We got an opening title sequence through the shark's point of view but there was small problem with that. The point of view shots also breached the water. Was the shark swimming about Amity harbor with its head out of the water?

If it didn't I guess we wouldn't know we are back in Amity. A small matter, I was willing to go for the ride. We got Mrs. Brody's big camera reveal with some stupid kitchen scene with a now grown Sean Brody who has become a cop like his late dad who succumbed to a heart attack sometime after the events of *Jaws 2*.

It's here where I pause, because before the movie started I heard people around asking how this movie would fit in with the events of the third one. It wasn't in Florida again, but did the whole Sea World and Brody brothers thing happen?

Early press announcements for *Jaws the Revenge* said it was the thrilling "third installment" to the shark series. I guess Universal was just pretending *Jaws 3-D* didn't happen. And who could blame them?

The opening of the film made it clear the Brody boys never went to Florida and the events of *Jaws 3-D* were to be ignored. Or maybe it was all a dream like "Dallas" pulled to give us another cliffhanger to rival *Who Shot JR?* The *Halloween* franchise would take a cue from this with its attempt to ignore time-lines and create new storylines. Thanks, *Jaws The Revenge*.

There was no applause at the end. There was a lot of laughter and it came when the shark inexplicably roared when it leapt from the water. Shocked by some electronic tracker and beacon inside it, Michael Brody would send a jolt of electricity through the fish, making it leap out fo the crystal clear blue surf. Whenever it did, the shark roared with this cheap 1950s monster movie sound effect. It had been used by *The Deadly Mantis*, one of those giant big bug movies from the 50s, and perhaps best heard as Spot's roar from the TV show, *The Munsters*. Remember the fire-

bre3athing dragon below Herman's staircase? That roar is the same exact roar used by *Jaws the Revenge* and coincidentally, both *The Munsters* and *Jaws* were properties of Universal Studios.

Sharks have no vocal chords or lungs. The shark in *Jaws 3-D* growled. This new one was spectacular all right, because it roared like some prehistoric monster. The sad part is that a real-life scientist was credited with advising on the film.

What the hell happened here? Was Dr. John E. McCosker paid to use his name for some kind of "We consulted experts!" kind of move? Didn't this guy look at the film and say, "Ummmm…sharks can't roar. It is physically impossible. They don't have lungs. They don't have vocal chords. Sharks can't swim in reverse. Sharks can't swim faster than a plane from New England to The Bahamas," or perhaps the biggest one: "Sharks aren't fucking psychic and have no conscious ability to enact revenge upon a family and hunt them down like some marine killer GPS system."

I would love to hear from Dr. McCosker, if he is still alive, to know exactly what his purpose was on this film. Maybe he consulted on snails.

The audience around me chuckled more than a few times, and this was more akin to sitting in *The Amityville Horror* amusement than when I saw the first two *Jaws* films with a theatrical group. The original ending had Mario Van Peebles die a bloody death, falling into the maw of a very fiberglass-looking shark. If you look at the edit, the skin tones of the stand alone, fake sharks comes nowhere near the skin tone of the platform mechanical sharks.

We also saw the mechanical arm of the platform shark right there on the screen. All they had to do was crop the image, simply enlarge it a little in editing and shift the picture down and film error eliminated. They had to have seen it, because it happened several times, but the issue is, no one cared enough to correct it. This is no different than the blatant boom shadow on Rod Steiger in the 1979 *Amityville Horror*. The filmmakers could have fixed it, even with a reshoot, but they knew they didn't have to. It was going to make money regardless.

This is "Cynema."

The audience around me questioned how Michael Caine could jump from his plane, into the ocean, swim 300 feet and climb aboard the ship perfectly dry. The answer was simple: no one cared. Peebles fell into the fake shark and was last seen struggling, bleeding out, in the monster's jaws below the water. That was is for good 'ole Jake. His death was the only time I heard any intentional reaction from the audience. There were a few "Awwws!" The movie ended with the shark leaping from the water and Mrs. Brody flashbacking to the end of *Jaws* (which she was not present for, as well as her son's death in the opening of the film) and impaled the great beast on the bowsprit of the boat.

There was a jumbled mess of editing and the audience let out a number of "Oh my God's," of disgust and disappointment. This ending effect was almost as bad as that infamous conclusion to *Jaws 3-D* with the souvenir shop shark gliding into the glass window.

We last see the shark sinking to the bottom, the bow of the boat stuck through its head, evoking again, the original film but in no way coming close to it.

The lights came up and people stood, shaking their heads. I definitely heard, "This was worse than the last one" from someone walking up the aisle. A lot of shaking heads in disbelief. When we walked out into the lobby one lady said to people waiting in line for the next show, "Get your money back now."

Universal decided to change the ending, as if this would fix anything. Being that Jake was about the only character people liked, they reshot his ending, allowing him to miraculously and inexplicably live. They also changed the way the shark died. It was still struck by the bowsprit, only now it exploded.

Why? We don't know. Did it matter? Who the hell cares? This is an actual frame of the new ending and the effect used.

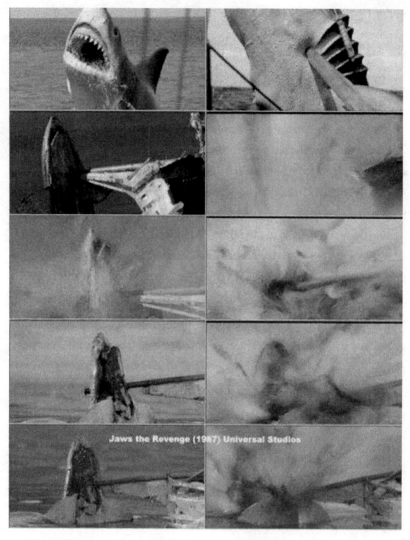

Jaws the Revenge (1987) Universal Studios

That still sums up the entire film and its dedication to quality entertainment.

Jaws The Revenge is not a film. I don't care what official stories are out there stating it was made with every intention of being a good film. This was a cynical cash grab and nothing more. It capitalized on the good will of its audience who trusted enough to return one more time in the hope of getting something good.

Jaws The Revenge is a breach of trust between filmmakers and audiences. It is a middle finger from the "I got mine" mindset that created it. A bunch of people got paid a lot of money to fuck around in The Bahamas for three months and couldn't have cared less about what made it to the screen.

Save the Hollywood bullshit. This was a hit and run cash grab. This never intended to "be about the people or characters." The sharks were built before there was a final script. When they did get a final script, it was revised when they couldn't lure Scheider and Dreyfuss back, they felt the psychic shark storyline was the best way to go.

Michael Caine said this about *Jaws The Revenge* in his autobiography: *"I won an Oscar, paid for a house and had a great holiday. Not bad for a flop movie."*

That's everything you need to know about the motivation behind the making of this.

There is a thing called "So bad it's good." *Prophecy* is an example. *Amityville 3-D* is another. These types of films are legion. Both are flawed movies, and silly in their premises but yet, they are a lot of fun. I enjoy the living hell out of them and many others just like them. "So bad it's good" is an entirely different thing than cynical. Roger Corman's "Galaxy of Terror" is so bad, it is wonderful. "Jaws the Revenge" is just shit and the definition of "Cynema." Why? Because "Galaxy" had almost no budget and made by a man who understood the schlock factor and gave us a clear "Alien" rip off while delivering sex-crazed worms and Sid Haig chopping off his own arm. Corman's goal was to entertain. It always was.

I don't believe Joe Alves, John Frankenheimer, Richard Fleischer or a number of other directors set out to make bad movies. A lot of things happened to make them that way, but they all had some wonderful elements to them that made them enjoyable. Remember what Sam Arkoff said about *Q: The Winged Serpent,* "The dreck was my idea."

That's terrific because sometimes movies are just movies to be enjoyed, not picked over and analyzed to death, looking to find every piece of minutia or fan Easter egg in them. A bad film isn't necessarily a cynical one.

The cynical ones know they suck from the start. They don't care about the script. They don't care about remotely being entertaining. They are made to capitalize by throwing enough shit against the wall in the hope of something sticking.

The cynical movies are made by committees, executives and filmmakers that have as much commitment to quality as a porn filmmaker. In the case of *Jaws The Revenge*, I might just give the porn director more credit than the powers that green lit that "film."

Now we have content everywhere. Just labeling entertainment as "content" now implies a fast food type of mentality. We just want our Big Macs. We want assembly line filmmaking that simply satiates us.

Just look at what Disney has done with *Star Wars* to understand what I am saying.

We can now watch our content on small phone screens, tablets and desktops. The biggest of flat screen TVs can't compare to the experience of seeing a great film (bad or terrific) with a large crowd. You just don't get the same thing in your living room no matter how good your picture and sound are.

I ended with *Jaws The Revenge* as I said I would. That was the film that closed out 80s horror for me. The decade ended on the other end of the spectrum from the way it started. Horror would recover but this kind of cynicism had taken root.

Fright Night got it. It knew the joy and fun of old time bad and cheesy movies. It also knew it was going way by the mid-70s. Cable and the home video revolutions were eroding the drive-in, big screen experience. An era was closing by 1985 which again, is why *Fright Night* resonated with me. It warned us of the coming cynicism as it was already in place and Peter Vincent told Charley Brewster this as the boy told him with sincerity that he believed in vampires even though few others did anymore.

We've reached the end of our walk. I leave you in the digital world of streaming and endless content, extended universes and the Cynema demons that await you if you venture off the path and onto the moors.

It is my sincere wish that theaters rise from the COVID aftermath and you get to experience a movie on the big screen with an enthusiastic audience of strangers that for one brief moment all become comrades in that blue flickering digital light. I hope you get the chance to stand and applaud a movie.

This was horror for me and I count myself lucky to have experienced it the way I have for it will never be quite like that again.

Except for *Jaws The Revenge*.

I take *Jaws the Revenge* personally.

SPECIAL THANKS

You always run the risk of missing someone when doing a public list of thanks. I'll do my best because…this is personal, like gag credits at the end of a film.

Thank you…

Lisa and Logan above all.

Nanny and Pappy—you're both dead and can't read this anyway, but thank you for the needed dose of the macabre in my childhood.

Bonnie. You took me to *Jaws* and started it all. I never stopped thanking you.

Toni. I might've gotten famous but it would've been better with her here.

My stepfather, Brian. You saved it all.

My brother—who always put on the dress.

Uncle JR, who got that Super 8mm film camera "hot off the truck" that snowy night.

The Stroudsburg High School Class of 1985 that defined me and special thanks to the ones that gave me some of the best times and memories of my life and believed in me.

The teachers who made the difference: Mrs. DeFranco, Mrs. Haddon, Mr. Moraski, Mr. Steen, Mr. Burnett, Mr. Powell, Mr. Beaver, Mrs. Schneider, and Mr. Barna.

Tommy Lee Wallace—from boyhood hero to Mayberry's Obi Wan Kenobi.

Willie Scott. You always said it.

KP—You're so cool, Brewster.

Chris—Pal o'mine.

The *Mad Monster Party* friends—you know who you are.

My Dear Count—March 18th, 1981.

Mrs. D's Catch and Release Wunderkinds and that "other horror kid." Shame!

Da Mone—No Wonder Rome Fell.

The Yarashi

Bob and Lydia

Phyllis and Louis—always there. Always kind.

Sal aka "Pop" who made the first one happen.

Count Fagula

Q Bruce—for always getting before and behind the camera and making me laugh.

Mr. Big wherever you are.

The Moron Twins, Earl, Edwina and Grenelda and The Marsh's. Enough said.

Spock—I have been and always shall be your friend. I also can't feel my face.

Aunt Barbara and Uncle Bobby Welser.

Chip—Handsome check.

Jackie Laster who got me lunch with Anthony Perkins and a job.

Mr. H…for hiring me and not firing me.

Lee Marshall. I should have listened to you.

Doug and Matt because Everything's Fire.

Cloris. Fuck you, you fucking fuck.

June. I can't move…

The Popper. Nice lid.

Fangoria. Better than *Cosmo*.

Felissa Rose—from The Sherman to partners and close friends.

Adrienne Barbeau—you ARE the voice of Antonio Bay. Always.

Dee Wallace—America's Mom and my adopted one.

Anthony Perkins—for being kind to me.

Stephen King—I wanted to write because of you.

Amanda Wyss—Your cat is on my fence.

C. Thomas Howell—my boyfriend ;)

Kane Hodder—See you in Hell but I won't do that.

Roy K and SOTA FX—The Best

Frank Hennenlotter—for taking my call.

George Romero—the under-appreciated Gentleman of Horror

John Carpenter—for being you.

Jaws: The Revenge—for nothing except a tagline from the worst movie ever made.

CPSIA information can be obtained
at www.ICGtesting.com
Printed in the USA
LVHW052257130422
716130LV00012B/336